# DOROTHY HEATHCOTE ON EDUCATION AND DRAMA

Dorothy Heathcote MBE was a unique educator whose practice had a vital influence on the international development of drama in education. For more than half a century she inspired generations of teachers and educators all over the world with her original and authentic approach to teaching and learning.

This new collection of the essential writings of Dorothy Heathcote traces the development of her practice over her long professional life. It combines the most important and influential articles from the first edition with more recent pieces to show the significant development in Heathcote's thinking and practice. The book reveals the increasing complexity of her engagement with Mantle of the Expert as an approach to the curriculum and revisits earlier themes that are central to her work in such pieces as *Productive Tensions* and *Internal Coherence*. In everything she writes she is concerned with introducing teachers to the power of drama as a means of activating the curriculum and giving them the insight and understanding to enable them to generate significant learning experiences with their students.

Each section is accompanied by an introduction, a summary of key points and an extensive list of resources. Edited by a leading expert in drama education and featuring a foreword by Gavin Bolton, this new collection of Dorothy Heathcote's work will be welcomed by academics, teachers of drama and student teachers.

**Cecily O'Neill** is an internationally acknowledged authority on drama in education. Her previous publications include *Drama Worlds: A Framework for Process Drama*, *Words into Worlds: Learning a Second Language through Process Drama*, *Drama Structures* and *Dorothy Heathcote: Collected Writings on Education and Drama* with Liz Johnson. She is a visiting lecturer and examiner at a number of universities in the UK and the USA. She holds a PhD from the University of Exeter and an Honorary Fellowship from the University of Winchester.

# DOROTHY HEATHCOTE ON EDUCATION AND DRAMA

Essential writings

*Edited by Cecily O'Neill*

Routledge
Taylor & Francis Group

LONDON AND NEW YORK

First published 2015
by Routledge
2 Park Square, Milton Park, Abingdon, Oxon OX14 4RN

and by Routledge
711 Third Avenue, New York, NY 10017

*Routledge is an imprint of the Taylor & Francis Group, an informa business*

*British Library Cataloguing in Publication Data*
A catalogue record for this book is available from the British Library

*Library of Congress Cataloging-in-Publication Data*
Heathcote, Dorothy.
Dorothy Heathcote on education and drama : essential writings / editor: Cecily O'Neill.
pages cm
1. Drama in education. I. O'Neill, Cecily.
PN3171.H3256 2014
371.3'32—dc23
2014008064

ISBN: 978-0-415-72458-6 (hbk)
ISBN: 978-0-415-72459-3 (pbk)
ISBN: 978-1-315-75721-6 (ebk)

Typeset in Bembo
by Cenveo Publisher Services

Printed and bound in Great Britain by
TJ International Ltd, Padstow, Cornwall

In memory of Dorothy Heathcote MBE, 1926–2011

# CONTENTS

# FOREWORD

This new publication is an exciting extension of the 1984 edition. While preserving some of the key chapters of that earlier collection, it takes the reader into new territory relating to Dorothy Heathcote's more recent work, opening up areas of exploration, offering further sophisticated examples of practice and a more detailed record of her latest experimentations, especially her refinement of 'Mantle of the Expert'.

Reading the book is curiously like having a conversation with Dorothy, as if she is talking to you, sharing with you her vision, her concerns, how she stumbles across ideas and then searches for a way of formulating them, making them accessible for others. And you, the reader, are taking part in this conversation, for you bring to each page what you already understand about drama in schools, what you yourself have already discovered from your own experience. And, let's face it, however 'expert' you may be as a drama teacher, there will be some aspect of your teaching that could benefit from further development. So you will pick and choose from the pages on offer. And that is just what Dorothy allows you to do, for she covers a huge range of drama teaching dimensions.

Do you want advice on how to 'read' a class of children, where they stand intellectually, emotionally, socially etc. or do you need help with how to adjust your chosen drama material to that particular stage of development? Or what about choice of theme and how to find an arresting and productive starting point? Should you find a shared role for the whole of the group? Should you yourself play a role? But how then do you get the group to take over responsibility so that the drama is their creation? And if it becomes theirs, how can you subtly change the level of what they are experiencing so that they are challenged to think, to express themselves, to respect one another, to give themselves over to the task in hand? Are you more interested in how to *plan* a drama session, perhaps drawing on Dorothy's useful tips on the categorization or grading of different dramatic devices such as 'conventions', 'framing', 'tension', 'theatre forms', etc.? Or are you concerned to develop ideas on how drama might relate to other aspects of the curriculum and to share educational projects with other members of staff? You may, of course, be searching for Dorothy's views on the nature of dramatic art or on her overall philosophy of education and drama's place within that concept. Or you may be concerned with the training of teachers. More academically, you may want to analyse the professional journey Dorothy herself has gone through on her way to becoming one of the world's most influential teachers.

In gathering together these articles, many of which are now difficult for us to lay our hands on from other published sources, Cecily O'Neill has produced a collection that combines both an overview and a detailed record of Dorothy Heathcote's remarkable contribution to our understanding of drama education. So, dear reader, please 'dip in' or 'dig deeply' – it just depends on the kind of conversation you want to have with Dorothy.

*Gavin Bolton*

# ACKNOWLEDGEMENTS

It has been a privilege to revisit Dorothy Heathcote's writings from *Collected Writings* and to encounter her later work for inclusion in this book. Dorothy Heathcote profoundly altered my practice and every time I use drama, I am strengthened by the memory of the knowledge and insights she has given me.

Recognition of the significance of Heathcote's work has been kept alive by the editors and contributors to the journals and conferences of NATD and National Drama in the UK and internationally by many other professional and academic organizations. These dedicated educators continue to safeguard her legacy and such events as 'Heathcote Re-Considered' (National Drama Conference, London, 2013) show that in spite of an inhospitable and at times openly hostile educational climate, there is an eagerness among teachers and academics to rise to the challenge of Heathcote's vision of teaching and learning.

I am extremely grateful to NATD, the Association for the Teaching of Drama, and the website www.mantleoftheexpert.com for permission to include the articles 'Notes on signs and portents', 'Productive tensions' and 'Contexts for active learning', as well as excerpts from 'Key elements in Mantle of the Expert', and the paper 'Creativity', written for the London Borough of Redbridge.

I would also like to thank the editorial board of *YARATICI DRAMA DERGİSİ*, the Turkish *Creative Drama Journal*, for permission to include excerpts from several articles published in a special edition of the journal, dedicated to Heathcote's work (*Creative Drama Journal*, Summer/Winter 2010, Volume 5, Issues 9–10). These excerpts appear in this volume as 'Conventions in Mantle of the Expert', 'Elements of Mantle of the Expert,' and 'Encountering power givers and power takers.'

Liz Johnson, the co-editor of *Dorothy Heathcote: Collected Writings on Education and Drama*, was unfortunately unable to be part of this endeavour. I want to thank her for her support and suggestions. Finally, I would like to thank Marianne Heathcote Woodbridge and her family for their support and encouragement, and for providing the image for the cover of this book.

# INTRODUCTION

Dorothy Heathcote MBE was a remarkable educator whose theory and practice have had a vital influence on the development of drama in education. For more than half a century her innovative and authentic approaches to teaching and learning inspired generations of teachers and educators all over the world. She died in 2011, aged 85, as she was about to receive the award of an MBE acknowledging her enormous contribution to education. Her influence lives on in all the teachers whose practice has been profoundly altered by her teaching and writing.

The landscape of education has changed profoundly since Heathcote began her work in teaching training in 1950. At that time, awareness of the need for a more child-centred style of education had been growing, and teachers, especially in primary schools, suddenly had the freedom to experiment with more progressive styles of teaching. It seems significant that in her first position at the Institute of Education in Newcastle Heathcote was entrusted with the task of introducing drama to primary school principals who were attending a part-time Froebel course. Without any background in schools or in the psychology or philosophy of education, it is likely that she would have felt the need to familiarize herself with the precepts of Friedrich Froebel, the German educator who developed the concept of the Kindergarten.[1] Froebel's belief in a holistic approach to education built on first-hand experience, collective play, talk and reflection would have resonated with Heathcote, as well as his recognition of the child as part of a learning community that included parents working in harmony with teachers. His approach to learning is aimed at developing the child's autonomy and relies on the skilled observation of children. It acknowledges young people as active, feeling, thinking human beings, seeing patterns and making connections. All of these principles have remained central to Heathcote's vision of teacher education.

The 1950s and 60s were a period of optimism and creativity in education. Teacher training courses increased in length and scope and provided a fertile climate for the growth of drama in education. There was increasing recognition among teachers and teacher trainers of the potential of drama in the classroom as a means of promoting creativity, spontaneity and self-expression. Peter Slade and Brian Way were significant figures in this development. Slade, who became Birmingham's first adviser on drama in 1943, established relevant courses in teacher education, including a one-year child drama certificate, and in 1954 published his influential text *Child Drama*.[2] Although he had a background in theatre, Slade believed that drama with children was an experiential art to do with spontaneous personal expression and one that was profoundly different from and opposed to performance. Brian Way's book *Development through Drama* soon became a popular handbook for drama teachers and helped to reinforce Slade's distinction between drama and theatre.[3] Way's work in developing participatory theatre for young audiences was also very influential, but in drama education Way was concerned with the personal development of the individual student and an increase in such capacities as concentration and imagination.

In the theatre, avant-garde directors including Joan Littlewood and Peter Brook used improvisation techniques in rehearsal and as a method of devising performances, and in their influential book *Improvisation* Hodgson and Richards claimed that the central activity of acting was improvisation.[4] An associated development in 1965 was the establishment of England's first Theatre in Education company at the Belgrade Theatre in Coventry. T.I.E, as the movement came to be known, drew on participatory theatre techniques and aspects of drama in education, including strategies that had been generated by Heathcote. All of these influences led to a growing interest among drama teachers in and use of improvisation, theatre games and exercises.

An awareness of Heathcote's work was also growing among drama teachers and advisers. The profound difference between her approach and what had previously been regarded as good practice was soon apparent. As Gavin Bolton makes clear, dramatic action for Heathcote was about attending to the meanings negotiated with her students and leading to action.[5] She was not concerned with theatre skills or personal development, but with creating work that carried *meaning* for the participants.

Among the most immediately noticeable of Heathcote's innovations was the use of Teacher in Role, which sharply distinguished her work from the trust and concentration exercises, brief improvisations and theatre games that were staple ingredients of the drama lesson at the time. She frequently initiated the drama by taking on a role, endowing the students with a generic role and a shared viewpoint, instead of allocating parts among individuals or casting the drama. The theme or situation to be explored was chosen after much discussion. Reflection before, during and after each lesson was always a major part of any drama session.

Heathcote's use of role was controversial and often misunderstood by those who failed to grasp its functional and generative characteristics. As Heathcote noted: 'There is a prejudice against using role because it is so efficient and looks so showy'.[6] She was sometimes regarded as a manipulator, interfering with the children's own creativity as she initiated the fictional world of the drama in role, supported and affirmed the students' contributions and profoundly altered the classroom relationships. However, Heathcote's ability to launch the work in the essential 'now' time of drama was impressive, as was the active response of the students as they joined in, opposed or transformed what was happening. This approach soon became known as 'living-through' drama.

In *Dramatic Imagination* she considered some of the labels that have been applied to her practice over the decades.

> Years ago I quoted Kenneth Tynan: Drama occurs when a person or persons are moving towards, or in, or emerging from a state of desperation.... people seized on it as Dorothy's 'man in a mess' stage. I can't escape the labels people hang round my neck.[7]

B. J. Wagner's revealing case study, *Drama as a Learning Medium*, first published in the United States in 1976, captures the depth and dramatic intensity of Heathcote's practice at this time.[8] A number of inspiring films and videos of her work documented the power of her approach to drama.[9]

In her paper 'Subject or System', first published in 1971, Heathcote defines the 'laws' of drama in education as the participants' attempt to create 'a living, moving picture of life':

> I define educational drama as being anything which involves people in active role-taking situations in which attitudes, not characters, are the chief concern, lived at life-rate (that is, discovery at this moment, not memory based) and obeying the natural laws of the medium. I regard these laws as being: a willing suspension of disbelief; agreement to pretence; employing all past experiences available to the group at the present moment and any conjecture of imagination they are capable of, in an attempt to create a living, moving picture of life, which aims at surprise and discovery for the participants rather than for any onlookers. The scope of this is to be defined by story-line and theme, so that the problem with which they grapple is clearly defined. I maintain that problem-solving is the basis of learning and maturation.[10]

It is possible to view the development of Heathcote's work in three overlapping phases. In what might be regarded as the first phase, when her practice was described as 'living-through' drama, the students were often invited to provide a theme or situation for the drama, but questioning and negotiation beforehand and reflection both inside and outside the drama were always vital elements. Although she frequently initiated the drama by taking on a role, she regularly halted the 'living through' to elicit students' contributions. By skilful questioning and speculation about the events of the drama she encouraged the students to reflect on the implications of what was happening. As well as creating the sense of 'being there' in 'now' time, she carefully positioned her students so that they became watchers of the event – self-spectators outside the action. This double stance allowed her to invite the group to contemplate the developing meaning of the work from *inside* the drama. She believed that experience without reflection was unlikely to lead to learning and that students are most engaged when they have a real voice in the work and when they have co-created the content. Her aim was to build on her students' knowledge and experience and to bring their existing understandings into awareness so that they became engaged in real learning.

Whatever role Heathcote adopted in the drama, she never ceased to be the teacher. She explained that she built respect for the role through the teacher and, for the teacher, through the role. It was this duality – where she functioned both as teacher and in a role – that enabled her to slow down the action, invite reflection and heighten awareness of the meaning of the event. She moved smoothly and effectively between stances, often halting the drama and inviting the students to monitor and modify her role.

Early in the 1980s I watched Heathcote at work with a group of London adolescents who wanted the drama to be about teenage delinquents in a secure facility. She asked if she could be the Warden. They agreed and the drama began. In a harsh voice she ordered the group to sit down and assigned each of them a number. They obeyed at once. Coming out of role, Dorothy asked if that was the kind of warden they wanted her to be. They eagerly agreed that it was. Back in role, she grew more authoritative, correcting them, insisting that they recite their numbers correctly and demanding to know the whereabouts of a missing inmate.

Then once again she stepped out of role and checked that this was the kind of Warden they wanted her to be. The adolescents enthusiastically confirmed that it was. By moving in and out of role she was inviting the students to monitor and modify her role, but also giving them time to observe and interpret it before rushing to a response.

In the early 1970s Heathcote began to move away from her previous 'living-through' approach. This might be seen as her second phase. Rather than responding to themes and ideas negotiated with the students, at this point Heathcote more frequently operated in curriculum areas that had been proposed by the teacher. Students were invited to become involved in situations where the background to the work had already been prepared in some detail. The papers in Part II show her increasing use of 'depictions', as well as the development of her 'conventions'. These strategies slowed up the action and meant that explorations of significant curriculum material could be undertaken in detail. But, as in her earlier work, there was always a double consciousness of immersion in the experience and self-spectatorship, combining engagement and distancing within the same context. Part II includes the most important of her writings on the use of conventions. Part III focuses on Mantle of the Expert, an integrative approach to the materials of the curriculum which is likely to prove the most innovative and influential of her contributions to drama and to education.

By the middle of the 1970s, as she moved into what might be described as her third phase, Heathcote began to work almost exclusively in Mantle of the Expert. This way of working was to become her most ambitious attempt to create a model of authentically holistic teaching. It employed all the modes of drama that she had already generated and refined, but in a prepared context designed to achieve particular curricular objectives. Heathcote explains that she developed Mantle of the Expert when she was trying to help teachers who didn't understand how to create tension in drama, and to eliminate the need for children to 'act' or behave 'like other people'. Mantle of the Expert has strong links with play but because students are invited to take on responsibility for purposeful tasks, they don't feel 'babyish'. They are also supported by the sense of community and the shared point of view which are key characteristics of Mantle of the Expert.

Heathcote's Mantle of the Expert and her Commission Model display her concern about learners who are rarely provided with opportunities to develop a sense of active citizenship in a world where many young people are increasingly disenfranchised and alienated from society. She aspired to create communities of learners both inside and outside the school boundaries, and to promote the skills of critical thinking, reflection, responsibility, collaboration and communication that are crucial for success in the world beyond school. She hoped that involvement in authentic learning would alter the learners' sense of themselves and their relationship to their world.

In the 1970s, as the teaching profession became almost entirely a graduate one, the training of teachers began to focus on academic and education studies rather than on teaching methods and extended teaching practice. There was a reaction against the 'progressive' methods of the 1960s, a call for teachers to become more accountable and an increase in central government control over teachers and schools. By the 1990s a National Curriculum had been established in England. This curriculum set out core and foundation subjects accompanied by programmes of study and 'attainment targets' – the knowledge, skills and understanding which children would be expected to acquire at each 'key stage' of their education.[11] Perhaps the most damaging outcome of these developments was that teachers and schools were relegated from being curriculum innovators to mere curriculum 'deliverers'. Regular revisions of the National

Curriculum and the introduction of league tables for schools embedded the regular testing of students at the centre of the English school system, and education became increasingly focused on the need to prepare for the tests. The time available to arts subjects and in particular to dance and drama, which had not been included as separate subjects in the National Curriculum, became squeezed in an overloaded and often unbalanced curriculum.

By 1989 drama in education and the work of Heathcote and Bolton in particular were under attack.[12] It was regarded as anti-theatre, focused on process and devoid of social and political content. In the same year, Heathcote gave a keynote address to NATD's conference, in which she sought to allay the anxiety that teachers were feeling about drama's place in the curriculum. She reminded them that by using drama they are bringing an enormous gift into a school:

> You employ systems that use materials in different contexts. You always work at affective tasks; you are always transforming ideas, information, forging language, formulating sign, and you can use frame, now and imminent time, resources and contracts to agree to fictional truths. Through these you create resonance and de-sanitize the curriculum. … You can teach people how to learn. You can help people understand empathy. You can help people realize what they know, to own their own knowledge.[13]

In the last decade the opportunity to undertake specialist teacher training in drama in the UK has been greatly eroded. The number of one-year postgraduate teaching training courses in drama (PGCEs) in colleges and universities has been diminishing each year, as has the number of students accepted on these courses. In teacher training at primary level, students often receive only a few hours' preparation in using drama in the classroom at a time when Heathcote's active, empowering and authentic approaches to teaching and learning are more essential than ever.

It is worth remembering that Heathcote saw herself primarily as a teacher and only secondarily as a drama teacher. Her major concern has always been to encourage every teacher to take advantage of the invaluable approaches to learning that drama offers, whatever the subject area or age level within which they work. She sees drama as a means of providing a human context for the curriculum, so that knowledge does not remain fragmented and subject-based but is rooted in human action, interaction, commitment and responsibility. Ironically, the pedagogy that Dorothy Heathcote had been promoting since the middle of the twentieth century resonates with a vision of twenty-first century education in which critical thinking, collaboration and cross-curriculum problem-solving are seen as essential skills for future citizens.

In the decades since the publication in 1984 of *Dorothy Heathcote: Collected Writings on Education and Drama*, Heathcote continued to refine her theory and practice.[14] In her talks and writings she constantly revisited the key elements of her practice that she had been articulating and elaborating throughout her professional life. In this new collection of Heathcote's writings, the purpose is to share and clarify the vital modes of learning that she developed over more than half a century. The chapters from *Collected Writings* included here are those that have proved the most significant in terms of the frequency with which they are cited in other publications, theses and dissertations. These have been edited to enable the key points in each chapter to emerge with greater clarity. Where quotations from elsewhere in that book are included, these are indicated by relevant chapter titles and page numbers.

In several cases the chapters from the last three decades of Heathcote's working life are accounts of keynote addresses or workshops which she gave in various international locations and which have been transcribed and published in drama journals and on websites. Again, these have been edited with a view to length and to avoid repetition of the many examples with which Heathcote illustrated her talks.

Her writings are arranged in three parts – 'Teachers and teaching', 'Drama in practice' and 'Mantle of the Expert'. These themes are not entirely disconnected, as some approaches, examples and strategies will occur in more than one part. However, although some details of Heathcote's practice may have been modified over the years, what has not changed is her commitment to drama as a medium for learning. The key purposes and essential characteristics of her approach to education have remained constant throughout her remarkable career.

In the present educational climate, where education is limited by narrow curricular objectives, where students' learning is predicted, controlled and tested, where teachers and schools are burdened by the tyranny of league tables, it is more important than ever to hold on to Heathcote's vision of education and to recognize its relevance. This collection of Heathcote's writings gives a glimpse of the significance of the kind of teaching and learning it is possible achieve through drama.

> The difference may be that we create a race of teachers who are unafraid to make relationships with classes, who are unafraid to admit that they do not know, who never stop seeking to learn more about the dynamics of teaching; who bring all of themselves to school and demand that their classes do the same; who can actually change their modes of work to suit the needs of their classes at any time so that learning is kept meaningful, who like to get on with the people they teach because they are unafraid of the dull, the aggressive, the unacademic, the 'naughty'; who are able to admit that they are tired today, so their classes can take some responsibility. It is surely worth trying a different way.[15]

As Bolton pointed out in his keynote speech at the *Heathcote Re-Considered* conference in July 2013, it is not enough to speak of Heathcote's work in terms of 'technique' or 'strategy'.[16] He reminded us that it would be a mistake to think her approach could be defined in terms of *methodology*. Her practice was deeply drawn from her own philosophy of life, her intuitive understanding of the meaning of people's behaviour, her astonishing skill in 'reading' other people's behaviour, the meaning of their beliefs and the rules of their culture. Her creativity was drawn from the *meaning* of art, of literature and of education and, indeed, of life.

I am confident that these visions of active, empowering and authentic education will continue to inspire, motivate and challenge new generations of teachers and learners.

Heathcote's work will continue to live in the present every time teachers use what they have learned from her in order to generate with their students a fictional world, an imagined space full of possibility, authentic learning and discovery.

## Notes

1 Friedrich Froebel (1782–1852) was a German educator who originated the kindergarten system.
2 Slade, P. (1954) *Child Drama*, University of London Press.
3 Way, B. (1967) *Development through Drama*, London: Longman. For an analysis of the development of drama during this period, see Bolton, G. (1984) *Drama as Education*, London: Longman, and Bolton, G. (1998) *Acting in Classroom Drama*, Stoke-on-Trent: Trentham Books.

4 Hodgson, J. and Richards, E. (1966) *Improvisation*, London: Methuen and Co. Ltd.
5 Bolton, G. (1998) *Acting in Classroom Drama*, Birmingham and Stoke-on-Trent: Trentham Books.
6 See 'Signs and portents' pp. 70-78, this volume.
7 Heathcote, D. (2010) 'Dramatic Imagination', *The Journal for Drama in Education* 26 (2), Summer.
8 Wagner, B. J. (1976) *Dorothy Heathcote: Drama as a Learning Medium*, Washington, DC: National Education Association. A second edition of this book was published in 1991.
9 See 'Resources' pp. 157–159, this volume.
10 'Subject or System' in Johnson, L. and O'Neill, C. (eds.) (1984) *Dorothy Heathcote: Collected Writings on Education and Drama*, London: Hutchinson, pp. 61–62.
11 The 'core subjects' were mathematics, English and science; six foundation subjects included history, geography, technology, music, art and physical education; a modern foreign language was included at secondary level.
12 Hornbrook, D. (1989) *Education and Dramatic Art*, Oxford: Blackwell Education.
13 Heathcote, D. (2012) 'The Fight for Drama – The Fight for Education', *The Journal for Drama in Education* 28 (1), Special Supplement, Spring.
14 Johnson, L. and O'Neill, C. (eds.) (1984) *Dorothy Heathcote: Collected Writings on Education and Drama*, London: Hutchinson. Later published by Stanley Thornes. An American edition was published by Northwestern University Press in 1991.
15 'Training Teachers to Use Drama as Education' in Johnson, L. and O'Neill, C. (eds.) (1984) *Dorothy Heathcote: Collected Writings on Education and Drama*, London: Hutchinson, p. 40.
16 Bolton, G. (2013) 'Digging for Dorothy', keynote address given at *Heathcote Re-Considered*, National Drama Conference, Greenwich, July 2013. Published in *Heathcote Re-Considered: Conference Echoes*, www.nationaldrama.org.uk.

# PART I
# Teachers and teaching

# EXCELLENCE IN TEACHING

*Dorothy Heathcote's professional life was dedicated to developing teachers who could generate effective learning with their students. She taught through example and her writings, lectures and keynote speeches, and the many master classes and school residencies she undertook had as their primary aim the development of teachers who are not merely competent but creative and inspiring.*

*This chapter includes many of the most significant principles that underpin all of Heathcote's practice. First published in 1978, the paper touches on a key element in all of Heathcote's work with children – the need to realign the relationship between teacher and students – to bring power to the students and to draw on their power. She makes clear that this requires mutual respect, constant attention to the students' attitudes and responses, and the ability to withhold judgement. As she puts it: 'Drama is a social art, and teachers are made during encounters with their students.' Heathcote knew that teaching is an 'open skill' that is demonstrated minute by minute in response to the changing circumstances of the classroom. She had a realistic understanding of the complexity of these interactions and the unpredictability of their outcomes, as well as the risks that might arise from this unpredictability. She encourages teachers to watch children at play and become comfortable with them. Are they able to assess the social health of their students accurately and modify their interactions accordingly? How do they view their students? Do they see them as clay, flowers, candles, echoes, friends, adversaries, crucibles, machines or vessels? Each different view of the child will offer a different kind of learning experience.*

*It is interesting that this is one of the last papers in which she uses the word 'improvisation' to describe her practice, defining it as 'essentially living at life-rate, in the present, with an agreement to pretend'. Excellence in teaching and the capacity to generate authentic learning experiences will always depend on attention to detail and the ability to negotiate with significance. To achieve excellence as a teacher may not seem a realistic aim, but to aspire to excellence is a worthy objective.*

*This is an edited version of the chapter published in* Collected Writings. *It was first published in 1978 in the New Zealand journal* Education.

## Relating to people

What do we mean when we say, 'That is an excellent teacher'?

For me, an excellent teacher is one who knows the difference between relating to things and relating to people. Both need great skill, but the greatest skill lies in how we relate to people.

If I am to aspire to excellence as a teacher, I must be able to see my pupils as they really are. I mustn't discourage them – I must accept them. This means adjusting myself to my pupils, and seeing things from another standpoint.

I must also preserve an interest in my students and, in this way, grasp something of their potential. I must see what they are in the process of becoming. When children come to us with labels – 'a slow learner', 'a non-reader' – we tend to shut our minds to change: but the ability to preserve an interest in children prevents teachers from stereotyping them in all sorts of ways.

As an excellent teacher, I must not be afraid to move out of my centre and meet the children where *they* are. The ability to go forward to meet people gives me the opportunity to vary my approach and my responses. If I do this, I will not be afraid to try unfamiliar things, because I'm not afraid of being rejected. Rejection is not part of trying to meet someone. Even if some rejection must take place, let that be of the *idea* and not of the *person*. I think we – the teachers and the pupils – often feel rejected in school when it's really our ideas that are being rejected.

I must also have the ability to see the world through my students, and not my students through the world. This ability can give a teacher a new perception, a renewal of energy and teaching style; there is a sort of regeneration when suddenly a class shows you a whole new way of looking at something.

As an example of this, I might describe what happened recently when I was working with some young men in a borstal institution.[1] I was in the tricky position of making the borstal boys take the role of prison officers while their prison officers sat watching us. I hoped that the boys would treat my prisoner just as their prison officers had been treating them. So I became an official from the Bureau of American Indian Affairs, and I put them in charge of Ishi, the last surviving member of his tribe. Ishi had really been found earlier this century on a railway station, and the bureau had decreed that this man – ill, sick, forlorn, speaking tongues nobody had ever heard – was to be put in the local jail until such time 'as he should be made city-like, and civilized'. Of course, the boys defied all my desires to get Ishi put in the jail. They said, 'You're not putting him in jail. We'll build him a house.' And they built him one – without any windows. I protested at this, but they insisted, and I realized we were looking at the house from two different points of view: for them it gave privacy, and for me it was a prison. I'm still pondering why they did it. Perhaps it was something to do with the fact that I couldn't look in and peer at Ishi. The fact that he couldn't see out either made no difference. It was what I might do to him that mattered. To understand this, I had to look at their house through their eyes, not through mine.

But, as a teacher who seeks excellence, I must also have the ability not to be lessened by my students, to withstand them, to use my own eyes sometimes, and be myself. One of the ways of avoiding being lessened is to refuse to give back what the pupils give you, especially if they are uncooperative. So often, it is easier to play tit-for-tat and be lessened.

I must have the ability to withstand certain pressures. I must be able to say, 'I respect how it looks from your point of view but I'm not giving in, because I can explain why I want it my way.' It's often easier to let the children get away with it, because it's too tiring to keep battling on. But the real battle is for a higher quality of response. I feel this ability to withstand is to know something of the clarity of one's purposes.

The ability to resist is a little like the ability to withstand. While withstanding may be to hold the status quo, resisting is to demonstrate, 'No further! That's it!' I've had to spend a lot of energy in my teaching to create circumstances in which I can resist without pain, either to me or to the class. All my strategies enable me to create a disciplined world and to find ways of using power without it being my power. Frequently I use the power of the subject to discipline a group. I say, 'It demands this of us' – not 'I demand this of you.' By resisting people, you help them to find guidelines and boundaries which can begin to function for all of us. Sometimes these boundaries are painfully constraining, and sometimes these moments when one says 'No further!' are very risky. There are times when I know a group of children could just laugh me out of the room, because, from where they stand, I am an idiot in an idiotic system. But then it's necessary to stand there saying, 'Why do you laugh and tear your own work down?', when it would be so much simpler to laugh with them and get out of the room safely.

If I wish to be an excellent teacher, I must also have the ability to dominate the scene for my students when it is necessary, and in the guise of one thing, do another, so that the pupils can grow. This is where you take risks in order to gain, where you approach the work by guile, by the delicate use of lures, and use oblique approaches to attain your goals.

I'll give you an example of how domination worked with delinquent boys. I once went to my class in a school, taking my three-month-old daughter with me. I walked in and, for some crazy reason, I expected the class to be doing *Julius Caesar*, because that's what the timetable said. So I wheeled the pram gaily in and was met by a line of black-browed, beady-eyed morons. There was anger all over that room! So, of course, I said, 'Oh, I thought we were doing *Julius Caesar*', and they glowered in return.

This was one day when I dominated – I was very tired at the end of it! I looked one of the boys in the eye and said, 'There *are* days like today. Why don't you have a pint on me?' And I offered him one. The lad took it (thank God he *did* take it!) and I drew pints all round and dominated the situation. The clouds did not lift, but the pints were not thrown back in my face.

So then I had to find a way of showing that I valued what they had done in just letting me be in the room with them. I said, 'You think *you've* got troubles? Have you seen my brat? I'm not going to see *her* father again. You think you've got troubles? Not one of you signs that notice saying you don't want my pub to close. It's going to shut next month. You've come in here and drunk my beer, but you'll let me lose my job, won't you?'

And they said, '*We* didn't know it was going to shut. We didn't even know it was going to open.'

'Ah, well it is, and not one of you've signed the notice, have you?'

'Well, we *would* have signed it, if we'd seen it.'

'I've heard *that* before.'

And then I stopped and said, 'There must be somebody worse off than us. Somewhere in the world there must be somebody worse off than me and this brat, and you with all your troubles. Tell you what, come to the bar, and don't tell the fellow next to you what's up with you, but see if you can find out what's up with him.'

And the crowd of black gloom drifted over to the bar (the teacher's table), and I stood there pulling pints, sloshing them down, and groaning about my brat. And I asked if they had found out anything about each other, and I heard incredible things. 'I've had a row with the wife this morning,' and, 'I've drunk all me wages,' and so on. And so the moaning and groaning went on. (They should have been doing *Julius Caesar* but I didn't dare draw their attention to that fact, because the gloom would have come down again.)

I said 'I wonder if anybody *could* come in here who was worse off than us.'

And one lad thought a bit and said, 'Yes, a tramp could come in here; a tramp that's got nowt could come in here.'

'Do you want to be a tramp that's got nowt?'

And he said 'Ay'.

And he put on a sacking coat and walked up to the counter that didn't exist, and I reached up and gave him a pint in one of the better glasses. He took the pint and had just begun to drink it, when I looked at one of the other lads and asked, 'Now what made him come in here, into this gloomy hole? I mean, we're all standing here like cheese at fourpence and yet he comes in here. There's nowt to cheer him up in here.'

And the tramp said something that was really to open all our eyes: 'All the other pubs have music.'

An amazing new view – it was quiet in here! And at that point I said, 'Well, the reason it's quiet in here is because we're doing *Julius Caesar*. We are, you know! And what's more tomorrow one of these silly devils is going to fight at Philippi. And the bloody generals are arguing over eighty bloody drachmas. And it's you and me that's going to be fighting at Philippi.'

And at that point, we became drunken ... e, we got on to the way ordinary private soldiers ... never come into the front line.

You know, that's as good an introducti... ... bout an hour, but I think it's a good example o...

As an excellent teacher, I must be able t... ... their power. This negotiation, this exchange of ... ...n are damaged too much in school, they won't ... want you to keep it, because that way they can ... ith her about. I can't do it the way she wants it do... ... to take power, and then give you back a bit, and t... ...a shame that we've set up our schools so that child...

But all this can be achieved only when ... attention to others and be slow to make judgements. ... a matter of respect.

Paying attention starts when I begin worki... ...alk in, how they look at each other. Do I see elements of se... ... other? This boy is tired-looking; that girl looks as if she's had a bad knock. I can't judge whether I'm right, but I can pay attention and, in so doing, recognize a little of the conditions of people.

The ability to withhold judgement is often seen as ambivalence in a teacher. We all know a teacher who never makes up her mind whether some student is good or bad. Why can't she? She *must* know! And often a lack of rigour is the reason why such teachers fail to make judgements. They have no proper standards by which to measure people. But one can be desperately wrong if one moves too soon.

Being slow to make judgements allows me constantly to renew my view of each pupil and to update it. I think this is one of the hardest things we must train ourselves to do if we aspire to excellence in teaching. We should stop believing things other people tell us about children, stop taking things for granted, stop saying that because we once knew nasty Jimmy Jones, and *his* eyes were close together as well, so *this* lad's going to be the same. One of the most rejuvenating

things is to give everyone a fresh start each morning. The ability to do this is part of the condition of innocence. I think innocence has a chance of bringing with it enormous gaiety and
trust, so that you walk into the classroom clean every morning, however mucky you are at the
end of the day.

## Relating to self

### Before we can relate to people successfully, we must first come to terms with ourselves

To keep my teaching in trim, I must first be able to look straight at myself and take my own
measure. I must be almost obsessed with myself. This isn't as selfish as it sounds, because, if
I know what I am, then I know what is needed to renew myself. Otherwise, I go into the
classroom tired, and I'm not paid to go into a classroom tired. Some people seem born tired,
and some people seem to become tired, but in the long run, nobody's going to make you tired
except yourself.

The ability to be obsessed by ourselves seems to me to be a marvellous gift. We are constantly
concerned and interested in ourselves – 'How funny! I wonder why I feel like *that* today.'

I don't think this is a bad thing. It leads towards interest in the outcome of how we feel
and what we see ourselves to be. We can use this interest in the classroom to see ourselves
through children's eyes. I remember that lovely story in Laurie Lee's *Cider with Rosie*, where
he says that he was furious with the teacher the first day he went to school, because she told
him to 'stand there for the present', and he never got the present!

Being obsessed with ourselves enables us to see what renews us, and so be able to renew
ourselves, and to accept the palliatives we need. I think we have to learn which palliatives
regenerate energy, and forgive ourselves, and use them with temperance. One palliative I
require is just five minutes to cook in peace. I also need to see that I am prepared for my
work. But I don't need the palliative of a long sleep – I can get up ever so early, as long as I
have a few minutes at the end of the day to take some sort of action in another direction: my
palliative is to change action. Another of my palliatives is my sewing. I think if we took more
heed, very consciously, of the kind of things that give us long holidays (because I don't think
it's necessarily long holidays that give us long holidays), we could experience a great gulf of
rest. Just the lifting of the pressures then makes us ready for something else.

Then we have the energy to work at ourselves. This, to me, is very important. My mother
used to say, 'Nay, I'd rather work out than rust out.' I believe the same.

I see working at myself as the ability to examine the journey of my life, to constantly review
it, and to perceive where I'm at in it. I foresee my death and I look forward to it, not in a
morbid sort of way, but by constantly recognizing my humanity. I seem to get a certain amount
of restoration when I look at the many parts of me and wonder what ancestor each part came
from. I find it infinitely exciting to look at children in this way too, even if one hasn't known
their fathers and mothers, and to realize that they are the product of so many forerunners.

Teaching demands that we give ourselves fully to the task in hand. To do this means that we
must be complete and completely self-knowing. This demand is one of the gifts of teaching that
isn't necessarily talked of by the unions. It is a repayment to a teacher that no one mentions.
And being forced to concentrate on the task in hand means that we can often temporarily forget
all the other things that are bothering us. There aren't a lot of jobs like that.

We need, too, to allow ourselves to be restless spirits − to be in the process of becoming. I don't mean darting about like a gadfly, trying first this innovation and then that. I'm talking about the spirit that says, 'I can see where they're at − I'll show them the next hill.' It's the restlessness that, while confirming what is understood, leads on to the next mystery. I find that very exciting.

But, in all this, we must have the ability to be ourselves and not a facade of ourselves. If we are ourselves, then we have the ability to accept the limitations of our situation. We don't have to agree to these limitations, but we can accept them until we can do something about them. This is why I'm a pain in the neck to people when I come to lecture for them. They say, 'What sort of a room would you like to use?' and I say, 'I don't mind. As long as it has a roof over it, it'll do.'

'Would you like a blackboard?'

'Well, I must have a blackboard.' (All other limitations can disappear, as long as I've got something I can write on and rub out on!)

'How big a class would you like?'

'Well, I don't mind.'

'What age of class?'

'Well, I don't really mind.'

'What would you like to do with them?'

'I don't really mind.'

You see, if we don't ask for a special set-up, then we have to be ourselves, for we have nothing else to draw on. Then we see what drives us, what kinds of teaching space and noise and discipline we can and cannot stand; and what our concerns in the classroom really are.

By being ourselves in this way we are able to affect others and to be affected by them. On days when all my skills function happily, I am in a condition of excellence. I am all right with myself.

But is achieving excellence in teaching a realistic aim? It seems to me that the reality is in aspiration, and that aspiration to excellence is a reality. Excellence still exists, and it always did. But the conditions that promote excellence rarely exist, and they rarely have. So we have a choice whether, in conditions which often scarcely contribute to excellence, to choose to aspire to it. We can practise choosing; we can renew and review our choice. We make our choices on excellence daily, minute by minute, each choice dictating the next. You can't reach excellence for a whole day; you can only reach it minute by minute. And this is one of the excitements of teaching − the constant exhilaration of recognizing the choice we have made at any moment. When we stop choosing, things go radically wrong with us.

In this work, drama, what we are trying to do is to make ordinary experiences significant, and that's a hard thing. That is the excellence we strive for. To distort experience into significance means that we have to get children to pay attention, and they may not have the vocabulary for it. I don't mean spoken vocabulary − they may not have practised the ability to pay attention. They do practise it privately, because they pay attention to the things that concern their survival, such as the mood their parents are in, or what'll happen if they hit the cat, or read that book that they shouldn't, or go out with their mates when they're supposed to be doing their homework.

All these things *make* them pay attention. But there's something a bit odd about saying to children, 'I'll create this depicted world so that you can pay attention to it.' Children often don't have experiences to make that work. And so we need the skill of high-level negotiation to help the classes we work with pay attention when we try to distort matters into significance for them. To do this we have to be able to create significance, and we cannot do this if we teach casually. We can only create moments when children stumble upon an authentic experience if we teach with attention to detail and its relation to the whole. This is the root of excellence. We sold our young teachers down the river when we told them to be nice and easy with the kids, and casual and friendly. We sold our profession down the river. In trying to get rid of distance and formality, we got rid of significance. If I could give young teachers anything, I would give them the ability to negotiate with significance. This, to me, is what high-quality endeavour means.

## Note

1 A borstal institution was a type of youth detention centre in the UK. The borstal system was abolished in 1982 and replaced by youth custody centres.

# THRESHOLDS OF SECURITY

*In this paper Heathcote addresses the needs of teachers who may be approaching drama for the first time. Although she never trained as a teacher and never held a teaching position in a school, Heathcote is extremely realistic about the challenges facing every teacher in the classroom. She points out that before any of us can relate successfully to others, we must first come to terms with ourselves and with our own needs. She reminds us that we teach as the people we are, and we need to meet the students as they are. Our humanity should not be separated from our teaching. It is our ability and willingness to be our authentic selves in the classroom that will lead to rewarding interactions, engagement and learning.*

*Heathcote recognizes the reality of the classroom and understands that other teachers are unlikely to possess her degree of skills or experience. She insists that to be effective in the classroom it is necessary for teachers to work within their own security levels and deals with what she regards as the fundamental matters that must be considered if teachers are to learn how to use drama effectively. All of the security thresholds she describes are intended to encourage teachers to reflect on their own individual strengths and weaknesses and recognize their own needs so they can serve the needs of their students more effectively. She explains her own choices in terms of class size and the kinds of space she finds comfortable before analysing a sequence of such choices and their outcomes.*

*She notes the fact that all teachers possess a variety of teaching registers as part of their 'survival kit' in their day-to-day interactions with students. Drama offers greater flexibility in the range of registers the teacher may use. Elsewhere she lists them:*

- *the narrator, who helps to set the mood and keeps an account of events;*
- *the deliberate opposer of the common view, who gives feedback and promotes clarity of thought;*
- *the positive withdrawer, who 'lets them get on with it';*
- *the suggester of ideas, as a group member;*
- *the supporter of tentative leadership;*
- *the 'dogsbody', who provides material and resources;*
- *the one who reflects the children's ideas back to them so they can assess them;*
- *the arbiter in argument;*
- *the deliberately obtuse one, who needs to be informed;*
- *the one who believes that the children can do it.*[1]

*This chapter is an edited version of 'Drama and Education: Subject or System?' in Johnson, L. and O'Neill, C. (eds.) (1984)* Dorothy Heathcote: Collected Writings on Education and Drama, *London: Hutchinson. It was first published in Dodd, N. and Hickson, W. (eds.) (1971).* Drama and Theatre in Education, *London: Heinemann.*

What do all teachers hold in common? We can assume the wish to communicate, or at least the responsibility for communication (if only of the one-way type). One can also assume interest in the subject area, presumably a modicum of concern with assessment of what has been communicated, together with some basic training for the job and the need to survive in the job. No one teaches a teacher how to teach. Teachers are made in the classroom during confrontations with their classes, and the product they become is a result of their need to survive and the ways they devise to do this.

One should be prepared to define one's terms. For the present purpose I will define a teacher as 'one who creates learning situations for others'. That is, a person whose energies and skills are at the service, during the professional situation, of the students.

I am concerned with two main aspects of teaching: the first is the way a teacher confronts the class and the way the two-way flow of communication takes place. This is the living, vibrating matter of teaching, firmly based upon mutual respect by each for the other's contribution. In the classroom setting the communication system between teacher and student is elemental. Communication is the centre of the educative system.

The second point concerns the areas of security that the teacher gradually acquires and depends upon in the job. Teachers need to understand their own security in order that they may gradually push back these security needs and accept more tenuous positions so that eventually they may teach from positions of *calculated risk*. I believe very few teachers discover their true teaching thresholds because of the pressure of timetables and a curriculum that prevents the discovery of a natural teaching pace and rhythm. This applies equally to the students. Many may never come to terms with their learning rate until after their school life is over.

The security thresholds for the teacher seem to include:

## The noise threshold

If we are going to teach at all well in any circumstances (and here I am not referring only to drama), we must understand the kind and the quality of noise we can take and the point at which we cannot take it. 'Are you comfortable in class when children discuss and leave you out of it?', 'What if children argue back, or shout at each other across you, or are shifting furniture?' are questions that are relevant here. Some teachers are very uncomfortable under one or other of these circumstances, and it would be wiser and more efficient for them never to become involved in such situations. Some are uncomfortable with even an appearance of disorganization. Headmasters looking through windows may have a very powerful effect upon that particular threshold!

## The space threshold

I make my contacts most comfortably when classes are close together and near to me. Others need to teach at a distance. This does not make either one a better or worse teacher. Value judgements are irrelevant here; the main consideration is that teachers understand why they teach at the distance they elect to use and the consequent effects of this choice. For many years I wondered at my stupidity in creating crowded situations until I understood this requirement and now can accept and employ it positively. I have to create situations in which classes can first throw their behaviour in my face in order that I may make an assessment of needs and therefore of starting points.

Also, for drama, I require that a class be made to feel like a group. Desks isolate individuals. Therefore my instinct is to discard them unless I need individual differences to emerge. Then I hurry to the desks in order that that behaviour may emerge. Eye impact and eye feedback are important. The teacher who needs the class to look (and feel) like a small number in a large space functions very differently from the one who prefers a class to seem a large group in a relatively small space. In fact both of these are valuable experiences at relevant times. Once this is consciously understood, changes may be made to employ both experiences when they best serve the needs of the class, of the material, and lastly of the teacher who may be more ready to risk-take because of this conscious knowing.

Teachers often request empty space for drama, but all areas are space; only some are interrupted upwards by pillars, cupboards etc., some symmetrically by desks, others circularly by floor patterns or lighting arrangements. Some may focus towards one end. The teacher and class will have a subjective response to all these factors which can be most profitably employed if they are consciously recognized in drama work so that strengths and weaknesses of form, for the purpose in hand, may be exploited or circumvented.

## The size of group threshold

While relationships are still tenuous, I require my classes to function as one group. For some people this is the least happy or convenient grouping. I require the large group for my personal comfort, because I need to make personal contact of eye and voice. I also require an immediate feedback of response (good or bad) from them in order to test the relationship and feel the temper of the class. Even when I first began teaching, I used this large grouping. The important question is what sizes of groups give you security? Often when teachers are in training or first attempt drama, the situation becomes closed just at the time when it should remain open. For example, advice is often given that one should begin working with small groups or even individuals or pairs, the assumption being that these latter are easier to deal with. In fact, to be realistic, the size of the group is entirely dependent upon the subjective view of the teacher. The medium is so flexible that it can begin anywhere and function under all circumstances. Every other rule is irrelevant at this point.

Once some security is gained, the size of groups can be directly related to the aim and purpose of the work. A whole class working upon a market situation will bring, receive and face totally different experiences from when working in pairs. It should be possible to help a teacher understand the differing consequences of saying, 'Find a partner and work this out', 'Divide into groups', 'Everybody is going to be the same character', 'Go away and lay out your market stalls', 'Find your houses', 'Listen to this story and then act it', 'Start with these words', 'Don't go in there.' It should also be possible to help a teacher understand the difference between progression that aims at burnishing the drama and that which undertakes to burnish the children. Both are sensible educational aims but there is no doubt in my mind which has priority, though sometimes the play may appear to be more important.

A further testing aspect of grouping emerges during periods of discussion. Some teachers require students to communicate through them. Otherwise they feel a loss of control when the children turn aside and speak to each other with consequent loss of audibility for the teacher. Trying to ensure that every word is heard by everyone else, except under specific circumstances, leads to loss of efficiency and boredom. Personally I am most secure when the students are ignoring my presence, discussing among themselves, and enabling me to tune in to the temperature and attitudes of their work and the messages I can receive through ear and eye. Thus I am informed of their next need. I can quickly get the gist of the discussion simply by asking. I gain much of my information about groups through identification and empathy and rely less upon verbal interchange. The main thing is that we need to know what we rely on, so that we can structure to get what we require, first for our security, and later in order to risk-take.

## Decision-making and leadership thresholds

Some basic questions here seem to be: How do you structure for leadership? Do you appoint your trustworthy and reliable ones proven by time? On what occasions do you require that you retain leadership yourself? At what stage, and why, will you challenge weaker personnel to lead? When don't you mind which person emerges? Obviously all these situations are of value for different purposes. The secure teacher can employ them all efficiently and skilfully and build in the security of a satisfying result for the class. All this is related to the types and degrees of selection a teacher can allow a class while still retaining a feeling of security, and also to the way decisions are taken. I need my classes to decide upon the material to be used in order that I may discover what types of themes interest them and at what level they need to work and how they will become involved. I also believe that decision-taking is an important educational experience and one means of ensuring involvement.

Group decision-taking is not easy but there is nothing quite so revealing of either the needs or resources of any community as making this demand. Drama involves groups in a vast range of decision-taking, and progression in this field is related to increasing subtleties of feeling, perception, language, social adjustment and drama expertise. I want my classes to learn to make decisions and to understand the problems and rewards of these decisions, so I regard it as my prime task to ensure that they clearly understand the choice between possibilities, the nature of the decision taken and the demands likely to be put upon them because of that decision. This is another reason why drama is such a wonderful educational tool.

## The subject interest of the teacher

This clearly will be shaped by the intellectual and emotional capacities of the teacher's personality, the quality of training received and the particular approach. It is obvious that the teacher's own interests in the field may be entirely irrelevant to those of the class. In drama it is especially important that teachers have no rigid rules about how to begin, what material is suitable, at what level it will be employed, and which dramatic forms are most acceptable and rewarding at any age. As the teacher and the class learn to use themselves and their ideas, and increase their capacity to grapple with and understand the medium of drama, further development is likely to be limited if the teacher begins by using rigid rules.

## Evaluation and standards thresholds

This relates to the ways teachers observe and the things they value and therefore look for as they observe their students. Some retire or withdraw in order to see their classes at work;

others intrude. Some identify; others enquire. A class involved in drama will throw up so much behaviour and so many teaching opportunities that it is impossible to observe everything or to seize upon everything. So it is essential that the teacher learns to be highly sensitive in observing the relevance of what is thrown up and to perceive the class's needs through their behaviour. This penetration of the surface facts in order to reach the relevant data is highly important, because the teacher stimulates and feeds the hidden or disguised elements in classes' or individuals' behaviour through drama work.

Another important area of observation is that of clearly seeing (that is, without bias and minus the blinkers of the teacher's previously devised intent) the present group, its mood and possibilities at any given moment. A clear example of this was seen when a boy with learning difficulties was rummaging through a dressing-up box to choose clothes suitable for a slave driver in King Herod's entourage. He selected a hangman's black mask and cap. If the teacher's response had been 'Wrong period; must intervene', how much would have been buried which was just on the point of emerging? In choosing the black mask and cap the boy was crystalliz-ing his ideas and feelings. The teacher waited, saw the boy work in the clothes in the drama and observed the enlarged attitudes that brought a sureness of approach to the boy and drew a clear response from the 'slaves' to the visual threat he fed them. At some stage the anachronism may be pointed out and a compromise made but the child's need should dictate the timing of this. This boy eventually said in response to an interest being shown in his choice of clothing, 'I'm not bringing these women much life, am I?' And thus some of the reasoning behind his choice became clearer to the boy, the class and the teacher. He had taken a reading of the situ-ation of which he was capable at that moment and this is at once both the very stuff and oppor-tunity offered by drama in education: to permit present readings to be exposed and explored and through that permission to widen into more subtle and generously based readings.

So, in the action of the drama these experiences become exposed for consideration – either by audiences, if that is the final objective, or by the group only, if that is the purpose of the work. The teacher needs to be unprejudiced and receptive to a vast range of readings, helping the situation by receiving, challenging, assisting in developing ideas and above all creating and preserving attitudes of receptivity, non-value judgements and artistic integrity in the students.

Surely it should be possible for us to devise situations whereby teachers may learn how to do this filtered through their own personalities. Because of my personality, much of the drama my classes work on is sociologically based, as I see a class of children trying to work together as a social group, so I give a strong lead in this area with a correspondingly weak one in others.

## Teaching registers

All teachers develop a range of registers as part of their survival kit. The difficulty is to be aware of the uses made of them and their real value to the teacher. Drama reflects registers of approach to and confrontation with other persons at times of change or crisis. Therefore the teacher requires sensitivity in this area and in particular must have a conscious command of the register used in confronting classes and understand the reasons for the selection at any given time. It is dangerous in any teaching situation to employ the 'I'm telling you' register too often – in drama situations it is suicidal. What of teacher as catalyst? (When I switch on the red light, 'it' has begun.) As reassurer? (Don't worry, put yourself in my hands.) As devil's advocate? (That's surely not true.) As good listener? (Good idea. What happens then?)

Register is related to authority and impact, and all teachers need to know what kinds of authority they dare not or cannot forgo at any price. The teacher with a range of authorities and ways of asserting them can employ them to serve the needs of the various classes rather than the teacher's own needs. For example:

1. *The authority of role.* 'I have my river pilot's licence and I am empowered by law to escort this boat and crew to the harbour bar.'
2. *The one who knows.* 'When you've decided what you require, I'll help you to find out about it.'
3. *The teacher leader.* 'I'm in charge here.'
4. *The authority of being in a position to switch roles.* To run with the hare and hunt with the hounds. Children rarely consider that they could also do this!

For me the most secure authority has always been from within the drama situation rather than the teaching one – the authority of role. Not only can I be more flexible in the use of registers, but also I am fearful of relying on teacher authority. I mistrust my ability to cope with situations that might arise where the teacher is in opposition to the class. The role authority gives me shifting power and a variety of registers to be at the service of the class. I may suddenly gather authority to deny or accede to requests, or lose power but have strong opinions or resist a class in order to strengthen its opinions and decisions. My belief in my attitudes supports their belief in theirs, but this type of teaching takes courage at first and is always a calculated risk.

A further facet of the authority spectrum is that of status and stature. Teachers who 'can be wrong' are likely to last longer and go further! This question of status is the most basic question of all and requires attention when we train teachers and not only for drama, though because drama brings the child's subjective life into the classroom, the problems of status and stature are thrown up very quickly and the teacher requires support and preparation to deal with them.

How does drama function as an educational medium? Improvisation is essentially living at life-rate, in the present, with agreement to pretend. Dramatic activities are concerned with crisis, the experiences of life, small or large, which cause people to reflect and pay attention. The role-taker draws upon all previous relevant experience, all information, factual and subjective, abilities, failings, blind spots and skills, character and personality. Thus when seeking to understand the 'pretend' situation, the role-taker draws all relevant information to the surface and puts it into action, while interacting with others who are also in the same situation. The important difference between real life and this make-believe life is that in the latter there is the opportunity for one problem to be faced at a time so that selectivity becomes possible, and different permutations of response may be tried.

As I stated before, it is prejudice that usually emerges first and often at first this is reinforced. I believe the teacher must accept this hazard, but also be prepared to do something about it in due course. However, the first drama discipline for the teacher is to accept the present condition of the group as revealed by their work. A group of boys chose to rob a security car, bringing to their work all their notions about the police, property, wilful damage and right and wrong. No one was arrested, even though the police saw the robbery – it was not within the boys' capacity to give the police the upper hand, even though their real condition, living in an approved school,[2] was living testimony to the true position. As teacher I saw no point at all in forcing the issue, other than offering a mild challenge to the authenticity of the situation, for groups must forge their own truths for themselves. It is therefore essential in educational drama that the teacher becomes skilled in helping to reveal the currently emergent truth to the group creating it.

All too often we plan the immediacy of the moment right out of the picture so that persons can never be confronted by themselves. We plan so that people know what they ought to do next, whereas in fact we should plan so that they discover what they did do next. The element of surprise is one of the most important bases of work in educational drama.

For classroom purposes the values of drama seem to me to be these: it is sociologically based, employing individuals within groups and the interaction of their active processes; it is also play-based, having a defined area of intention (as in games – a football team knows it will not end up playing at darts!) and employing elaboration. We often deny our students elaboration time. In fact it is often prevented by the teacher's own worry or impatience. Elaboration experience probably contributes more than anything else to the process of becoming a mature person.

The rules of drama are definite but they are so infinitely flexible and basic that they offer a very wide range of elaboration. In football the brilliant player 'plays' the rules to their limit and good drama experience is as concerned with its rules as with the exploitation of them. So improvisation is really an elaboration procedure that employs all relevant knowledge – factual and emotional information – and tests it in action.

Theatre is a game of elaboration within a strict framework of intent. Drama is not a teaching process in the conventional sense. It comes about by a series of confrontations between persons and their ideas. The game provides the safe framework for such confrontations. One of the reasons why teachers may experience a feeling of failure in using these procedures is that they either do not understand or fail to perceive the initial phenomenon of group inertia. A group of persons gathered together, facing another person, generate a kind of inertia of expectancy and look to the one isolated person (the teacher) to solve it. We must consciously train our teachers not only to expect it as a natural phenomenon but to deal with it fruitfully and at least cost to themselves. The first element in solving this group inertia problem is that of having a wide range of focus to offer. The group must become focused in order that it may begin its work. Out of this focus can emerge that moment of arrested attention that launches that work. So the teacher projects energy first to focus attention, and then to direct it towards the defined area of intent. It is at this stage that teachers must know the size of groups, spaces and other risk areas they are prepared to cope with at this moment. To clarify this let us take an ordinary classroom situation that often arises. We will define the teacher's thresholds thus:

1.  *Space* – There is only a classroom with moveable but not stackable desks. The teacher prefers a hall.
2.  *Noise* – Another teacher on one side of the classroom prefers *not* to hear the dramatic work! The drama teacher tries to respect this and anyway worries a bit if the children begin talking or moving rather freely.
3.  *Decisions* – The teacher prefers to plan but is learning to risk just a tiny bit. However, as yet he always introduces the idea they will work on.
4.  *Size of group* – The teacher prefers children to work in groups of about five but is aware that the classroom makes this rather difficult to achieve.

5.  *Teaching registers* – The teacher likes to be friendly but the children know the voice of authority that appears when they take too much into their own hands. For example the teacher will always prevent a 'fight' developing, see it 'a mile off' and deflect it, unless it can be planned and known in advance for example – (a) who will win, (b) how many will take active part, and (c) what all the others will be doing. The class is a group of lively ten year olds – equally divided between boys and girls – and the teacher is male.

6.  *Understanding of the medium* – He realizes the significance of selecting a problem, but is not yet good at or swift in helping children's own ideas to take the lead but wants this to happen and recognizes the extra quality present in work where ideas and disciplines are acquired together.

7.  *Subject chosen* – The Easter Story because it might be pleasant to 'work it up' for the other classes to see. He knows it is exciting, especially the entry into Jerusalem, the Last Supper, the arrest in the Garden of Gethsemane, the trial and Peter's denial and finally the carrying of the cross. He sees that the material is relevant to girls and boys but he doesn't wish to foist a heavily moral viewpoint upon them.

Now, remember, he has as yet no space, he doesn't wish to make much noise, he doesn't want the children to become too excited but he *does* want to use this theme and initially with smallish groups. So he must find first a focus that is relevant to boys and girls so that their attention will be arrested. Because he wishes to work with small groups, he must have decided before he even opens his mouth whether he will choose mixed-gender groups or whether he will allow the boys and girls to select their own groupings. If he does this, he knows in advance that his groups will be composed of either all boys or all girls! So *that* must be settled before he decides that the time has come when girls and boys must start working in mixed small groups. He therefore must examine his theme to find a focus that requires mixed small groups.

*Any* theme will yield problems to suit any type and condition of class. These immediately leap to my mind if one looks at the Easter Story: families out in the evening in the Garden witness the arrest of Jesus, groups of soldiers and women at the well during the entry into Jerusalem, witnesses confronting Peter and accusing him, a disciple's family at any of these events, the room below that in which the Last Supper takes place with women preparing food and disciples occasionally entering to collect and return dishes and to report what is happening in the upper room. It can readily be seen that because of the teacher's group size and noise thresholds, most of the conventional visions of the Easter story must be bypassed. This is not necessarily a disadvantage but he must be extremely flexible in conjuring up small group areas to be explored. He will be at a distinct advantage in using small groups to explore some of the personal agonies, fears, and bewilderments arising out of the larger panorama of events, but he cannot do these large panoramic events, because he has 'cut his crowd scenes' by selecting small groups.

All of the small group scenes mentioned, however (and there will be hundreds of others within the theme – What of Joseph of Arimathea? Did his family welcome the idea of a notorious stranger occupying their beautifully constructed tomb?), may provide a nucleus of experiences which may be then fed into the larger panoramic view and this can be another advantage to him.

So before he meets his class, he must already have examined his theme to discover the size and intensity of his small-group problems. He then must present his theme through focus on 'family' situations. For example, should he choose to focus attention by using a picture, say, of the entry into Jerusalem or the Last Supper, he must *not* discuss the crowd situations. Instead he must lead immediately into a study of smaller 'kin' groupings (for example friends, families, shared feelings); otherwise his focus will be irrelevant to the development he can afford to permit. He has created for himself one enormous problem, which, if he does not realize it, will cause all the work to be hard graft instead of a pleasurable exciting evolution of ideas gradually crystallizing into form.

The problem is that because he has chosen small groups, he is placing an emphasis upon language in the main and to a certain extent upon the more subtle relationships and emotions. His ten-year-old students may be at a loss to do more than touch the fringes of these problems, and he and they may be disappointed and frustrated. One of the early tasks of the teacher is to create experiences of intensity (not necessarily of depth), because these are the ones that will commit the class to further work, because they give the feedback of instant success. Only the teacher can ensure that no failure is experienced – the group cannot. It is at once simpler and more economical to achieve this for the whole class. If we look at our Easter story again, which are the moments when intense experiences may be easily created? Usually these are easiest and most powerful when all the group are focused upon one aspect, for example a crowd watching a Christ carrying an obviously too heavy cross will have a reaction; whether it is obvious or not is irrelevant. A crowd watching a soldier take a crown of thorns, pass it amongst them, and then place it upon the head of Christ cannot avoid a kind of involvement, though it may be inactive. A crowd of happy citizens suddenly hearing the voices or marching feet of troops in the Garden in the evening will have their attention arrested even momentarily. If our teacher understands this, he will naturally see that tensions of this nature are within his small-group situations. It can readily be seen now that his focus, whether spoken, seen, handled or heard must have this element in it. Strangely enough, this element of experience is the one most often omitted; yet this is the very experience that will release energy to generate further similar experiences.

Another tool in the hands of our teacher will be his ability to employ a flexible range of linguistic registers. He does *not need* to be an actor or possess hundreds of dialects and accents in his repertoire but he does need to indicate attitudes, different strata in society, periods and style, by his own choice of words, tone, pitch and pause when he makes his contribution. *Remember we do not ask of the children that they act in the stage actor sense, only that they take up attitudes and viewpoints and for the time believe in them.* Ability in this area gives the teacher the opportunity to become one with the class, because he can without apparent effort select words which are in the children's own register, put them at their ease or draw their attention to what is necessary. A variety of registers is also essential for helping groups to capture mood, quality and type of tension, social strata of personnel, period and style, provided these are hints and not performances

I recall an extremely bright class of forty-two ten- and eleven-year-olds living on an ice planet called Isagon who developed an original verbal style in keeping with their culture, because as their leader I slightly stressed the 'S' sounds in words. This was taken up by them and gave rise to a whole new conception of motor development. We travelled via a type of hover-system and it arose entirely from the slight sibilance of my words.

The last important linguistic area is that of knowing what not to say and when not to speak – the hardest area of all. This is only achieved when our teacher is so secure that all his attention, except that necessary area of detachment that is his teaching lifeline, is focused upon the students and not upon his own image and status.

So we focus, then we define our area, then we elaborate and out of elaboration comes the next stage: the demand, which I believe is basic in all human beings, for form to be achieved. Again it is the teacher's responsibility to perceive when pressure towards form may be made and at what level that form may be achieved. A class of six-year-olds making a tournament achieved form by ordering the events, the places in which the events would happen, the processions to and from the winner's and loser's prizes and the harmony of the headdresses of the ladies. This was 'doing' form. A class of fourteen-year-olds, working on the voices of the Sybil in the cave, worked entirely on juxtaposing and texturing sound effects. Form in educational work must be achieved in conjunction with the needs of the class.

What is form? As with drama we all understand it when it happens. The first component would appear to be reducing miscellany to order. In drama this miscellany is all the variety of life experience available in the group, and their range of ideas for solutions to the current problems, all their differing ways of approach, and the way they actually perceive their work. Elaboration reveals the miscellany.

The second ingredient would appear to be a process of simplification. In *Imagination* Harold Rugg notes: 'The essence of creative activity lies in a simplifying process which automatically involves not only the selection and rearrangement of the available material but its modification in process of developing a simpler form'.[3] Form has been defined as a kind of organization to which nothing can be added and from which nothing can be taken.[4]

Third, form is 'fitness of purpose' of all the material contained in it. Form-making is not a process of finishing something; it is a forward moving procedure constantly simplifying, seeing more clearly. It is not a static repetition, for we can never exactly repeat an experience. Would it be worthwhile?

So in the creative work we have focus, definition, elaboration and form. There is a further area – that of maturation and completion. Maturation in educational terms seems to me to be 'the total end possible at this present time'. Some creative work can be preserved and lived with daily, met freshly and savoured over and over again – clay pots, short stories, paintings, recorded music, fabrics – and though these can be naturally set aside in favour of other visions, they are not lost things but ones that are no longer needed at the moment. Positive completion is a feature of living, and in the drama field it may take many forms. Showing to others, humbly or with great style, is the most often used.

Sometimes, however, the material achievement is such that it requires to be written up as a record (for example the class of girls working on a drama of 'How to select a husband' decided to create an advice column as the end product, crystallized into an economical film, developed into a series of lectures).

I find the best kind of guide to help me in considering material is a short basic list:

- drive (what makes a group want to do something);
- feedback (what satisfactions are achieved by doing it);
- signals (the range of communication within the group);
- rituals (the experiences which seem to be required to be made again and again);
- content (the level at which children can work).

The more flexibly teachers can learn to approach material the better, if only to achieve constant rejuvenation rather than diminution of self and their ideas. It is a matter of the teacher finding the level and area that will stretch a class, yet give satisfaction in those five areas of the list.

I have dealt with what I believe to be the fundamental areas we should be considering if we are to help teachers to employ drama creatively in school: to confront their thresholds in basic drama 'rules' in the classroom, and finally to choose material to use in relation to age and ability levels in classes. Good material serves all classes and circumstances. One selects an area of the material upon which to work that will serve the needs of the children. All material will be concerned with 'people, now'. Variations will be used depending upon the strata in society, and the verbal, emotional development and imagination of the class. Harold Rugg, again in *Imagination*, says:

> the principal function of imagination is to enable the human being constantly to build thought models of the real world. The inventor conceives in imagination new arrangements of his machine-parts to bring about described movements. The creative dancer conceives in imagination the right movements for the objectification of his or her imagined conception. The mathematician imagines alternative hierarchies of symbols of relationship.
>
> The steps involved in thinking point to the crucial role of the imagination: the capacity to delay responses; to manipulate symbols in imagination; to sense and hold the direction dictated by perception and recall; and to generalize, that is, to form and use concepts. The chief distinction between men and animals is this capacity to work out solutions to problems symbolically, in imagination. In Koestler's phrase, 'Artists treat facts as stimuli for imagination, whereas scientists use imagination to coordinate facts'.

So it would appear that in helping teachers we need to devise situations free of tension which will enable them to define their present teaching needs as far as thresholds are concerned, to understand as well as they may precisely what makes drama work, to be flexible in selecting, presenting and handling their material and to observe honestly their teaching results. Obviously the operative words in the above sentence are 'free of tensions', so value judgements and relationships concerned with status are not relevant here. Until we can train them so that they become open to receiving positively classroom experiences, teachers will go on teaching behind the closed doors of their classrooms. This means that teachers must be able to discover and healthily recognize their real strengths and also to understand those strengths and positive qualities that embody their darker sides – punctuality in a person can make them intolerant of others who are less time-conscious, for example; to teach as much by intake from their classes as by output to them; to forgive themselves for their failures and start afresh; to *structure* their drama lessons rather than plan the children's contribution out of them and so spend precious time trying to keep to the plan; to observe clearly what is really happening as the children dramatize; and lastly to bring to school not just their knowledge and information. This way the 'realness' in the teacher can keep alive and present the 'realness' in the children.

## Notes

1 'Dramatic Activity', in Johnson, L. and O'Neill, C. (eds.) (1984) *Dorothy Heathcote: Collected Writings on Education and Drama*, London: Hutchinson, p. 59.
2 A secure facility for young offenders.
3 Rugg, Harold (1963) *Imagination*, New York: Harper and Row.
4 Danz, Louis (1932) *The Psychologist Looks at Art*, New York: Longman, p. 80.

# CREATIVITY

*The teacher's function in the classroom can be a consistent but limited one – the one who knows and can therefore tell or instruct. Heathcote saw this function as too restricted and limiting. She believed that as long as teachers come to school to teach and students come to be taught, the creative energies of both are deflected and neglected. Paradoxically, if teachers could find a way not to use all their energies in merely instructing students, she felt that they would become free to operate creatively. The result would be that students would become less dependent on teachers and teachers would become free to exploit learning opportunities so that their knowledge and skills would be needed and welcomed.*

*Heathcote insisted that if we are to give more than lip service to creativity in children, we must actively support that of the teacher and come to recognize fully the creativity of good teaching.*

> *We want people who are original, creative, spontaneous, and innovative. But we want them to be produced by teachers whom we condemn in a hundred ways to be overworked and uninspired, unrespected and underpaid. So, also, we would like children – as a product – to be creative and to learn about creativity, while we make the best chance they have to learn and to respond to teaching as lacking in creativity as we possibly can.*
>
> *There is only one sure way to develop creativity in all the different kinds of children in our schools. We must cherish all the way through the creativity of those who have elected to become teachers because they want to teach, whether in the school and the teachers' college, in the way the teacher's job is set up, in the freedom granted to the teacher to teach while others perform the thousand chores which are no essential part of this task and this art, in the time given the teacher to read and explore and think and plan and search for new materials.*[1]

*In this edited version of a paper, written for the London Borough of Redbridge in 2010, Heathcote reflects on the challenges of teaching and compares it to a kind of alchemy. She describes an innovative approach to preparing teachers in training to encounter children in a safe and creative setting. The experience is aimed at giving student teachers the knowledge and confidence to understand and embark on that unique relationship that can exist between teachers and learners. The significance of close and accurate observation is made clear, as is the importance of teachers becoming capable of creating shared learning experiences with their students. For Heathcote the skills required to achieve this were not mysterious. They included:*

1.  *imagination;*
2.  *the ability to sense the general mood of a group;*
3.  *the capacity to put the children's needs before the teacher's plans;*
4.  *the ability to employ sensitive changes of register in communication with the group;*
5.  *the ability to* look *— to perceive the real situation;*
6.  *the ability to* listen *— to perceive the real statement.*[2]

*Heathcote considers the qualities of the creative personality and lists the characteristics of different kinds of teachers, all of whom have a contribution to make. She introduces her paper with a poem that could serve as a mission statement for her life's work.*

## Making involves transformation and alchemy

> To make something
> Requires a vision to serve a need.
> First the raw elements are taken,
> Then the process begins of
> Forming that which must work fitly for purpose.
> All making involves energy — of fire, water, tools,
> And the minds, will and sinews of humans serving
> To exploit and explore.
> So you here,
> Existing in your time,
> May continue the making and the forming
> In the service of our own kind. See that you
> Honour the earth's elements, and the mind's exploring purpose
> But remember always, Earth and Humankind serve each other,
> In order that all may flourish.

The very word 'creativity' frightens me; it is much overused like 'expert' and I suspect that it is biased towards the arts rather than the sciences. It seems that there is more evidence from the arts but I don't think they own the field by any means. I tried to find models to see if I understand the practice of being creative and to find some useful definitions. Dictionaries offered little help!

I remembered when I was working with some six-year-old 'scientists' in America who wanted to find a cure for cancer. Their desire led us into close observations, detailed explanations and using evidence. They cured their patients by winding them through rollers and were very pleased with themselves. Their next fictional assignment came from Mr Nixon (who was that very week to resign as President of the USA) and was to discover what was causing plants to get sick. You can fail as scientists with plants! Some of the teachers did not like either of these serious endeavours. Was I being 'creative' in switching from sick people to sick plants so that I could provide a protected experience for that group of six-year-olds where they could fail as scientists? And were they being creative when they suddenly accepted that the plants continued to fail and discovered seeds?

Are we being creative when we drive forward through an impasse? And does this impasse summon old knowing in a moment of illumination which throws a switch and suddenly two knowings fuse, because we will abandon one path and find another, seemingly at a tangent to the first? Being interested in teaching and therefore learning, I have an investment in seeking how we teachers may help ourselves to be creative thinkers and doers.

The negative image of creativity is that of the loner who veers towards destruction, so perhaps positive creativity follows the path of light – the instinct to give, share, seek contact and explore all around them, even as they stand out from the crowd. Michelangelo said, 'I saw the angel in the stone/marble and set him free.'

As a teacher I have to accept that the word is a gift word you cannot use to describe yourself. 'Teacher' is more than a functional title. It has leanings towards alchemy – that mix of parts that occasionally gives birth to new knowings in self and others. So some days I teach and now and again I feel myself to be a teacher. As teachers we make nothing tangible. We plant ideas, offer models, create links with seemingly disparate notions, differences and likenesses, patterns and formings, often comprehended through the tasks we perforce invent to enable understanding. We have one huge problem. We are rarely there when growth from a seed we planted is recognized by those we work with. This realization haunts us and gives rise to the black dog of lack of confidence in ourselves and others, and often in the people we teach.

So we need a wholeness in our teaching personae as well as an enthusiastic interest in the curriculum ideas that we use to engage our students. Teaching personae need attention. Schools are like beehives and the cells and types of workers within are many and various. Some teachers are good lecturers and synthesizers. Some work most 'creatively' as private tutors. Some are creative listeners who give inspiring feedback. Some are hunters and guides – research fellows. Some are outsiders who do not aspire to be teachers but who bring talents, attributes and knowledge that those within the beehive have long ignored. And some are journeymen, solid and reliable information planters.

If we could shift the pattern of clock, subjects, and one adult to each class, we might fulfil something of Sir Edward Hall's assertion:

> Education should be related with transformation rather than information only. To keep adding curriculum labels – more maths, physics, art, citizenship, world faiths, as separate subjects will not transform. Our schools have been deprived of soul – of spirituality – a sense of the grace of life.[3]

The architect Sir Richard Rogers has echoed this assertion, claiming that our years of schooling should be used to examine and enquire into citizenship and community, linking physics, biology, physiology, art and history. He believes that much of our quality of life as members of a community depends upon getting this right. The mantra 'learning how to learn' is at present singularly lacking in inner substance in explaining how to bring this about. I find myself relying on my own resources and it can feel daunting sometimes, partly because of the black dog of self-doubt which all teachers encounter when it is least expected. One of the steps towards trusting our own inventiveness or creativity is getting rid of two fears – that of children working in tribes who may rise up and challenge us, and our fear of failing in creating classroom tasks which engage them and provide learning outcomes.

Thinking about this paper reminded me of an experiment we carried out in Northumberland College during the first five days of a teacher education course. We wanted the would-be teachers to discover something of their own instincts for relating to children in a learning, teaching situation, so we brought in sufficient numbers of ten- and eleven-year-old children so that each teacher could work with one child.

The autumn weather was fine and the college grounds with mature trees, lawns and a stream, invited exploration. If rain came, the college with its resources was available and open for use. We tried to support the 'teachers', while avoiding the intrusion at this early stage in their careers of the expertise of their lecturers. There would be no overt instruction and all tutors would meet the students without any labels naming subject areas of interest. We aimed for encounters and reviewing of these, by sharing their personal responses and making plans for the next day's encounter based upon that of the previous day. The children stayed for one hour only at first. Towards the end of the week, the buses came for them after an hour and a half.

## Monday

Each student was to 'find a child' as they left the buses. After the hour spent with their child, we would be interested in:

1.   What system did they use to acquire their companion for the hour?
2.   What happened during the time?

They were provided with small notebooks to keep a brief journal of the week – a page for each day – of their impressions of these encounters, and any notes regarding what they had learned about their child after each encounter, as well as some development they thought they would find reasonable to consider in advance. They were also provided with a bag of pencils, crayons, papers, and a clipboard for their child to use, should the need arise, but they were not obliged to use these. The children came and went, and we settled down to find out how each adult had acquired their child.

Many and varied were the techniques:

* standing and smiling close to the bus;
* showing they had bags with interesting things in;
* rushing forward to be sure they captured their child;
* standing well back to survey the field and then approaching a 'lost' one;
* noticing who was left out and approaching them before they became nervous.

One or two confessed they looked for people who looked intelligent! Brave souls. From this first encounter they progressed through the remaining four days so that by Friday they had enabled their child to become their teacher.

## Tuesday

* What did the teacher do to pick up their Monday relationship?
* Did they continue the same activities begun on Monday?
* Did they bring any reminders? Or blandishments (i.e. lollipops!)?
* What development occurred from Monday's activities?
* Had they initiated these? On what basis?

## Wednesday

Each teacher was to have made a plan that could logically develop Tuesday's activities and discover in the process how they introduced and managed these developments. So before this meeting they had all planned a 'lesson' and listened to each other explaining their plans, and then they tested these plans at the Wednesday encounter.

## Thursday

Using Wednesday's experiences, they were asked to consider further developments and prepare any 'tools' they considered helpful, such as paints, books of any kind which were relevant, objects, scissors, rulers – indeed anything at all – even dry leaves and glue. Before this session ended, they were asked to plan with their 'colleague' something which they would try to learn by being taught by their child-teacher.

## Friday

And on Friday…they became 'pupils', helping their 'teacher' to help them learn. This help may have included having suitable materials ready. At the end of this session each pupil was given the original bag of pencils, papers and crayons, plus a short note written in advance as a 'thank-you letter' but *which would include positive truthful comments about the work shared and what they had perceived about their child's abilities*. There was also paper and an envelope addressed to themselves, for their child to write a note which would be forwarded to the college, so they would receive it in due course.

Throughout this week tutors provided listening and supportive comments with no instructions or expert subject advice beyond locating useful materials for the morning sessions. All the teachers discussed in groups – to save time – there were 80 of them – their experiences of the morning encounters. Tutors could comment in these group sessions, reminding them all that they had begun their discoveries about teaching and planning. The teachers consulted their journal papers and read to each other any interesting questions or observations they had recorded. These journals were then completed and the following week they were available in the college library to be read by each other if they wished. These short spontaneous journals were often referred to later, as the teachers began to recognize them as their first steps towards relating with a child, and seeing with hindsight what lay behind the 'teaching' decisions and preparations they made. Many important questions were first tentatively formulated on these few papers.

I planned this week's introduction to being a teacher because I am convinced that too many 'experts' too early in the process simply continue the propensity in our schooling system for students to become teacher-dependent. Early 'raw' safe encounters and the number in the class – one child – could perhaps begin the process of building in the would-be teachers some knowledge and the confidence to embark on that unique relationship between teachers and taught. Of course I do not know how this week affected the teachers that these young people grew into – the teacher's blight of 'delay in realization' and the 'black dog' again!

After the experiment some tutors regarded it as a foundation stone for the whole course, a reference point. Some were doubtful about the time spent and the apparent randomness of the work, plus the class size of one pupil only. They considered that nothing had actually been taught about teaching. Well, we've heard that often haven't we?

In *A Thomas Jefferson Education*, Oliver Van Deville cites the abilities which mark the independent creative learner:[4]

- the ability to define problems without a guide;
- the ability to ask hard questions which challenge prevailing assumptions;
- the ability to quickly assimilate needed data from masses of irrelevant information. It takes thinking to separate the important from the rest;
- the ability to work in teams without guidance;
- the ability to work absolutely alone;
- the ability to persuade others that your course is the right one, but to listen to those seeking to persuade you of theirs;
- the ability to reorganize information into new patterns;
- the ability to discuss ideas with an eye towards application;
- the ability to think inductively, deductively and dialectically.

Then he identifies these qualities which enter the domains of bonding and ethical morality, the soft sciences:

- the ability to establish, maintain and improve lasting relationships;
- the ability to keep one's life in proper balance;
- the ability to discern truth and error regardless of the source or the delivery;
- the ability to discern true from right;
- the ability and discipline to do right;
- the ability and discipline to constantly improve.

We teachers can create tasks from within contexts which will make opportunities for all participants, including ourselves, to focus upon and recognize the territories that drama opens up to us to explore.

## Notes

1  'Subject or System' in Johnson, L. and O'Neill, C. (eds.) (1984) *Dorothy Heathcote: Collected Writings on Education and Drama*, London: Hutchinson, pp. 61–79.
2  'Role-taking' in Johnson, L. and O'Neill, C. (eds.) (1984) *Dorothy Heathcote: Collected Writings on Education and Drama*, London: Hutchinson, p. 58.
3  Hall, E.T. (1959) *The Silent Language*, London: Anchor Books.
4  Van Deville, O. (2000) *A Thomas Jefferson Education*, Salt Lake City, UT: George Wythe College Press.

# PART II
# Drama in practice

# INTRODUCTION

The papers in this section deal with Heathcote's most significant and lasting contributions to the practice of drama in education. Among these contributions, Teacher in Role is a strategy that has had a profound effect on the work of drama teachers in many different settings throughout the world.

At first, Teacher in Role was often misunderstood and misapplied. However, it came to be recognized as a significant principle of teaching as well as a strategy for promoting learning, in which the power structure between students and teacher is perceived as negotiable. Teacher in Role is not just an efficient, intriguing and enormously useful strategy. It is also an economical way of initiating collaboration, of beginning to share power with the class. No invented world, whether in the theatre or in the classroom, can flourish without collaboration as its foundation. But it's important to note that this collaboration implies a 'sharing' and an 'exchange', not a 'transfer' of power. In the classroom, collaboration demands a change in the traditional relationship of teacher and students. Teachers who insist on holding onto all their accustomed power and authority are unlikely to achieve true collaboration.

Sometimes the greatest resistance to the concept of power-sharing comes from the students. They may oppose any alternative to the familiar and often undemanding power structure of the classroom, where the teacher is the main source of information and authority. They may refuse the invitation to accept any power, which means they are also resisting the engagement and responsibility that comes with that acceptance. But students' engagement and acceptance has to be voluntary.

> I realized that every single teaching strategy I've ever invented has been because I can't bear to be in a position where I have to 'tell people off'. If I reach that point I am breaking a deeply felt rule to do with power used to disadvantage. To get collaboration from classes, who really owe you no attention you haven't won, needs subtle and honest strategies, which forge bonds rather than confrontation.[1]

One type of resistance to collaboration is when the class tries to provoke the authority stance of teacher power by their behaviour. Another is what Heathcote vividly describes as a 'beady-eyed, rat-like spectatorship' – an apparently innocent conformity to the teacher while they make certain that she sees the privately shared sign for classmates. The teacher has to choose either to ignore this behaviour, which would be an inauthentic response, or to react with teacher power by coercing or threatening students. Teachers are often concerned that they will lose their authority as teachers by taking on a role in the drama. But as Heathcote points out, there are always two stances available to her. She does not abandon her stance as a teacher, but builds trust in the drama by negotiating as teacher, while she builds trust in the fictional state when she operates in role. The role helps the students to *do*, and the teacher helps them to *see*.

> For me, the most secure authority has always been from within the drama situation – the authority of role. I can be more flexible in the use of registers. The role-authority gives me shifting power and a variety of registers to be at the service of the class. I may suddenly gather authority to deny or accede to requests, or lack power but have strong opinions, or resist a class in order to strengthen its opinions and decisions. My belief in my attitude supports their belief in theirs.[2]

Heathcote stressed that teachers who operate in role in the drama must never act in the sense that an actor does, because they have a different task to do. Teaching in role never means merely joining in the work as an 'extra' on equal terms with the rest of the group. As she explains in 'Signs and Portents':

> One does not become merely a person in the play, because one is teaching as well as signing. Ask yourself this question. The last time you worked in role were you really only adding to the number in the cast?[3]

The task of the teacher in role is to bring the students into active participation in the fictional event. Because the teacher's role is publicly available to be 'read', interpreted and interrogated by the students, they are immediately caught up in contemplation, speculation and anticipation. The teacher in role operates as an 'anti-corrosive agent' by deflecting students' embarrassment and preventing them from feeling 'stared at'. Instead, they are drawn together in attending to the emerging dramatic world as they discover their place within it. They gradually come to realize the nature of the relationship of their roles to that presented by the teacher and the responsibilities of the roles with which they've been endowed through that relationship. Students become engaged in the work because they have been placed in a significant relationship with the action, a relationship that brings with it an attitude and responsibilities.

Reflection on the event has always been a significant element of Heathcote's work in drama. In addition to the experience of 'being there' in the 'now time' of drama, she made sure that a sense of self-spectatorship – of being outside the event – was generated in the participants.

> Drama teaches people by demonstrating interactive social behaviour, and encouraging critical spectatorship, because art releases the spectator/action possibility in people.[4]

This sense of spectatorship was heightened as Heathcote's practice began to shift away from drama at 'seeming life-rate'. Although there had always been a degree of pre-planning, negotiating, and questioning in 'living-through' drama, the work sometimes moved too rapidly for students to become deeply absorbed in and committed to it. In order to 'slow down time' and enable students to get a grip on their thinking and review their responses, Heathcote began to employ 'depictions', or 'conventions' as she called them, in which the students encountered persons in role, images or objects of significance. Some of these conventions are representations of an 'other' – a person in role with whom the students may interact or to whom they may respond. In some of the conventions, the 'other' is brought into being through writings, reports, and letters. In other conventions, symbolic objects may be used that are closely associated with or evoke the presence of the 'other'.

As well as slowing down the action, the use of conventions elicits a different kind of response, a different kind of engagement involving a degree of detachment. The students' engagement is determined by the *task* of responding to the depictions, rather than by involvement in a particular role or situation.

As Heathcote puts it:

> The 'spectator' in (the students) must be awakened so that they perceive and enjoy the world of action and responsibility even as they function in it.[5]

It is a strategy that promotes close attention to detail, reflection and interpretation, and the beginnings of an understanding of form. The students' responses to these depictions or conventions require a change of gear, an elaboration of understanding filtered through a different kind of experience. There is a balance between engagement and detachment that protects the students from uncritical absorption in the emotional dimensions of the work. This balance is a characteristic of aesthetic experience, which always possesses a cognitive as well as an emotional element.

In her development of this approach Heathcote was employing the key aesthetic element of *distance*, using the persons, images and objects represented in these conventions to suspend the 'now' time of drama, in order that contemplation and interpretation became possible.[6] One of the ways in which Heathcote manipulates different degrees of distance in the work is through the use of *frames*. As she points out, in any social encounter there are two aspects present. One is the action necessary for the event to progress forward towards a conclusion. The other is the *perspective* from which people are coming to enter the event. This is frame, and frame will be the main agent in providing tension and meaning for the participants.[7] Depictions and conventions invite many complex framings which immediately generate a variety of language styles and purposes. Heathcote based her understanding of 'frame' on Erving Goffman's *Frame Analysis*.[8] Through the careful use of frame, teachers can place their students in very precise situations that will demand different kinds of thought, depiction, interaction and use of power.

She elaborates on the concept of frame in 'Signs and Portents', included in this section. This is one of the most influential pieces of writing that Heathcote ever produced and it is widely cited in other publications and in academic studies. It was specially written for *the Journal of the Standing Conference of Young People's Theatre*, and originally published in 1980. At the time, Theatre in Education – T.I.E – was flourishing in the UK. In 1965, the first ever Theatre in Education company had been created by the Belgrade Theatre in Coventry. At the Belgrade, a team of actor/teachers used theatrical performances that typically included a significant degree of participation and interaction with the audience and explored cultural, social, political and moral issues. The format was soon adopted by other theatres in the UK and abroad.

However, because of financial and political constraints, a number of T.I.E companies were forced to close during the 1980s. Although a number of T.I.E companies are still in operation, the term is often used to refer to any theatre work that takes place in schools or is aimed at school audiences. Much of the philosophy and practice of T.I.E continues to be significant in the practice of what has become known internationally as Applied Theatre.

Heathcote regarded the use of 'sign' as one of the teacher's essential tools. Sign is at the heart of human communication, whether between individuals or in the virtual world of the theatre. In 'Signs and Portents' she explicitly relates her background in theatre to her recognition of the importance of 'sign' in the classroom. Her theatrical understanding is obvious in her revealing account of the problems faced by T.I.E teams when they try to negotiate two different positions, as performers inside the action of the play and facilitators or workshop leaders outside it. The team has to alter its signing systems when its members operate both as actors and as facilitators or workshop leaders with students, and, as Heathcote notes, theatrical signing is so not easily laid aside. Students become aware that their involvement in the work is of a different kind from that of the actors. There is a message here for teachers who mistakenly believe that if they create an elaborate role it will be more effective. Instead, such elaboration is more likely to turn the students into passive spectators rather than active participants.

Theatre as an art form is entirely based on sign, and Heathcote's development of her thirty-three conventions displays her deep understanding of theatrical processes and the ways in which they may be employed in the service of drama in education. In *Dorothy Heathcote: Drama as a Learning Medium*, she is quoted as saying:

> Classroom drama uses the elements of the art of theatre.... The difference between the theatre and the classroom is that in theatre everything is contrived so that the audience gets the kicks. In the classroom the participants get the kicks. However, the tools are the same: the elements of theatre craft.[9]

In 1968, in the first phase of her practice, she listed some of the teacher's essential functions when using drama, and in the examples given in the following chapters it is possible to observe these functions in action:

- creating a climate in which value judgements do not apply, but where the honesty of individual contributions is valued and respect is shown to each individual's ideas and methods of contribution;
- employing children's ideas and making them 'work' positively, while using the natural laws of the medium;
- creating a working situation of integrity, employing the adult world within the situation, while allowing the children their own world of concepts and values;
- promoting teaching objectives without destroying the children's contributions;
- understanding the way drama functions in promoting the release of varying and conflicting attitudes within the group;
- understanding that drama is not stories retold, but confrontations between individuals, lived at life-rate;
- being able to prepare and plan, while retaining the necessary 'surprise-confrontation' element for the children.[10]

Although the majority of these functions have remained consistently in operation throughout Heathcote's career, it is interesting to note that in her later writings and practice the last three functions in the list were considerably modified. 'Releasing conflicting attitudes' and 'exploring confrontations at life-rate' ceased to be a major focus as her practice moved towards the use of conventions and later the task-based approach of Mantle of the Expert.

She also began to rethink what she had seen as the 'necessary 'surprise-confrontation' element of the work. In 1971 she had warned that the immediacy of the moment was too often planned right out of the drama.[11] However, within the next few years any element of surprise in the work began to be negotiated and pre-planned with the students.

In a paper published in 2010 she writes:

> The most essential element in productive tension is that the outcome must be agreed before the experience is embarked upon. Knowing the outcome from the start slows time into experiential time. If everyone is trying to reach resolution they rush towards resolving the dilemma. By knowing the outcome they all create the dilemma at a pace they find reasonable.[12]

Heathcote's notion of drama happening at life-rate and involving confrontation was modified as the sense of spectatorship became more dominant in her practice. This development can be traced in the papers included in this part of the book.

## Notes

1 Heathcote, D. (2012) 'Contexts for Active Learning', *The Journal for Drama in Education*, Special Issue, Summer.

2 'Subject or System', in Johnson, L. and O'Neill, C. (eds.) (1984) *Dorothy Heathcote: Collected Writings on Education and Drama*, London: Hutchinson, p. 69.

3 'Signs and Portents', in Johnson, L. and O'Neill, C. (eds.) (1984) *Dorothy Heathcote: Collected Writings on Education and Drama*, London: Hutchinson, p. 162.

4 See 'The authentic teacher and the future' pp. 94–108, this volume.

5 Bolton, G. and Heathcote, D. (1999) *So You Want to Use Role-Play? A New Approach in How to Plan*, Stoke-on-Trent: Trentham Books, p. 18.

6 For an in-depth study of the significance of distance in drama education, see Eriksson, S. A. (2009) *Distancing at Close Range*, Vasa: Abo.

7 'Signs and Portents', in Johnson, L. and O'Neill, C. (eds.) (1984) *Dorothy Heathcote: Collected Writings on Education and Drama*, London: Hutchinson, p. 163.

8 Goffman, Erving. (1975) *Frame Analysis*, Harmondsworth: Peregrine Books.

9 Wagner, B. J. (1976) *Dorothy Heathcote: Drama as a Learning Medium*, Washington, DC: National Education Association.

10 'Role-taking', in Johnson, L. and O'Neill, C. (eds.) (1984) *Dorothy Heathcote: Collected Writings on Education and Drama*, London: Hutchinson, p. 51.

11 'Subject or System', in Johnson, L. and O'Neill, C. (eds.) (1984) *Dorothy Heathcote: Collected Writings on Education and Drama*, London: Hutchinson, p. 70.

12 See 'Productive tensions' pp. 55–61, this volume.

# NOTES ON DRAMA

*These notes were originally published in the Resources section of* Collected Writings. *However, their clarity and simplicity of expression has made them extremely useful and popular with teachers. As well as outlining different modes of drama, they anticipate Heathcote's further development and elaboration of Mantle of the Expert.*

## What is drama?

Drama is the selective expression of human interaction in which codes and patterns of behaviour may be examined because:

1. The area can be selected for review. In life it cannot, for we are busy living.
2. The theatre has developed over many years the different styles and modes that can be employed to review people's dilemmas and problems.
3. The actual moment in time can be isolated, tried again, turned around, and replayed with different solutions, because we can accept the conventions.
4. The theatre does this constantly. It shows life in action, the way people fill the spaces between themselves and others – it can appear to show what the *reality* of life is but *seems* to be the opportunity of art, to *distort the view productively*.
5. Theatre can uphold the moral code or challenge it with equal facility.
6. We can learn through theatre because we can measure our own experiences against others in an identifying way.
7. We can identify our experiences with those selected ones we are shown.
8. Using a process of identification can we employ this 'looking at life' for teaching?
9. Can this change behaviour patterns?
10. Can we learn how to identify? If so, with what do we identify and how?
11. Can theatre and drama help us examine ourselves, our own codes, our own patterns of thinking and behaving?
12. When drama is used in learning establishments what has to be present to make it succeed?

13. There is no moralizer present in the room, only the circumstances. Old jaded views must be given a new look of shocking proportions. Somehow prejudice must be bypassed to let in new light upon old matter. So these elements must come into play:

| | |
|---|---|
| **A** A problem must be seen in action. | It must be interesting for the participants. |
| **B** The new element. | Old familiar matters appear in new forms to 'shock' into awareness. |
| **C** Decisions must be called for. | There is an active commitment to action and the solving of problems. |
| **D** Experience is employed productively not passively. | Relevant previous experience comes into action. |
| **E** Getting feedback – not to be avoided! | There is no escape from the immediate outcome and results of decisions. |
| **F** Conscious examination of changes, if any. | Reflection – a standing back from the action to review present conceptualization. |

## Drama in education

The word drama seems to explain one kind of activity – it looks as if it is about the reconstruction of life. In this form it is familiar to us on TV and in theatre and film. When we see it, we can recognize human behaviour, sometimes like our own and sometimes shockingly different. We are usually outside this drama, so we are in a position to predict to a certain extent what is going to happen. To a certain extent we can enjoy the agonies, joys and pseudo-agonies of those whose 'lives' we eavesdrop on. We can also anticipate, and this is an important part of the pleasure.

So when teachers say they teach drama, we tend to think that we know what is going to happen. But actually using that blanket term isn't much use to us in school, because blanket words are not much use to a teacher. The elements of an activity have to be discovered first, before teachers can put this activity to use meaningfully.

What are the elements in drama that make it a possible learning tool? How does drama work?

1. People have to work out together the lives they are pretending to live.
   *Drama demands cooperation.*
2. People have to employ what they already know, about the life they are trying to live.
   *Drama puts life experience to use.*
   *Drama makes factual experience* (information) *come into active employment.*
3. People have to be able to live in two worlds at once and not get them mixed up.
   *Drama uses fiction and fantasy but makes people more aware of reality.*
4. People have to agree to sustain a common understanding of what they are making together, no matter how separately they may appear to be thinking. Footballers have to do this too – they don't end up all playing different games!
   *Drama stresses an agreement among participants to sustain mutual support for each other while allowing everyone a chance to work differently – to bring personal ideas to the whole.*
5. People have to express thinking, feeling, and actions to each other. If they don't do this, then no one in the group knows what is going on.
   *Drama makes people find precision in communication.*

6.  Drama uses objects but often in a symbolic way. Chairs have to become thrones, but also these 'thrones' become the symbol of the king when he is absent.
    *Drama stresses the use of reflection. Symbols become ordinary, but the ordinary also is seen to be symbolic.*
7.  People have to interpret the actions of others but often in unfamiliar circumstances. You don't meet dragons every day; you don't have to be skilled goldsmiths; you don't have to battle with kings – or hospital matrons! You don't have to argue with warlocks; you don't face the rigours of great journeys or cope with enemies who seek to take your life.
    *Drama allows you to live out crises in a testing kind of way. It tests attitudes and present capacities.*

What use are all these to teachers? The least usable part of the picture is the 'making plays up' bit. That is for making plays – all the rest is about developing the skills of being a person in a community. To make this work in teaching will demand that new forms are used in schools. New outward forms that is, where the play is not seen publicly but inner demands can be made on the class. We have been experimenting with some of these forms:

1.  One class teaching another one by the ways they simulate events and stress a certain problem, perhaps to avoid the confusion that occurs when too much information is given at once.
2.  Using one person in role to meet the class – Julius Caesar, Florence Nightingale, a tramp. Know your students' need and devise the role to meet it.
3.  Setting up *'working as'* rather than *'learning about'* situations in other subject areas. (A group of Year 1 children who collected antiques might then run a museum service in the school – it *isn't* crazy and they *can* do it.)

## Types of drama

You can approach learning through drama in various ways. Each way makes a different journey, a different kind of demand on your planning and a different kind of demand on your students. Each approach makes a different kind of learning happen.

1.  *Roles:* where a person is the challenge.
2.  *Mantle of the Expert:* where the class is set a task in such a way that they function as experts.
3.  *Analogy:* where one problem, a real one, is revealed by an exact parallel to it.
4.  *Text:* where interpretation of someone else's work is the means of learning.
5.  *Dance forms:* where emphasis on non-verbal signals, experiences, and explanations are the means of discovery.
6.  *Simulation:* where a simulation of life is made.
7.  *Games:* where the rules lead and control the play.

All these outer modes are 'respectable'. What makes them 'shabby' is the quality of the interior experience that is planned into them. Good 'interior form' can never have a 'wrong' external pattern.

## Roles

When you use a role you gain:

- a person for the class to respond to;
- a lifestyle which comes into the room;
- a holding device which attracts interest;
- something to inquire into that acts as a focus;
- a specific example of emotional/intelligent life and attitudes to challenge;
- a pressure exactly where you want it.

But you must decide:

- what that pressure is to be;
- exactly how the role will exert the pressure on the class;
- which symbolic objects will be essential to communicate the lifestyle;
- exactly what you want your class to experience through meeting the role.

You can't get away with 'shabby' planning ever! Using a role can:

- teach facts;
- challenge attitudes;
- pose questions;
- demand understanding;
- help you question yourself;
- modify class behaviour;
- make students want to read the book/play again.

## Mantle of the Expert

'*Mantle*' meaning: I declare that I will uphold the lifestyle and standards of my calling.

'*Expert*' meaning: Furthermore I will undertake to take seriously the acquisition and using of those skills deemed necessary in that lifestyle I have entered because of my calling.

When you use this approach to drama you gain:

- A commitment from the children to learn the information and skills they will need, for example an expert mariner must function within a framework of the sea, journeys, and the tools and skills of the seafarer. Because of the need for information it allows the teacher to use drama directly to run alongside and feed off the curriculum.
- A discipline for the class that provides a framework in which the attitudes are contained without the teacher imposing rules and demands. For example, a mariner must obey the laws of the sea; a mariner must obey the pressure of the oceans' ways; a mariner must obey the social hierarchy within the vessel; a mariner must learn the trade.
- A task-orientated situation, where the job in hand must be done first. So, doing the job and fulfilling the task are the vehicle that starts creative ideas flowing. Children

employ what they know and no information will be fed to them first. Which means that:

- Teachers can diagnose what children already know.
- Teachers can feed information when they see that the class needs it.
- Teachers are forced to demonstrate that they can differentiate between 'force-feeding' facts and creating a climate where facts, skills and understanding can grow together.
- Teachers who 'know it all' can't teach well through the 'Mantle of the Expert'. They can't wait for real learning to happen. They can't recognize real learning when they see it.

## Analogy

You can't use this mode if you won't decide:

- exactly what you want to teach about;
- what aspect of your theme or concept you want to parallel;
- how to make the connection ultimately between the real situation you need to open up for consideration and the analogous one;
- exactly how to parallel the *inner form* and not the storyline.

Every theme or concept is capable of having an exact parallel if you understand that it is this inner form that is important. Analogy is the best way of making something fresh and worthy of consideration when it has become too cliché-ridden, too familiar and too full of prejudice because of memory and past weariness. It provides a new face for old material.

## Dance forms

This mode can be used when you decide your statements are complete without the need for words. You have to be prepared to interest yourself in:

- which concepts and ideas truly do not need words;
- which statements are clearer because the dance/movement form is employed;
- the labour of clarity and precision in thought and act.

## Simulation

Simulation means holding the mirror up to nature. You gain:

- an exploration of interaction, and a chance to see the results of your action on other people;
- an opportunity to work with feeling and thought simultaneously;
- a chance to form your ideas into some kind of order.

The problems are:

- Everyone can bring in any idea they fancy – this may make it difficult for the inexperienced teacher.

- All these ideas have to be sorted out into working patterns.
- You have to be able to make the rules of theatre work immediately.
- You have to be able to win belief in the big lie, the Art Form, the agreement to pretend.

## Games

Every lesson needs a spine – the central idea to suggest the task and the actions flowing from the task. In using games:

- Rules help the teacher to avoid being the arbiter of behaviour.
- Rules allow the teacher to be an equal player.
- The task is clear.
- The goals are clear.
- The method of doing the task is clear.
- Rewards and punishments are formalized.
- Status – at any point – is related to task, chance and rules, not to individual stature in the group.
- There is an end product to be seen.

*Games* formalize life interaction processes and can allow a problem to be seen clearly so that another look is possible because the game allows us to sidestep. Thus a temporary relief from emotion and muddle can reveal the spine of the problem. Out of this insight comes energy and clearer purpose. Like *Analogy*, games work best when the central spine of the game opens up the central spine of the real problem exactly.

Whatever mode of drama you use, the first central part of each lesson is the *focus*. Out of the *focus* the task can be found and set. Out of the task arises all the potential learning on which the teacher can focus for further tasks. The task provides the opportunity for assessment of needs. This brings modification of the task. The teacher must decide how to use the focus and the task in terms of:

- social learning;
- factual learning;
- reflective learning;
- curriculum pressures.

The progress of the drama lesson can be described metaphorically:

1. The ship = the teacher plans how to make the focus work.
2. The tidal currents = the class behaviour, knowledge and understanding dictate the teacher's ongoing function during the lesson.
3. The voyage and discovery = these are made according to the way the teacher steers within the tidal currents.
4. The map = the map is not the plan; it is the outcome.

In every drama lesson there will be a general idea which will lead to the focus out of which must be brought *Reflection* and the *Universal*, without which there is no learning from the experience.

It must be remembered that:

- It is not the doing – it is the considerations underlying the doing.
- It is not the saying – it is the effect of the saying.
- It is not merely telling people what you want them to learn – it is the experience arising out of the action that enables them to learn.

## Aims in drama

During any first session my aim is threefold: first, I want the children to recognize that I am putting the onus upon them to have ideas. Second, I want them to realize that I am prepared to accept their ideas and to use them and make them work. This decision-making, where children watch their own choices worked out in action, seems to me to be one of the important services which drama renders to education, where we are trying to encourage children to think for themselves. Third, I want the children to work from the very beginning within a true drama context, that is not a vitiated art form watered down for them but the real thing with the real disciplines which drama requires, for example group problems jointly worked out in the present. All too often drama presents children with a story form with the emphasis upon events – whereas in fact drama reveals events through the feelings and attitudes of people. We would not ask children to paint with wrongly mixed pigments. The same applies to other art forms too, so, while accepting the ideas of the children, I am also 'mixing' these ideas so that they are usable by the children.

It is important from the start that all the children's needs are respected as far as possible, and therefore I must give those without confidence the opportunity to hide and be reserved, and those who are too confident the necessary challenges to make them work more thoughtfully. Some children learn most at this stage by being 'onlookers', rather than 'ideas people', that is, responders rather than initiators, and I must respect this.

Finally, I regard the *effort made* to be of more importance to me as a teacher than the resulting drama, but at the same time the children are working for *their* result, which may be great personal pleasure, or the satisfaction of their play needs, or many other things including the achievement of having made something happen.

## Questions to consider

What *precisely* do I want the dramatic input to do for the children, the learning area and me? It cannot be a *general* answer. It can usually be quite clearly named as a skill, for example 'to enable children to realize that old-seeming documents often deal with the same matters modern people are concerned about' or 'to realize that things like books are *still* written slow and hard'.

Am I aware of how I use my *voice* in teaching? Can I feed information while apparently asking for it? For example, 'I'm looking for some marble but I'm not certain if the Carrara quarries will be best – have you any Carrara in? They say the green is very good, but I like the rose myself.'

There is *no need* to think I must know everything about the subject in hand before I start the work!

Have I clarified the simplest starting point? And have I considered the stages in building belief in the *authenticity of the task?*

Have I divided the task suitably?

Have I thought carefully about how symbolic material will be used? For example, *charts* of plans, designs, maps, etc. No work can *actually* be done, but it needs authentic record keeping. For example a herbalist needs reference material, diagrams of a garden, ways of *recording* measurement, receipts, recipes, drawings of shelves and jars – all the last five will be made as the work progresses – plus lists of ailments and charts of the body, etc.

People must be given the opportunity to work in small groups – because *talk* about the work is most essential for development. And groups need to cross-refer as the work continues.

Can I tolerate *not* giving direct instructions and answers before people have a chance *not to be told?*

# DRAMA AND LEARNING

*This chapter outlines the key characteristics of drama and the kinds of strategies and techniques likely to promote the effective use of drama in schools. Heathcote explains her use of teacher-in-role, the need for reflection both inside and outside the drama and the importance of slowing down the action so that this reflection can take place. She deals with such factors as tension, time and progression in drama and examines the limitations of theatre exercises. Heathcote emphasizes that drama for discovery is not about ends. It is about journeys whose destinations are unknown. As she points out, drama is not the most efficient means of teaching facts, but it allows facts to be understood in action.*

*This is an edited version of the chapter in* Dorothy Heathcote: Collected Writings. *It first appeared as 'Drama as Education' in* Children and Drama, *edited by Nellie McCaslin, published by David McKay & Co. Ltd, New York, 1977.*

It seems sensible to me that, if there is a way of making the world simpler and more understandable to children, why not use it? Drama makes it possible to isolate an event or to compare one event with another, to look at events that have happened to other people in other places and times perhaps, or to look at one's own experience after the event, within the safety of knowing that just at this moment it is not really happening. We can, however, feel that it is happening, because drama uses the same rules we find in life. People exist in their environment, living a moment at a time and taking those decisions which seem reasonable in the light of their present knowledge about the current state of affairs. The difference is that in life we have many other things to consider at the same time and often cannot revise a decision taken, except in the long term. So drama can be a kind of playing at or practice of living, tuning up those areas of feeling-capacity and expression-capacity as well as social-capacity.

I often work in role at first because it fixes emotional reaction. I find much prejudice against this way of working, though I maintain it is the equivalent of good paint or clay and proper tools. The proper tools of drama are emotional reaction and the state of being trapped, a state from which one can escape only by working through the situation.

I am much criticized for 'stopping to consider', especially when 'it's going nicely, thank you', but it is for this very reason that I can stop. I know that the event can be rediscovered.

Reflection about the work is one of the best ways I know to elicit trust, for I can stop the work in order to show enthusiasm, to challenge, to demand more, and to show my own involvement as well as my non-interest in value judgements.

These are the procedures:

1. We make the world smaller by the isolation of an area of concern.
2. We involve groups of people who, in turn, are involved in group decision-taking. Groups can work in fantasy or real-life situations. These are the same; only the rules are different. But whichever the students choose, they must realize that in drama there must always be the acceptance of the 'One Big Lie'. This is an agreement to pretend that we are in the situation we have chosen. The truths are the truths of how we see the situation, our own behaviour, our own language and expression, our own significant actions and the truths we find to be important to us in that situation. I have discovered that all people understand the idea of the One Big Lie. It eliminates the silliness that often characterizes children's work at first. One reason for self-consciousness is, of course, that the person of the child is used as the material; another, that the rules are hard to perceive.
3. We establish certain ground rules:
   (a) First the situation must be defined.
       There must be a beginning that each person can recognize as true to the situation. In games the rules stand at all times when the game is played, and the players learn them once and for all. Drama rules may appear to change because the actual start must use the present capacity of the class to relate to each other. In drama what is important is the social health of the class, and the nature of the game – which will change with each playing.
   (b) Group views must be put to use so that the drama starts where the groups are (simply because you cannot start from where you aren't).
       This means that the leader/instigator must find a common starting point. If the common starting point is negative, then the negative must be used – positively, of course. To get classes to commit to the work, however, requires strategies.
   (c) There must be some instigation to review progress.
       Drama often disguises progress or shows it falsely; for example, if the action moves quickly, the result can be mistaken for quality. A slower approach may suggest lack of progress. I usually take on the responsibility for reviewing progress at first, because it is difficult for a member of a group to get the ear of the class. Once the social health of a class has improved, however, it is easy for others to assume responsibility and they should be encouraged to take it.

       The first leaders are often those who have language confidence, though not necessarily the most ability. Later, the demands shift from talk to action, from the repetition of facts to the understanding of feelings, by the demand for skills of different kinds (often not socially acceptable, such as picking locks or brazening out a stand against authority).

       As I have said, I am much criticized for instigating early review. I do it because one thing that must happen in learning is the development of a sense of commitment to the work. I will not guarantee that classes work; what I will guarantee is that I will always keep the work interesting. Reviewing, to me, is a strategy.

(d)  Strategies must change according to the class and the drama.

Because I often work in role at first, there is an assumption that that is the way I shall continue to work. In an organically changing situation such as teaching, one is constantly seeking to make the first strategies redundant, while seeking to serve the class in other ways. I am weary of explaining that I do not do the same things every time; I start where the class can start and from then on, as we become more understanding of each other, I try to build a working relationship in which we can take more liberties with feelings, make more demands upon each other and move more as a team.

A class with poor social health requires a more delicate strategy than one in better health, where there can be some self-help. So, strategies are of two kinds: those that stimulate the class to working and those that further the action in the drama. Progression lies in the growing ability of the class to accept the discipline of the drama form and to put the work before personal interest. Concern for each member of the group, ability to take more thoughtful decisions, the courage to risk making and rejecting suggestions – all these are progressions.

There are also the art-form progressions. These are closely related to the above, of course, but there are the extra dimensions of awareness of the overview: the avoidance of anachronisms, the checking of facts, the groping with unfamiliar skills and pursuing them past weariness, never giving up until it feels right. In other words, sometimes the work matters more than the individual.

(e)  The work must go slowly enough to give a class an experience.

This is very difficult with classes of poor social health because they do not want to go slowly. Another reason for strategy! I never object to any ideas the class wishes to work on, but I do interfere with the pace. I cannot say that this is right, but I believe pace is an important aspect of work and I do much to ensure that it contributes to the best experience. This is an area that a class cannot manage for itself.

(f)  Tension of some kind must be present in the drama.

Teachers rarely understand how to provide it. The simple factor in making tension work is that something must be left to chance but not more than one thing at a time. So long as there is that one factor and no one in the room knows precisely when that thing will occur (though everything has been set up so that it must occur), we have tension.

Subtle tensions are useless in a class that will only respond to cruder ones. An example of such a tension might be waiting in the dark for an intruder to enter a room. Or a less crude one, demanding more patience, waiting one's turn to be interrogated, knowing that one of the group will be found guilty. The pressure must come from within the situation, not from the teacher/role insisting that it be done right.

Every conceivable situation can provide the tension to suit any type of class. I remember a group of delinquent children (fourteen-year-olds) who moved very quickly through a series of such tensions, each one making the group work harder than the preceding, because each one demanded more of them, while allowing them satisfaction. The first was a mugging; the second a verbal threat to a lady of wealth to blackmail her son; the third a painful forging of a document that would fool the guards; the fourth a telephone call made under the nose of the police, warning a friend of a police raid; finally, the wait outside a temple to find out whose baby – yes, baby (and they themselves were the mothers) – would be chosen as a sacrifice in a prayer for rain. They also did the ritual mourning.

(g) Feelings and thoughts that exist inside persons have to be made explicit to the students so that they can see and respond to the expression in the group.

Drama is about filling the spaces between people with meaningful experiences. This means that emotion is at the heart of drama experience but it is tempered with thought and planning. The first is experienced through tension, the second, through the reviewing process. Out of these we build reflective processes, which in the end are what we are trying to develop in all our teaching. Without the development of the power of reflection we have very little. It is reflection that permits the storing of knowledge, the recalling of power of feeling, and memory of past feelings.

All too often we phase out emotion in our classroom work as if it were unimportant. (Certainly emotion is harder to deal with than thinking, because children do not expect to use their emotions in school.) If we take the emotion out of drama, there is only the burden left.

Teaching drama is often done through the theatre exercise. But exercises have a built-in, self-destroying force, particularly when used with uncommitted classes. They have a drive towards ending themselves. True drama for discovery is not about ends; it is about journeys and not knowing how the journeys may end. When drama is exercise-driven, the natural discoveries that come from emotional involvement cannot arise. Exercises exist to take emotion out, so that coolness and repetition can exist. I know you can devise exercises for emotion, but why should you with children, who have the real thing so readily available just waiting to be tapped? The value of exercises lies in the way they help to isolate a factor and let special attention be paid to it. I say that exercises are for those who have already tasted the riches of a tough and real experience. Far too many classes never get to the reality of their art because of time spent on exercises.

Drama, then, teaches in the following way. Taking a moment in time, it uses the experiences of the participants, forcing them to confront their own actions and decisions and to go forward to a believable outcome in which they can gain satisfaction. This approach brings classes into those areas that in the main are avoided in school: emotional control, understanding of the place and importance of emotion, and language with which to express emotion. We expect good parents, partners, honest citizens, fine, sensitive friends, tolerant and understanding neighbours to emerge from the classes we teach but we have done very little to prepare them for these roles.

Drama is not an efficient means for straight factual teaching, but it provides a rich ground for making facts understood in action. The basis of all my class contacts seems to depend more and more upon a few relatively simple techniques:

- I plan the areas where the class will make the decisions.
- I also plan strategies that I shall use to get the class committed to work. This planning is always done from an inside experience approach rather than from an external tasks approach.
- I try to know the impact of every verbal statement I make as I make it.
- I select all signals with extreme care and sensitivity, even when working with my back to the wall with what I call 'dragon's teeth' classes.
- I spend much time examining the uses of questions and the types of questions asked.

- I recognize a dud question and set about recovering from it immediately. One dud may take ten or more other good questions to make a recovery.
- I decide when and why I shall leave role and become interrogator-leader. People assume that because I use role early, I mean to go on with it.
- I use role in order to teach the class that emotion is the heart of drama. Talking about emotion is no substitute for feeling it. This is the advantage of being in role but, of course, it is a complicated tool and it takes some patience to learn how to use it. I have not yet met a teacher who cannot use it and who does not learn more about the use of drama in their teaching as a result of its use.
- I seek rather than plant information.
- I never mix plans. In other words, I decide very clearly what the lesson should achieve. It may be an unplanned session when I deliberately decide to test the class in order to find out where it is; all subsequent sessions can be based on what I learn in the beginning. It may be a session especially designed to introduce some aspect of learning, or it may be to help study how the text comes alive on the stage.
- I select all the best artefacts, literature, and reference books I can find (adult materials for the most part, as I find them superior).
- I do not withhold information if I can find a way to impart it. I believe far too much information is withheld from classes, or children feel that it is being withheld, which has the same effect.
- I work slowly in the beginning. I do not move forward until the class is committed to the work. This does not mean that I stand still; it means that I use many strategies to keep in the same place while apparently moving forward. The social health of the class dictates this commitment, and it is my belief that all the real difficulties of drama come from social ill health.
- I work to stretch classes. I expect students to work very hard, and I show that I work hard too. I never withdraw help nor do I ever praise falsely.
- I give positive comment at all times, and when I want to urge further effort, I often quote my own experiences (always true but often edited to make the strongest impact and timed so as to shock the class into new awareness).
- I do not expect classes to like drama automatically.
- I guarantee that I will do nothing to make them feel foolish, but neither will I allow them to get off the hook.
- I use the rules from the beginning and especially make the point that all signals, whether positive or negative, affect the work.

Finally, I stress that the teacher will have to initiate, guide, time the work, and be the guide and mentor throughout. Children have not been trained to trust their own ideas or their own ways of approaching work. Therefore, for the time being, we have to carry the burden not only of working against the stream but also of creating classes who will revel in taking decisions, in using emotion productively, and in exercising their skills.

# PRODUCTIVE TENSIONS

*According to Heathcote, moments of tension must be felt, seen and experienced, if drama is to be effective. She insists that tension is not a matter of huge terrifying events such as earthquakes, mutinies and armies. It is more a matter of finding a lever from within the drama situation which puts pressure on the participants.*[1]

*In the previous chapter, Heathcote insists:*

> *Tension of some kind must be present in the drama. Teachers rarely understand how to provide it. The simple factor in making tension work is that something must be left to chance but not more than one thing at a time. So long as there is that one factor and no one in the room knows precisely when that thing will occur, though everything has been set up so that it must occur, we have tension. Subtle tensions are useless in a class that will only respond to cruder ones. An example of such a tension might be waiting in the dark for an intruder to enter a room. Or a less crude one, demanding more patience, might be waiting one's turn to be interrogated, knowing that one of the group will be found guilty. The pressure must come from within the situation, not from the teacher/role insisting that it be done right.*[2]

*Although the original title of this paper was* Productive Tension: A Keystone in Mantle of the Expert Teaching, *I have chosen to place it in this section. The fertility of Heathcote's dramatic imagination is displayed in the many levels of tension she proposes in this paper, and the examples she provides come from many phases of her work and exhibit the varied modes of drama she has employed throughout her career.*

*This is an edited version of the paper prepared by Luke Abbott for the website www.mantleoftheexpert. com. It first appeared in print in* The Journal for Drama in Education, *NATD, 26 (1), Spring 2010.*

## Drama and productive tension

In the theatre it is always 'now'. This means:

* Immediate expressive behaviour (as in life) *but*
* Highly selective in order to invite others to 'read' human behaviour within defined areas of experience.

- It progresses through observed episodic encounters.
- These are selected by playwrights to serve specific intentions.
- Actors observe these – in order to be as true as possible to those intentions.

*But* actors interpret these intentions in their own time and style so that they constantly aim to renew the concerns of the author. Actors are 'shape shifters' who, within the selected agreed contracts, have the freedom and discipline to create human characters facing the dilemmas placed before them by the text. Therefore actors enter their encounters and interactions with a point of view. Their artistry is the way they express individual points of view – body, voice, gesture, stillness, behaviour, and spatial placement. Each moment brings about its own future through *deliberation* and the intent to engage the audience. Actors carry the messages of their roles in the total playing out of events in social agreement with colleague/artists. The safety of the actors and their audience lies in the fact that they know at every moment that they are at one and the same time creator/doers and monitoring self-spectators.

Drama as education is based upon two keystones. The first is that drama time is necessarily experimental and it temporarily 'loses' the clock time of studentship and so embraces responsibility for outcomes and considerations of morality and ethics.

The second keystone is the changing relationship between teacher and taught. The materials of dramatic exploration are social interaction and the sharing of experiences regarding human behaviour. The teacher is no longer seen as the main fount of information and students are no longer seen as mere absorbers of that knowledge. Within drama processes, teacher and students can explain what it is to be human to each other within the framework of security that teachers provide for individuals in the group, as well as necessary protection from revelations regarding private matters.

Drama, like theatre, is like another time-space-room that all the participants recognize is available to enter. Which brings me to productive tension and why understanding how to make it happen in classrooms is enormously important for students and teachers. I can only explain it as far as I as yet understand it. I'm learning by trial and error and careful observation.

Dramatic action is expressed through the human person – thought/feeling expressed in a now and immediate time that invokes its future. To the human presence(s) are then added other aspects of 'sign' – surroundings, properties, light/shade, clothing, sounds, music. The drama element occurs when human action involves groups and interaction becomes necessary. Theatre demonstrates this group interaction driven by the varying motivations of those present, caught within the circumstances of the fictional world of the play. Drama for learning also works by creating fictional worlds that allow human events and motivations and outcomes to be explored, thus widening our experience of the capacities of human beings to learn, endure, overcome, accommodate to and empathize with others. It may, but need not, involve performance to and for audiences.

Playwrights introduce tensions into the action of their plays. These tensions have the effect of building their characters into the events, which forces them towards outcomes. These outcomes occur because of individual motivations and resulting actions. Thus the actors are 'nursed' by the playwright's inbuilt structures to find the play's resolution.

Productive tension is quite different from conflict. It is the key to deepening the exploration of motive that influences the action and therefore the journey. Conflict is a shallower concept, for it tends to lock people into negative repetitive responses during the interactive process and prevents more subtle exploration. In the classroom the teacher can select from a range of tensions starting with crude encounters that first attract the group to participate and explore, so that deeper work can follow. The main challenge is to create the binding circumstances that hold the group in the fictional world at a level of attraction that catches their interest. If the attraction holds, then the attention, interest, investment, commitment, concern and productive obsession will progressively deepen and widen the range of interaction. Involvement follows and promotes reflection about being human.

A simple working description of productive tension would be 'leaving something in the situation to chance which cannot be controlled entirely'. This does not preclude planning in advance in case a particular element crops up. There must be no cheating or surprises from the teacher without contracts.

## Levels of tension in order of subtlety

The defining parameters of a situation must first be established. This can be assisted by a combination of the *iconic* (drawn/images, etc.), the *symbolic* (language written/verbal charts, maps, etc.) and finally the *expressive* – the principal action. The current action/circumstance must dominate and take the interest of participants at a degree of attraction that they can understand and appreciate at a thinking level. Immediate tasks must be focused within the containing parameters. This makes it possible for the first action(s) to be launched.

I give below the levels I have tested.

Level 1. *The danger named but not entirely controllable, e.g. unusual forces.*
    A. Six-year-olds starting French language studies. As detectives they must secretly enter a French chateau to capture an evil chemist who is poisoning Coca-Cola in supermarkets in Paris. The gate is unlocked but a notice states: 'This chateau is guarded by a lion which bears a silver transmitting claw. The lion roams freely.' What to do?
    B. Macbeth is escorting the king to Macbeth's castle (15–16-year-old boys with low IQ in an approved school).
    This was tried out 3 times:
    The boar in his lair asleep – no sounds must be made.
    The boar has been spotted by a guide, but is there another way to reach the castle?
    The boar has been so close that the dogs with Macbeth's party may have been scented; they are agitated and barking, which may alert the boar.
Level 2. *Dangers known in advance and yet entered bravely, e.g. to find something and escape or release someone.*
    C. Nine-year-olds exploring aspects of King Arthur's legends. Teileman, the harpist, is immured in a Norman castle. Friends and companions of Arthur are to enter and bring him and his harp to safety. Friends are 'catchers of dungeon rats' with passes to enter but all are checked as they exit with rats. The harp and one rat-catcher must be carried out in sacks among the captured rats, while Teileman replaces the hidden rat-catcher. He is taller than all the friends and the guards are vigilant and can count!
Level 3. *Duty in the face of distractions. Including unpredictable territories – ruins, wastelands, treacherous sands, caves, tides. These territories demand that participants must be able to sustain their imagery of the place, and respond appropriately.*

D. Police and firemen (12–16-year-old pupils excluded from school) are trying to recover a body (a blind girl) from a moorland bog. Her guide dog is contantly howling, won't leave the site and cannot be caught. The witness – a farmer – heard her cry out while penning his sheep at dusk, then the howling of the dog, but has not seen where she entered the bog. This work was a prelude to discovering 'The Bog People'.

Level 4. *Herculean tasks. Surviving pressures of time, adverse climates, dangerous roads. These must be built into the tasks.*

E. 14–15-year-olds using a genuine handwritten diary of a British soldier fighting the Turks. The diary tells of the dilemma of Big Bertha, a giant cannon mounted so as to fire on the British ships, should any party try to land to put the cannon out of action so that the territory may be taken. There are two moonless nights on which to try to launch the small boat and scale the heights to silence the cannon. (*The Guns of Navarone* film deals with this episode.)

Level 5. *Danger from guile – possible betrayal or spy infiltration.*

F. Approved-school boys, as prisoners of war, plan to escape but can they be certain that a new prisoner brought into the hut is not a spy? Their escape plan is ready to be put into action that night.

G. Thirteen-year-olds beginning French language studies. A French scientist is held prisoner by the Germans. A young Englishwoman who knows the building from earlier, but has no French language, must be equipped to penetrate the guards and pass a secret verbal message to the prisoner giving precise instructions as to what to do to collaborate when a rescue party plans to release him. All her equipment must have French origin marks – her clothing, luggage, rail and bus tickets, identification documents, books and transit documents must withstand scrutiny. Her scarf (silk) is patterned with a map and basic French phrases well hidden to assist her in reaching the prisoner's street and finding the house she has known before the war, when much younger. In case of difficulty she carries a folding white stick and dark glasses, only to be used in dire emergency. The group is teaching her how to speak, behave and remember the instructions so she may stand a chance of assisting the rescue. They have to rehearse every single possibility and hazard she may face so as to be successful, and prepare all in the French language.

Level 6. *Threats because of stupidity: foolish carelessness, losing or forgetting critical information.*

H. A class of learning-impaired students, aged 12–14, focus on mathematics, weights, dimensions, critical timing using watches. A gang has surveyed a bank and discovered a weakness in security at the back of the premises, which are approached through a narrow archway leading to a quiet cul-de-sac. They are measuring their map – distances and times. They have getaway cars and the truck labelled 'Water Board', which will be parked early; the crew in overalls with correct identification will be working over a sewer. The watches, disguises, cars and routes and timings are all synchronized. The truck is discovered to be too tall/wide to be driven through the arch and is firmly stuck in position – choices – abort? Risk damaging the arch as they push? Leave it and run? Their client is not going to be pleased…

Level 7. *Extremely critical time limitations.*

I. Theatre students studying Bram Stoker's *Dracula*. Their companions in their coach hastening to Transylvania know that 'he' is travelling by sea, and Lucy, who has incomplete and transitory visions, is their only link with where his boat is currently travelling. Here, the students are not acting an episode – they are working as writers, creating two tense journeys to be portrayed in tandem with constant reference to Stoker's narrative. Their journey will use a Chamber Theatre format–'show me a story'. This involves use of the exact literary text with demonstration of the action.

J. The same students learning about Chamber Theatre using the book *Ursula Under* by Ingrid Hill. Ursula, a young child, has fallen down a disused mineshaft and a team of rescuers with a microphone has located her – precariously poised on old rubbish accumulated through the years. They plan the Chamber Theatre text to create the tensions of many groups, duties and interests (the press, engineers, the girl who is slender enough to finally descend on the rope to bring the child to the surface). It is the tension between literary form and Chamber Theatre form here – because this format is able to create the impression of simultaneity that the group will test when they have grasped the range of interests which are present and which must all be accommodated in their final presentation.

Level 8. *Pressures from sickness, woundings, accidents, traps seen too late.*

K. The six-year-old detectives (see example A) are trapped in a room which is being cleaned and feather-dusted by an old lady. The room is full of statues so they are forced to add themselves to the marble figures and withstand her feather duster without moving or sneezing. She is speaking in French trying to put the correct titles on each statue from a folder and obviously there are twenty-five too many statues. Shall they capture her and tie her up? Offer to help her so as to get her assistance to find the evil chemist? Can they trust her? This needs a role to do the dusting and contracts must be made so that all agree that the detectives will resolve this immediate problem some way, for they must stop the poisoning of the Coca-Cola.

Level 9. *Breaks in communication – the failure of messages, technical resources, lights failing.*

L. Being lost in a maze because the map is incomplete and doesn't therefore show which statue is the correct centre.

Level 10. *Missing signs or misreading them.*

M. Seven-year-olds who have found a baby and are trying to discover who is the likely mother from an assortment of 'ladies', demonstrated by the teacher:[3] a deaf person, a too busy mother with lots of children, a blind lady, a bookish lady, a witch who has always wanted a baby. Obviously the last role must be planned together, because the witch must be as 'dangerous' as they think they can cope with! The basis of this work was that the head teacher was anxious (because of the location of the school) that strangers should not be approached. This is highly delicate, because alerting them should not frighten – hence the exaggerated 'funny' ladies and much glee when they chose wisely and took the baby to the police station after breaking the witch's spell.

Level 11. *Breakdowns in relationships causing doubts that threaten support systems.*

N. Approved-school boys (BBC *Death of a President* 1966). The killer is being 'watched' by his companions on a radio contact as they listen to the account of the president's exit from church and await the gunshot – they hear the bullet has missed and the gunman escaped. 'He has muffed it!' They await his arrival knowing their associate will have been followed to their hideout, so all are in danger of arrest.

Level 12. *Loss of faith in some companions. So-called honourable betrayals or changes of heart or faith in a cause.*

        O. Canadian high school students studying the dissolution of the monasteries and an incident when Cromwell's troops are searching for a priest's hole in a large mansion. All the household is assembled to be interrogated. Into the assembly wanders the small child of the gatekeeper who has hidden the priest, seen by the child. Will the child tell? How to avoid troops noticing the child has entered?

You can probably start to invent your own examples for the following levels of tension:

Level 13. *Missed appointments can have positive or negative effects.*
Level 14. *Limitations of space.*
Level 15. *Requirement to be silent in difficult circumstances.*
Level 16. *Requirement to leave no evidence for others to find.*
Level 17. *Impenetrable codes or languages.*
Level 18. *Too many choices – cupboards, pathways, caskets, keys.*
Level 19. *A blocked exit.*
Level 20. *Disguised entrances/exits.*
Level 21. *Expected guide is helpless – bound, drugged, dead, asleep, hurt, late, a betrayal.*
Level 22. *Some important element is missing – ladders too short, ropes too thick or thin.*
Level 24. *Leader can no longer take command. Expertise essential but captured, delayed, drugged, hurt, dead.*

Any of these tensions can be combined, as for example pressures of time in the face of adverse territory or a need to improvise when an essential tool is lost. It will be important to:

- define the containments;
- define the immediate motives and purposes;
- define what must be left to chance and why it is uncontrollable except through the group exercising powers won in process – doing, not just holding meetings!

What can a teacher draw upon for help in planning for productive tension in order to develop involvement and commitment? Well, the first aid is to be in role, creating the 'now' time and immediacy, but obviously not by taking on the role of the powerful leader. More useful support will be brought about if you are the messenger (messengers have access to information from others beyond the group facing the task). Another aid is to bring in the 'stuff' but you are not certain what it consists of 'till we examine it'. 'Stuff' can be a letter, a phone call – which you will pass to the others as soon as you can – a diary, map, rail timetable, address, car to be collected, coded information 'you're not certain of' or properties you've collected or you all find waiting. And remember, you and your class can negotiate all this and make contracts.

    You have other factors to assist your planning for high focus. All factors are considered in order that the one uncontrollable element is defined, even if it does not immediately emerge when the episode begins. There should be no tricks played by you, but when emergencies arise they will be shared by you, so you and the participants can sort it out together. This allows you to keep in touch with the social health of the group and avoid those long static discussions that I fear bedevil much of Mantle of the Expert and other modes of drama work.

These are the human structures I draw on in planning for productive tension. The most essential element in productive tension is that the outcome must be agreed before the experience is embarked upon. Knowing the outcome from the start slows time into experiential time. If everyone is trying to reach resolution, they rush towards resolving the dilemma. By knowing the outcome they all create the dilemma at a pace they find reasonable. An example of this outcome-versus-dilemma was when a group of nine-year-olds in Birmingham were the 'local people' looking for a child missing from a supermarket. Their choices – Is the child dead, injured or safe? They elected for the last so the search was much more productively tense when they had located the place where the abductors were holding their victim. As with the witch earlier in example M, the students will have to create, by previous agreement, the circumstances which prevail when the searchers find the hideout. At this point, the frame distance of Convention No.1 (see 'Signs and portents') of active searching changes the frame distance to Convention No. 2 ('We can guide the press about the rescue, for we were there.'). Paradoxical as it may appear, frame distances and the use of conventions often create more meaningful experiences and understanding than enactment at frame distance No. 1 ('I am here. It is happening.').

## Notes

1  'Training Teachers to use Drama as Education' in Johnson, L. and O'Neill, C. (eds.) (1984) *Dorothy Heathcote: Collected Writings on Education and Drama*, London: Hutchinson, p. 34.
2  'Drama and Learning' in Johnson, L. and O'Neill, C. (eds.) (1984) *Dorothy Heathcote: Collected Writings on Education and Drama*, London: Hutchinson, p. 52.
3  See DVD *Making Magic*, Newcastle University.

# CHAMBER THEATRE

*Chamber Theatre is a method of adapting literary works using extracts from the original text in minimal settings. Narration is included in the performed text and may be delivered by more than one performer. Chamber Theatre was developed by Robert Breen at Northwestern University in 1947.[1]*

*Heathcote regarded this formal and explicitly theatrical device as one of the strategies appropriate for use within Mantle of the Expert. She sometimes prepared short Chamber Theatre texts for participants to animate as a way of deepening or extending their understanding during a Mantle of the Expert process. It is interesting that in the preceding chapter, 'Productive tensions', she provides examples of the use of Chamber Theatre where the tension lies in the struggle to accommodate the formal, presentational quality of Chamber Theatre and existing literary form. The strict rules of Chamber Theatre make it almost the reverse of any kind of lived-through, experiential drama happening in 'now' time.*

*In working with literature, Heathcote advises teachers to search for literary passages that contain evidence of social encounter, action and responses, evidence of place, mood, atmosphere, visual description and third-person narration.[2] 'Porphyria's Lover', the example she gives in this paper, is a very good illustration of a text that possesses all of these characteristics apart from the inclusion of a third-person narrator.*

*What follows is an edited version of the paper dated 24 January 2005 and published as* 'Chamber Theatre: A Bridge Worth the Forging' *in* The Journal for Drama in Education, *21 (2), Summer 2012.*

Chamber Theatre, sometimes called story or narrative drama, illuminates literary text by linking *telling* with *showing*. The writer's words are closely respected but can be demonstrated in action for onlookers. The process fulfils the laws of theatre, using sound, silence, movement, stillness, light and dark and the presence of actors in a symbiotic relationship with the written account that guides the process.

Teachers interested in reading and literature will have had satisfying experiences of lifting meaning from print, often at high speed, so the process of information and visualization feels seamless. If only teachers could provide a means for their students to achieve this! Literature is written for readers who must provide internal images plucked from the text in the very act of reading the words as they are presented by the writer. The ordering of events is constructed to cause meaning and comprehension as solitary readers enter their own mind space.

Texts imposed by curriculum demands can seem impenetrable. Adding the theatre strand can help readers to develop their mental images and aid them to become mature, sophisticated readers. This is surely the aim in schools when literacy and literature are placed so clearly at the centre of the curriculum. Chamber Theatre is a useful tool with a wide range of ages and abilities but this disciplined yet flexible form has been slow to become popular.

All work in the arts involves process in the making and form in the product. Chamber Theatre treats the original literary text as being 'holy'. This means all the text will be honoured in the process of lifting the words into a relationship with the action. If the words of the writer are not honoured, they will be seen as a restrictive corset rather than an intriguing terrain to be carefully explored and shaped into a satisfying fusion of words and demonstrating action.

Chamber Theatre is not interested in transforming fiction into drama: it resists the temptation to delete narrative descriptions and rewrite summaries as dialogue. No effort is made in Chamber Theatre to eliminate the narrative point of view which characterizes fiction; indeed, the storyteller's angle of vision is emphasized through physical representation on stage.

I propose several questions to myself before deciding to use Chamber Theatre with students.

1. Do these readers need Chamber Theatre in order to 'own' the text for themselves?
2. How may I test their ability to access their inner-eye vision? How do I normally do this when teaching?
3. How do I avoid falling into the trap of my personal enthusiasm for Chamber Theatre overriding the students' abilities?
4. Can I honestly say this approach is in the service of literature and student appreciation and pleasure in reading?
5. Do I have to give the literary text a full treatment or can I work on a 'taster' to help make the material accessible?
6. Will Chamber Theatre help the students to work on their own image-making so that it speeds up their grasp of the text instead of having to skim-read because of lack of time in a crowded timetable?

If I am satisfied that Chamber Theatre will be useful, then I have to face the first question, and, where possible, work in collaboration with the other readers. This is definitely not a time for parading my knowledge, which disempowers students and breeds student dependence on the teacher. The text is there for all of us to interrogate without my intervention.

The question that launches the interrogation is: Who is telling the story? The 'who' we select through discussion must be the person, or persons, who will be in a position to know all that the story requires. This is the first discipline, for not a word, nor any punctuation, nor any dialogue or analysis of motivation may be eliminated or altered. The text is holy. Thus the first bonus of Chamber Theatre is that it is active. The text must be read in order to discover 'who would know all this', but because the concentration is deflected into 'who would know', it provides the motivation to get over the barriers of unfamiliarity.

Browning's poem 'Porphyria's Lover' is a useful vehicle for exploring time shifts in a narrative. It will probably require two 'lover' roles: the one who tells of Porphyria's visit and its outcome, and the other who demonstrates the action of her visit. At the beginning of the poem, the narrator's words indicate the recent past ('set', 'was', 'tore'), but he also says 'tonight'. Thus the very recent past is firmly established. Then the narrator – the lover – tells us of Porphyria's arrival and the details of all her preparations watched and noted by her lover.

Now comes one of those fascinating challenges of Chamber Theatre, one that demands deep study of the written words in order that the lover's position can be expressed. Should there be two lovers – the one who sees and notes all the events and the one who is seated from the beginning, or comes to sit beside Porphyria at the phrase 'she called me'? There is a line indicating dialogue – 'murmuring how she loved me'. Another interesting challenge is in the final line – 'And yet God has not said a word.'

Porphyria's Lover

> The rain set early in tonight,
> The sullen wind was soon awake,
> It tore the elm-tops down for spite,
> And did its worst to vex the lake:
> I listened with heart fit to break.
> When glided in Porphyria; straight
> She shut the cold out and the storm,
> And kneeled and made the cheerless grate
> Blaze up, and all the cottage warm;
> Which done, she rose, and from her form
> Withdrew the dripping cloak and shawl,
> And laid her soiled gloves by, untied
> Her hat and let the damp hair fall,
> And, last, she sat down by my side
> And called me. When no voice replied,
> She put my arm about her waist,
> And made her smooth white shoulder bare,
> And all her yellow hair displaced,
> And, stooping, made my cheek lie there,
> And spread, o'er all, her yellow hair,
> Murmuring how she loved me — she
> Too weak, for all her heart's endeavour,
> To set its struggling passion free
> From pride, and vainer ties dissever,
> And give herself to me forever.
> But passion sometimes would prevail,
> Nor could tonight's gay feast restrain
> A sudden thought of one so pale
> For love of her, and all in vain:
> So, she was come through wind and rain.
> Be sure I looked up at her eyes
> Happy and proud; at last I knew
> Porphyria worshipped me: surprise
> Made my heart swell, and still it grew
> While I debated what to do.
> That moment she was mine, mine, fair,
> Perfectly pure and good: I found

A thing to do, and all her hair
In one long yellow string I wound
Three times her little throat around,
And strangled her. No pain felt she;
I am quite sure she felt no pain.
As a shut bud that holds a bee,
I warily oped her lids: again
Laughed the blue eyes without a stain.
And I untightened next the tress
About her neck; her cheek once more
Blushed bright beneath my burning kiss:
I propped her head up as before,
Only, this time my shoulder bore
Her head, which droops upon it still:
The smiling rosy little head,
So glad it has its utmost will,
That all it scorned at once is fled,
And I, its love, am gained instead!
Porphyria's love: she guessed not how
Her darling one wish would be heard.
And thus we sit together now,
And all night long we have not stirred,
And yet God has not said a word![3]

Suppose a camera team are filming the story? There might be a scriptwriter explaining to the sound and lighting crew and the director as they 'work' the actors through the event. You can see how literary texts beguile us into thinking again, and each idea takes us to in-depth reading. The final choice must not indulge in sentimentalism for its own sake. Remember, the text is pure!

Whatever experiences we provide for our students, it is imperative that they recognize the processes they are engaged in and can apply that awareness to future learning. If they cannot own their understanding, they remain teacher-dependent. Chamber Theatre demands, by the very process of *tell* and *show*, that participants must self-spectate whatever has to be made clear, and so it enables them to develop the way the showing and telling will be achieved through the correlation of dramatic action and the words spoken.

Self-spectatorship is not an embarrassed self-consciousness. As students clarify for themselves what must be made clear to others, they begin to be consciously aware of the process with which they are engaged. They may often need help in order to recognize and clarify their ideas. At this stage, notes will help memory. But there is another aspect to self-spectatorship. This is what all artists and creative workers do – whether painter, dancer, actor, writer, musician – they recognize their processes of action, using their medium of expression. Dancers' and actors' bodies and voices are their only medium of expression. It follows that their self-spectator is constantly alert regarding their intentions, their practice and their achievement in communicating. In Chamber Theatre also, the artist-participants judge and self-correct their choices.

One important factor by which Chamber Theatre prevents self-consciousness is that all the action is *demonstrated* to the audience. This relieves the actors from having to generate emotion from within themselves, because the writer's words provide that emotion and the words and action together make a seamless, believable statement. Getting this right further involves participants in monitoring and reflecting on the narrative, In order to illustrate the text more effectively they stare at the 'it' of the text and their own process of doing 'it', and thus they interrogate the author's intentions. Staring into the text stops them from feeling stared at – the self-spectator constantly engages with and monitors what they are doing because they know their intention.

I have already mentioned multiple roles, and Breen gives many subtle examples of how actors can represent different psychological aspects of roles within a narrative through the 'selves' who will be born of the artists' artistry in connection with the narrative. As he puts it, the juxtaposition of author, reader and the demonstrating actors combine the novel's narrative and the theatre's privilege of examining human motivation at the moment of action.

## Notes

1  Breen, Robert S. (1986) *Chamber Theatre*. Evanston, IL: William Caxton.
2  Heathcote, D. (2010) 'Dramatic Imagination', *The Journal for Drama in Education* (26) 2, Summer.
3  Jack, I. and Fowler, R. (1997) *The Poetical Works of Robert Browning*, volume III, Oxford: Oxford University Press.

# APPROACHING *HAMLET*

*I have introduced these notes on 'Approaching* Hamlet' *with a passage about Chamber Theatre from an account of a workshop given by Heathcote in Turkey in 2009.*[1]

    *This list of different ways of approaching a classic text displays the fertility of Heathcote's imagination, her innate sense of theatre and her command of a variety of powerful strategies for bringing literature to life. Several of these approaches could be described as Chamber Theatre, since they allow the text to be encountered in action without exposing participants who may have limited performance skills. It was originally published as 'Pages from a Teacher's Notebook' in* London Drama Magazine *6 (8), 1983.*

Chamber Theatre, or story theatre, fills an important gap between narration and theatre performance, which demands a degree of skill in revealing characters in the process of interaction, as happens in life encounters. This places heavy burdens upon students who may be self-conscious or inexperienced. Chamber Theatre frequently demands all the six theatre signs to be in process consistently – relevant selective sounds, pauses and silences, all gesture and interactive movement, settings and clothing as well as appropriate properties. These together 'hold the mirror up to nature' by suiting the action to the word and the word to the action, as Hamlet advised in his talk to the visiting players.

    Chamber Theatre operates by using a symbiotic relationship between the teller of the story and 'animators' who show the behaviours required by the story form. These animators can represent more than one character in the story, and sometimes a character can be shown to exist in a different time scale while contemporary time is revealed by another animator. The term 'animator' is suitable here because participants do not act the part of fully developed characters: they demonstrate only the behaviours spoken by the 'wise' narrator, the holder of all knowledge of the event. Seeking for the 'wise commentator' is one of the most useful ways of inducting students into deep reading of literary materials. Dialogue is used where essential and is spoken by the animator, who echoes the dialogue in the story.

1.   A '*Huis Clos*' situation
     Gertrude, Claudius and Hamlet are in limbo.

Scenes from the text come out of their queries, tensions and accusations. These can be played out of sequence. Three different explanations are given as each character directs the same scene, emphasizing different aspects. These scenes can be interrupted by any of the other characters who want to argue, accuse or question. Other characters join in as necessary.

The ghost may be used as interlocutor, general accuser, or the person responsible for the others being in limbo.

In a further elaboration we hear the views of a number of experts on the tragedy – psychiatrists, mediums, military experts.

2. A medium is employed to get at the truth of the tragedy. The same scenes are enacted from different points of view, as in the Japanese film *Rashomon*, e.g.

    (a)   Gertrude saw …
    (b)   Hamlet saw …
    (c)   Claudius saw ….

3. Ghosts of the dead appear, chained endlessly by their memories to rooms, things and places. They explain their situation and re-enact their lives and deaths.

4. The players visit another castle after the tragedy and turn the events to their own advantage by presenting their view of what happened at Elsinore. The story can be presented as farce, a detective story or a pathetic love story.

5. Personal body-servants, companions or friends of the different characters argue over their interpretations of the characters' behaviour, and scenes from the play are performed.

    They may see possibilities they previously missed and seek explanations for the behaviour of the great ones.

6. The events of the play are interpreted in two different ways – by a company of actors and a company of scholars.

    The first group react to 'the moment' and to emotion, and draw upon life for their evidence. The second group are dry, intellectual, seeking evidence and historical accuracy of detail. They clash and argue over their interpretations of the play. The 'man in the street' judges the truth of what they have presented.

7. The castle itself may speak its stories, taking on a personality, frozen in time, constantly retelling its story to every subsequent visitor or occupant – soldiers, servants, courtiers, kings, travellers, politicians. Each visitor will be from a different time period, with different interests and attitudes, and will see different meanings in the events of the play.

    A simpler version of this would be a guide showing tourists round the castle, and as each room is entered, relevant scenes are played.

8. Crucial scenes are re-enacted, but the 'dead' are chained to the live actors, and as the lines are spoken, the dead speak their thoughts with hindsight and insight. There are difficulties here, particularly of matching the linguistic style of the 'thoughts' with the lines of the text.

9. The work might begin with the players' scene – 'It all began with this' – and the dead gather to watch while the living present scenes relating to the players' scene.

10. Scenes are linked with comments by:

    (a)   Fortinbras and his followers;
    (b)   Horatio and his friends;
    (c)   a storyteller or commentator working though 'alienation', as in Brecht;
    (d)   a fairy-tale storyteller, or a storyteller in the 'saga' or 'myth' idiom;
    (e)   Hamlet's diary;
    (f)   a stagehand, as in Chinese theatre;

(g) the gravediggers;

(h) a commentator speaking in a modern idiom, changing from a humorous style to a spell-binding one as 'dead' actors take over. If a rack of clothes and regalia are hanging in the palace as relics, tourists can move into the scenes. Their guide can be magic, or a 'con-jure-man'. He can call up death or be 'taken over' by death. He can be a mystery figure who is mistaken for a guide, or a real guide, or the spirit of Elsinore.

11. Allegorical characters, e.g. power, lust, truth, kingship, loyalty.

A scene is played with real people, then with these allegorical figures, thus reducing it to fundamentals – If it had all happened otherwise....

12. First a particular scene is played; then improvisations are prepared to show versions of the way events might have turned out, e.g.

(a) if the ghost had not appeared;

(b) if Gertrude had only had an affair with Claudius instead of marrying him;

(c) if Ophelia had not died by drowning.

## Note

1 Heathcote, D. (2010) 'Mantle of the Expert Work in Ankara: Workshop with Secondary School Students, November 2009', *Creative Drama Journal* 5 (9–10), p. 203.

# SIGNS AND PORTENTS

*This is an edited version of the paper specially written for and first published in the* Journal of the Standing Conference of Young People's Theatre, *Spring, 1980. It was reprinted in* Collected Writings, *pp. 160–9, and is perhaps the best known of all Heathcote's writings. It has been acknowledged as influencing a generation of practitioners in the field of Theatre in Education. Heathcote considers the common denominators that apply when working in role and the ways in which this approach can empower both the teacher and the students. She discusses the significance of 'sign' in both theatre and classroom, and the value of conventions in T.I.E and drama in education.*

*Gavin Bolton explains how these strategies reveal Heathcote's theatrical artistry:*

> *However 'still' in reality, there must be for Heathcote a metaphorical movement to the depiction, always going beyond itself, a memory activated, a future indicated or circumstances reflected upon, considered and interrogated.*[1]

## Signs

Living in the actual world and theatre, which is a depiction of living conditions, use the same network of signs as their medium of communication – namely the human being signalling across space, in immediate time, to and with others, each reading and signalling simultaneously within the action of each passing moment. We cannot help signing so long as there is another human being who needs to read the signs. Actions become sign whenever there is more than one person present to read the action.

Balanced between *actual living* and *theatre* are the forms known as *drama in education* and *Theatre in Education* (T.I.E). I should like to explore the relationship of these four kinds of events in this paper.

When I first began teaching, I had no training in the 'proper' ways to make contact with my classes. Coming from a theatre training, I therefore used the thing I knew most about, which was how to make it interesting and exciting to be present at an occasion marked by the *conscious* signing of intent. As I had not been 'taught manners' as you might say, I didn't know about the complexities of classroom communication, where the person in charge uses the mouth as the main means of communication, with sometimes the blackboard as an additional aid to coherence. However, coming from the theatre, I got to thinking it would be important that the word and the gesture, and the relationship with the furniture and the book, and indeed anything which at the moment assisted in the total picture should become available to be 'read' by the class. I also knew that you don't ask questions to which you already know the answer. That is not how theatre works. You signal across space meaningfully, to get a response that will have been born from your own signal, as the person(s) alongside you read the sign. So of course you listen with all your body for the messages.

Coming from the theatre also, you don't consider sign to be bad manners. I still meet colleagues who somehow manage *by their* signing to indicate to me that there is something rather ungenteel about behaving like that in classrooms. However, I must say that I am glad that more teachers are braving these critics and trying to employ sign more coherently in their teaching. Students deserve the best systems of communication we can give them. I wonder if we would have fewer 'slow learners' if we used a more meticulously selective and complete signing system as our means of communication with such students. Individuals read signs very differently, and therefore decipher the code more easily if it is rich, full and highly selective for its present purpose.

This is the interesting variation on life and theatre signing which the classroom and the T.I.E team can exploit. In the theatre all actors sign for the benefit of the audience. In life we sign for the other person out of the need for a response. In teaching we make our signs especially interpretable, so that the children are able to read all signals with the least possible confusion. We deliberately sign for the responder to come into active participation in the event. If, therefore, as teachers we send out some signs to be part of the event, but demand of children that other signs, which are also present, are to be ignored, then we baffle them by the confusion of what they should ignore. The most developed skill that children bring to school is that of making sense for their own purposes of sign in their immediate environment. So we do not need to apologize for 'showing off', which is how working in role in the classroom is often seen. One can understand why people criticize it, because the medium of expression is the human person.

## Some common denominators in working through role

We probably all agree that when we say we work in role, we mean that we become part of the action of the 'play' and have a voice in the dramatic encounter. There must, by now, be some emergent theory born of practice, which could be brought together so that we can see what the rules are in order to apply them better. What follows are only the basic common denominators which I have isolated; they are not complete, because I don't myself understand it all yet.

### Now and imminent time

The factor that distinguishes a dramatic exploration of ideas seems to be the way in which time becomes different from the usual classroom time. During a discussion of ideas (though we ourselves exist in real time) the circumstances we are planning to generate and attempt to cause to exist in are still in another time state. We talk about, 'They would be this or that', because although we are generating the future action of the event, we are still only in the planning stage.

I am constantly amazed by the miracle of the way *thinking* about a dramatic idea can in an instant become that of *carrying it into action*. There is a world of difference between someone in a class saying, 'Well, they would take all their belongings with them', and saying, 'Let's pack up and leave'. That is the switch I work for, to enable a dramatic exploration of ideas to take place. It stands to reason then, if I want to assist in this switch to imminent time, the most efficient way is to start very carefully to use my contribution to the discussion in this *now* time state. That is role at its simplest. *I talk as if I'm there.* There is a lot more to it than that of course. One never becomes merely a person in the play, because one is teaching as well as signing. Ask yourself this question. The last time you worked in role were you really only adding to the number in the cast? If so, you've made a start in using the power of role, but there's a very exciting journey ahead if you care to investigate.

## Role as contract maker

I have already indicated that social encounters need sign – the sign of the person, in action, using all objects, significant space, pause, silences, and vocal power to make the meaning available to others in the encounter. This total acceptance of signing allows children to bring their profound experience to bear in interpreting the scene. A class on the defensive, which has developed resistant techniques to classroom practice, is particularly good at reading signs for its own ends. When the teacher begins to accept the total signing system as open for the class to interpret, an erosion of the position of negative spectatorship that we all develop under stress or criticism can also begin. In role I give myself two kinds of encounter. One is the power to get out of the familiar and expected teacher system of relating with the class. The other is the opportunity to make contracts as myself and encounter the class signing system through the role I artificially and totally consciously take up. So role can work as an anti-corrosive agent.

## 'The other'

This is a somewhat fanciful name to give to what might be perceived merely as something to deflect the attention of the class. I spend a lot of time preventing classes feeling stared at. Everything else in the world except oneself is 'another'. The actors in the theatre, the T.I.E team and the teacher have all made a contract to allow people to stare at them, but the children have not made that contract. And teachers of drama who take it for granted that children have given them this permission spend useless time in eroding the embarrassment that happens during drama lessons where children feel stared at.

   The obvious way of avoiding this is to give them something so attractive in the room that they feel *they* are staring at *it*. Role is one of the most efficient 'others'. Do not mistake what I am saying: I do not mean something that is merely interesting or entertaining; it may have that outer appearance, just as the teacher in role might fool an onlooker that the only thing the role is doing is acting. Roles must never act in the sense that an actor may, for they have a different job to do. What I am discussing here is that 'the other' be the gateway to all the full depth of exploration that will follow as the class becomes involved with the issues. When teacher in role is used, it can set the frame very quickly, because the very fact that someone has entered into a full signing system, in drama time, automatically places the rest of the people present into roles themselves, for they must be addressed as if they are those roles. It is much harder for the same shift or the potential for such a shift to be brought about by other means, simply because other objects used in this way cannot enter this special 'now' time of drama. There is prejudice against using role because it is so efficient and looks so showy.

## Sharing and giving of information

Teachers are noted for their propensity to share their understanding by a process of *telling* in one form or another. This often tends to look like one-way transmission. A teacher in role can undermine this approach because the theatre gets its message over more indirectly through the range of signs that come into play. Many kinds of information are available simultaneously when role is used, especially that of *frame* and of *attitude*.

Recently I was in role as a manager of a gold mine with a London class:

> The new issue of picks, shovels, screens and pans is due today. See that they are signed for, and you'd better check that they are the correct size this time. Those big meshes are useless for this soil. We've wasted too much time at the panning tanks re-screening. I just hope we haven't lost any nuggets through these wide meshes. Where's the storekeeper?

Put baldly like this, with no pitch, pause, gesture, position in relation to all the others, and a general demeanour of authority to speak while others listen, it seems like a one-way flow. What is not conveyed in print is the opportunity for the teacher to observe the class response to the variety of topics introduced. Neither can it explain the reasons why the role made that particular statement.

In this case the class was demonstrating in a fairly patient way that they were expecting to get into action and dig. It is possible for a teacher to ask all kinds of questions about such matters as, 'Where would the tools be kept?', 'Where is the actual shaft?', 'Who are we?', 'What are our jobs?' When they are asked questions like this, the children take interesting decisions but not *as if they were* miners. The fictional time state of drama cannot be induced through that type of question. In the pit manager's role there are also disadvantages. You cannot ask experienced miners (which in this drama is what the children will be) where they keep their tools. Everyone would know. Neither can you ask how they do their jobs. Nor can you ask who the storekeeper is. You would know. But you can induct all the miners into different kinds of information by the statement about new tools which will be arriving, the need to check these tools against wrong and useless ones, problems at the tanks, the introduction of one technical term which is *only* used in the mining of gold, as well as giving some indication of the existence of another authority figure who can supersede your power. With this approach the children have a chance to become seasoned miners in action, or at least in response, because everything can be assumed, yet explained quite explicitly. A request for the storekeeper (even if he or she isn't present because no one in the group wants to take on the responsibility) can yield the whereabouts of either keys to stores or a place where stores are currently kept; this in turn will yield a shaft where miners collect their tools. Rules of behaviour can emerge as they join their mates at the shaft head. Laws about matches, pocket contents, searches of the miners after shift – all these will become natural developments from 'Where is the storekeeper?' This is the excitement and subtlety of role work – thinking like a cat, while apparently signing crudely.

## *Negotiation*

Artists work from two positions of power. The *doing* position, where they are involved in the action of their art, and the *seeing* position from which they perceive what is happening and what might need to be done. By sometimes working in the action of the play and sometimes from the spectator position I can give this power to the class. Role helps them *do*, and the teacher helps them *see*. In the early stages, contracts and decisions are often best taken from the spectator position so that everyone can see there is no confidence trick happening. This is one of the secrets of sincere work. In a paradoxical way, then, I build trust in the drama by working as a teacher, negotiating within the real world, while in role I build trust in the virtual world. This is a very comfortable way to work for both teacher and class, for it enables all the rules to be seen as they come into action, and especially it gets rid of the teacher's power to *tell* directly.

## *Shifting the position of the class*

By taking up a role one not only offers a point of view to the others, but places them in a position from where it is assumed that they will also find a point of view. Note that I have said 'assumed'. One cannot endow people with commitment to a point of view, but often by being placed in the response position, they begin to hold a point of view, because they can see it has power. The crudest power to give others is that of disagreeing with the role, spotting the weakness in the role's position, or even opposing the role. If a class really wants to oppose a teacher, it can often be somewhat bitter in tone, open to the accusation of rudeness (at the least), but opposition to a role places a class in a very safe position from which to disagree, and it establishes their *right* to oppose the teacher's power. No one loses face. But the best thing of all, the *role*, not the *teacher*, can respond to the communication, thus holding it in the 'no penalty' zone. In this way good relations can be built on a very sure basis.

## Theatre in Education teams

So far I have been mainly looking at teacher in role from the point of view of the teacher in the classroom. What of T.I.E teams? The first advantage they have is that, under theatre conventions, they are accepted as total signers. They have given permission to others to stare so they can employ significance from the start. It is accepted as normal for the actor/teachers to employ such aspects of sign as clothing, properties and settings for the action. This is not so easy for the teacher because of different expectations of behaviour. One of the most fundamental decisions which T.I.E teams have made is that of working with classes both from inside and from outside the action of the play. However, often their weakest area is that they have the problem of having to change their signing systems to indicate and accommodate to these two positions. This is because of the very strength of their sign position when they are in the action of the play. A teacher, by her or his inability to sign strongly on clothing, setting and accuracy of properties, can sign mainly in the areas of language and body position, and these are more easily shed than the clothing and props signs of the T.I.E actor. Thus it is, I think, that the T.I.E teams often find difficulty in their negotiations from outside the action of the play or when they are seeking to bring their audiences into the action. Children can't help being reminded that they are in the action in not quite the same way that the actors are.

## Conventions

So we come to the fascinating area of conventions that can be used to enable children to become involved in drama experiences of many types. The ability of children to achieve truthful behaviour in both T.I.E and classroom drama, and to become committed to the decisions they are enabled to take during the action of the play is phenomenal. The conventions I shall outline seem to me to be a most useful addition to both types of work.

Avant-garde theatre has always used them, and film can wonderfully exploit these conventions. I use them more and more in my classroom work, and they are comparatively easy to manage with a little care and practice. They exploit the use of signing and significance in a very special way, because most of them shift the way in which the contact with role and 'immediate time' works. Most drama that moves forward at seeming life-rate is too swift for classes to become absorbed in and committed to. The conventions offered here *all slow down time* and enable classes to get a grip on decisions and on their own thinking about the issues they are dealing with. All the conventions function as 'other', but in relation to people:

1. The role actually present, naturalistic, yet significantly behaving, giving and accepting responses.
2. The same, except framed as a film. That is, people have permission to stare but not intrude. 'Film' can be stopped and restarted, or rerun.
3. The role present as in 'effigy'. It can be talked about, walked around, and even sculpted afresh, if it has been so framed.
4. The same, but with the convention that the effigy can be brought into lifelike response and then returned to effigy.
5. The role as portrait of a person. Not three dimensional, but in all other ways the same as effigy.
6. The role as portrait or effigy activated *to hear* what the class is saying. This produces selective language.
7. The role as above but activated to speak only, and not capable of movement.
8. The role depicted in picture: removed from actual life, as in a slide, a painting, a photograph or a drawing of the role. This includes those made by the class, as well as prepared depictions.
9. A drawing of someone important to the action seen in the making, for example on a blackboard.
10. A stylized depiction of someone. For example an identikit picture made by the class in frame as detectives.
11. The same, except made beforehand, so it is a *fait accompli*.
12. A life-size (cardboard) model with clothing (real) of a role. For example, 'framed' as if in a museum or salerooms. 'This is the dress worn by Florence Nightingale when she met Queen Victoria after Scutari.'
13. The same, except the class is dressing the model so as to see 'how it was' on that day when these events happened.
14. The clothing of a person cast off in disarray. For example, the remains of a tramp's presence, or a murder, or escape as in a highwayman situation.
15. Objects to represent a person's interests. This operates as in the Convention above, but more intimate things can indicate concerns rather than appearance. For example, a ring belonging to a Borgia.

16. An account of a person by another person in naturalistic fashion. For example, 'Well, when I saw him last he seemed all right. I never dreamed anything was wrong.'
17. An account of a person written as if from that person, but read by someone else. For example, a diary.
18. An account written by the person who now reads it to others, for example a policeman giving evidence or a confession. The role is present in this case but in contact through their writing, as an author might well be.
19. An account written by someone of someone else and read by yet another.
20. A story told about another, in order to bring that person close to the action. For example, 'I saw him open a safe once. It was an incredible performance. I'm not sure if he would assist us, though.'
21. A report of an event but formalized by authority or ritual. For example, an account of bravery in battle on the occasion of the presenting of posthumous medals.
22. A letter read in the voice of the writer. This is an emanation of a specific presence, not just any voice, communicating the words.
23. The same, but the letter is read by another with no attempt to portray the person who wrote it, but still expressing feeling.
24. A letter read without feeling. For example, as evidence, or an accusation in a formal situation.
25. The voice of a person overheard talking to another in informal language, that is, using a naturalistic tone.
26. The same, but in formal language.
27. A conversation overheard, where the people are not seen. Deliberate eavesdropping, as in spying.
28. A report of a conversation, written and spoken by another.
29. A reported conversation with two people reading the respective 'parts'.
30. A private reading of a conversation, reported as overheard.
31. The finding of a cryptic code message. For example, from tramps or spies.
32. The signature of a person found. For example, a half-burned paper.
33. The sign of a particular person discovered. For example, the special mark of the Scarlet Pimpernel.

All the above can be used to make classes feel involved with the immediate time of the action, and in touch with the human person, but these will not be achieved if the negotiations do not endow the class with the power to influence, not just to watch. This means that the participation needs to be framed.

## Frame

There are many ways of providing 'frames' for the action but the most important factor is that the participants have to be framed into *a position of influence*. In T.I.E it would seem an advantage to consider the many frames from which audiences might enter the action. If spectators are asked to use their judgement, as themselves, or to share in an endeavour with the actors, No.1 on the conventions list would seem to be the one that would feel right. But if they were asked to *comment on* the action as if it were in frozen time (as in a museum), then the frame can be different. For example, the actors may become portraits in a gallery and the participants may then be asked to reactivate them and make them 'play it again' in another way. Or, when teaching a Shakespearean play, a T.I.E team might play a scene of some seminal importance to the study, but then in an effigy or portrait convention, each protagonist in the situation might be 'hung' in a gallery and the children invited in groups to take one such painting and activate it to walk the scene again, asking it at each stage to explain itself.

I take it as a general rule that people have most power to become involved at a caring and urgently involved level if they are placed in a quite specific relationship with the action, because this inevitably brings with it the responsibility and, more particularly, the viewpoint that get them into an effective involvement in the event. By doing this, the social encounters, either during or after the main action of the play, become more complex and various. It *is* often done, of course, when, for example, the audience is invited to be a jury or soldiers at a firing squad, or indeed any situation where they may join in the moral or action decisions. However, the participation often functions in action time, the seeming life-rate of the theatre. The list of conventions above has only one such convention happening at life-rate – the first one. All the other encounters listed with people, their behaviour and motives, are in another kind of time. The roles exist to be rebuilt in one way or another and in one form or another. The class can be invited to reconstruct or reinterpret, and this has the remarkable effect of getting them hooked into the power to think about influence and hold a viewpoint, because the action is a process of *rebuilding* not sharing someone else's materials. Unlike television with its fast moving actions/images these other conventions function more like still photographs or photographic slides, causing infinitesimal decisions to be made by the children.

Theatre proper finds it difficult to cause audiences to reframe themselves, because this is not the mood in which most people come to the theatre. They anticipate the security of being spectators of the action. Likewise, the teacher who prefers to teach *about* things often uses the consciously cognitive approach. This type of teaching can avoid the immediate decision time of drama. T.I.E and classroom role work, however, are ideally suited to exploit these types of work and it pays well to explore them further.

I said at the beginning of this paper that if you only join the cast of the play, as it were, it adds very little to the kind of meaningful action that can take classes through the layers from mere attraction, to interest, to attention and finally to concern. The whole negotiation of role involves delicate linguistics in vocal sign, plus the equally selective body and space sign. Both areas of signalling demand that power is passed over to others. Let us take an example to try to make this clear.

Suppose the students are working as members of the team run by the Scarlet Pimpernel, rescuing an aristocrat from the revolution. The action has involved a teacher in role as one of the revolutionaries in order to place the class in danger as the 'brave rescuers'. The first episode may be dealt with in lifelike style; but see the difference in thought and the social demands that will be made if the second episode has to deal with the aristocrat being brought into an inn, where on the wall is the portrait of that aristocrat and the loyalties of the innkeeper are not known. The convention of *portrait* makes it possible here for a new look at danger, and the complexity of signing (which the class will of course handle without difficulty) creates an entirely new social and linguistic encounter. Obviously, whichever convention is selected, it will always be designed to serve the particular ends of the work.

Finally, having spent a long time wondering why I have for years been irritated by the cry of 'Let's have more drama in our schools', I now realize why I always wanted to say, 'Don't lobby for dramatics: lobby for better learning!' It is, of course, because the heart of communication in social situations is the sign. *All* teachers need to study how to exploit it as the first basis of their work. The theatre is the art form that is *totally* based in sign and adding drama to learning gives the urgency that is possible through using the now/imminent time of theatre.

## Note

1  Bolton, G. (1998) *Acting in Classroom Drama,* Stoke-on-Trent: Trentham Books, p. 191.

# NOTES ON SIGNS AND PORTENTS

*This paper was prepared by Heathcote with the help of Maggie Whitelaw for use on a British Council international drama course. It expands on the 33 conventions listed in the previous chapter. The implications for using each of the conventions and their impact on students are very usefully explored.*

*It first appeared in* Drama in Education, *a document published by The British Council in 1985.*

## The thirty-three conventions

1. **The role actually present, naturalistic, yet significantly behaving, giving and accepting responses.**
   (a) Practical considerations − Another person(s), who is 'locked' into role (unlike the teacher, who may shift from being a facilitator into a twilight role and back again). Costume, props etc. that are significant must be considered. Also, the signing of the person playing the role.
   (b) Impact on students − Very direct, multidimensional, personal, unpredictable, fluid and naturalistic.
   (c) Some implications for learning − The role demands attention and interaction from students. There is not much detachment, so the reflective element must be built in by the teacher's intervention in this interaction. Students' 'doing' will tend towards role rather than anything more abstract (i.e. the project the teacher may have in mind).
2. **The same, except framed as a film. That is, people have permission to stare but not intrude. 'Film' can be stopped and restarted, or rerun.**
   (a) Practical considerations − As for Convention 1.
   (b) Impact on students − Once seen, it is predictable, direct and multidimensional, but no personal interaction is required. It invites staring and comment.
   (c) Some implications for learning − It is available to stop, start and rerun the sequence. It provides scope for reflection on role. It is possible to notice how details build up, and perhaps how we know things on subliminal levels, i.e. 'I noticed that look she gave him but didn't know I'd noticed because he was demanding most of my attention; but when we ran it again slowly, I saw what it was I had seen.'

3. **The role present as in 'effigy'. It can be talked about, walked around, and even sculpted afresh, if it has been so framed.**
    (a) Practical considerations – As for Convention 1.
    (b) Impact on students – Mainly visual, impersonal, direct, static; invites staring and comment.
    (c) Some implications for learning – The effigy comments on what people found memorable about this person. It is not the *actual* person 'frozen'. Therefore, we are dealing not just with the person but also with an interpretive layer of the effigy-maker. If students are to be allowed to sculpt afresh, they will have to have some information or opinion about the role in order to do this with significance. The teacher may want to use this resculpting as a diagnostic tool to assess what students do know about the role.

4. **The same, but with the convention that the effigy can be brought into lifelike response and then returned to effigy.**
    (a) Practical considerations – As for Convention 1.
    (b) Impact on students – Multidimensional, alternatively inviting staring and interaction. Students have power over the duration of the interaction and can choose when to comment in 'private' by deactivating effigy.
    (c) Some implications for learning – The reflective element is inherent. Even when activated, it is not the same as Convention 1, as an effigy is made after a person dies, by somebody else. An activated effigy can tell the effigy's story, not the person's (although, of course, the effigy may know about the person it represents). Thus one may tap into how public interest in and opinion of the role has changed over the years (i.e. the effigy may have been moved from a prominent position to a dark corner where nobody notices it, etc.).

5. **The role as portrait of a person. Not three-dimensional but in all other ways the same as effigy.**
    (a) Practical considerations – As for Convention 1.
    (b) Impact on students – Visual; movement into the symbolical; invites staring and comment.
    (c) Some implications for learning – Again one has the added element, not only of the person, but also of the way the person was seen by whoever painted the portrait. The two-dimensional aspect allows for significant background and significant arrangement of artefacts/symbols on each side of role. (A glimpse at some Holbein paintings will give plenty of ideas as to how this may be done.)

6. **The role as portrait or effigy activated *to hear* what the class is saying. This causes selective language.**
    (a) Practical considerations – As for Convention 1.
    (b) Impact on students – A move from what we *see* to what we *say*. The focus moves from role to students' selves without appearing to.
    (c) Some implications for learning – Students have to really think about what they say, especially as there is no response. Because what is said does not invite interaction, it must be sufficient unto itself. This provokes thinking. It invites inner work, and therefore the teacher must be aware of whether students have sufficient social health to maintain this kind of response. It demands great belief.

7. **The role as above, but activated to speak only, and not capable of movement.**
    (a) Practical considerations – As for Convention 1.

(b) Impact on students – Visual, auditory, personal, immediate, non-threatening, as the role is clearly limited and restricted.

(c) Some implications for learning – Interaction is now possible. The role must speak as portrait not person – as with effigy – so there will be a certain amount of decoding for students to do. Because the role is static, permission to stare is continued throughout the interaction. This allows a mixture of personal and impersonal response. The role is both object and person.

8. **The role depicted in picture: removed from actual life, as in a slide, a painting, a photograph or a drawing of the role. This includes those made by the class, as well as prepared depictions.**

(a) Practical considerations – The teacher must prepare a picture and consider how it is to be displayed. Are students going to be allowed to handle it and study it closely or will it be mounted on a wall or board to give distance? If students are to make the picture, appropriate materials must be provided thoughtfully. (For example, would the drama be served better by a painting made in various shades of blue or a collage from magazines? Consultation with the art department may help here.)

(b) Impact on students – We are now dealing with 'things', not 'people'; so we are moving much more into the realm of the symbolic and visual. Or they could be creating their own picture; there is a 'busyness of doing'.

(c) Some implications for learning – When objects are used, there is more distance, which allows for affective exploration in a non-threatening way. Students are not asked to interact with the *actual* person but with the *meaning* of the person. This does not have the immediacy of Convention 5, but there is more scope for the symbolic, abstract and representational, which will demand more decoding from students, or, if they have made the depiction, a coding in of significance.

9. **A drawing seen in the making, of someone important to the action, as on a blackboard.**

(a) Practical considerations – A blackboard is by far the best medium for this, as lines drawn on a blackboard are not permanent, so a drawing can evolve and change through observation and discussion without being messy.

(b) Impact on students – The act of joint creation – a visual evolving. Teacher-talk is important here to keep the students empowered: 'Does that look like you want it?', 'I'm not sure what kind of eyebrows a person like this would have', etc.

(c) Some implications for learning – This offers a great opportunity for the teacher to create consciously a climate in the class that shows the students that they will be heard. The evolving of the picture taps into the element of mystery and suspense. Students can choose what they will have to deal with. This means that students should be inducted into the implications in their choices so that an understanding of the nature of foreshadowing is fostered.

10. **A stylized depiction of someone. For example an identikit picture made by the class in frame as detectives.**

(a) Practical considerations – Paper, pens, paints, crayons, etc. will be needed. The teacher must also ensure that the style of depiction and frame in which the students are working will complement each other.

    (b) Impact on students – Creative and visual. This Convention is discursive in the making and building of the depiction. Cooperation is required and an ability to forge consensus with each other.

    (c) Some implications for learning – Stylization will relieve anxiety about drawing ability. Also it opens the notion of 'genre', as each style of depiction carries different and specific implications, for example a design for a mosaic of a person or a newspaper cartoon of the same person. Some styles might help to date the depiction – 'That looks medieval' – or to classify where the depiction might be found: 'You get drawings like that in children's books.' Students must be able to decode. Style can also confirm frame, as in the example of an identikit picture made as detectives.

11. **The same, except made beforehand, so it is *a fait accompli*.**

    (a) Practical considerations – As for Convention 10, but teacher controls the signs that are laid in.

    (b) Impact on students – Visual – discursive through the forging of understanding.

    (c) Some implications for learning – As for Convention 10. The difference lies in teasing out rather than laying in meaning. The teacher may prefer to do it this way if there is a need for a tight control of the input.

12. **A life-size (cardboard) model with clothing (real) of a role. For example, 'framed' as if in a museum or salerooms. 'This is the dress worn by Florence Nightingale when she met Queen Victoria after Scutari.'**

    (a) Practical considerations – A cardboard model, or a dressmaker's model will do. Use could be made of the school costume-cupboard here without the fear that the students will spoil the clothes or get involved in meaningless 'dressing-up'.

    (b) Impact on students – Visual, immediate, through the reality and presence of the article. It is also tactile if students are allowed to touch the clothing. (This would depend on frame.)

    (c) Some implications for learning – It opens up the whole importance of what we wear (an issue that youngsters are highly aware of), and presents them with an opportunity to recognize the universal aspect of their expertise in this area instead of the emphasis being on the externals of changing fashion. Subtleties in appearance can also be engaged with. For example, noticing that 'the dress was very worn but the collar was of the finest lace'.

13. **The same, except the class is dressing the model so as to see 'how it was' on that day when these events happened.**

    (a) Practical considerations – As for Convention 12.

    (b) Impact on students – Selecting sign in arrangement of dress. Visual and tactile.

    (c) Some implications for learning – An affective and immediate exploration of what particular clothes may signify on a particular day. The person becomes accessible through the students' understanding of the choices they made. For example, 'Wearing this tie lets people know that I went to a good school, and that will be important today.'

14. **The clothing of a person cast off in disarray. For example, remains of a tramp's presence, or a murder, and escape as in a highwayman situation.**

    (a) Practical considerations – Clothing, which must be carefully chosen as to what might logically have been left behind.

    (b) Impact on students – Visual, tactile, with muddle evolving into meaning.

(c)  Some implications for learning – Making sense out of apparent chaos – a realization that the most unpromising mess often holds the most fascinating story. Students might be framed as 'detectives' with a puzzle to solve. Does what was left give any clues as to what was taken? Does the way it was left tell us anything about the manner of leaving?

15.  **Objects to represent a person's interests. This works as in the Convention above, but more intimate things can indicate concerns rather than appearance. For example, a ring of a Borgia.**

(a)  Practical considerations – Teacher must foresee the implications in the chosen objects.

(b)  Impact on students – Visual, tactile, kinaesthetic, with the class framed so as to be able to handle objects. (It is worth noting that neither handling nor not handling objects is 'best' – what you gain in intimacy you lose in distance and vice versa.)

(c)  Some implications for learning – Clothing is to do with how we choose to present ourselves to the world. Objects can serve this public function too (as in the 'status symbol') or they may be much more private, for example a pressed flower given many years ago by a lost or secret lover. Objects can symbolize events or intentions in a life and can be endowed with a great significance by their owners. For example: 'She once went back into a burning room for that little statuette, and I wouldn't have said it was worth much.' In such cases, objects are *keys* into what drives their owners.

16.  **An account of a person by another person in naturalistic fashion. For example, 'Well, when I saw him last he seemed all right. I never dreamed anything was wrong.'**

(a)  Practical considerations – There are several ways to do this. Obviously the teacher can give the account in role and can probably slip into that role quite easily. Another possibility is to have a secondary role present to give the account. In this case they must be clearly briefed that it is *their account* rather than *their role* that the students should engage with. In other words the role is very limited. A third possibility is the use of a taped account, which can be prepared beforehand and will leave the teacher free in the role of facilitator. Each way will give a slightly different emphasis that should be considered before choosing.

(b)  Impact on students – Immediate – limited to the account, the role is a vehicle for this. The use of a recording will focus on auditory signs; using a role introduces the potential for other signing systems.

(c)  Some implications for learning – The account gives an external validity to the person it is about – somebody knows them. At the same time, students are engaging with another person's perception. They therefore have to make judgements about how they feel about the person telling the account. If they have already encountered the person the account is about, this convention enables students to weigh their perceptions and judgements against another's.

17.  **An account of a person written as if from that person, but read by someone else. For example, a diary.**

(a)  Practical considerations – As for Convention 16.

(b)  Impact on students – Auditory and personal. Limited to the account.

(c)  Some implications for learning – Writing that is not specifically designed to be public gives insight into the personal thoughts and feelings the writer is willing to give permanence to. The way the account is read can layer in the judgements and attitudes of the reader. There is the possibility for covert information about the relationship (if any) between reader and writer.

18. **An account written by the person who now reads it to others, for example a policeman giving evidence or a confession. The role is present in this case but in contact through their writing, as an author might well be.**
    (a) Practical considerations – The role is present, but limited to reading the account.
    (b) Impact on students – Multidimensional. It is limited to the reading of the account. The interaction is with the account, not the role. Therefore the role is purely functional and not personal.
    (c) Some implications for learning – The account was written knowing that it was to be public and this will influence what is put down. Learning is possible in noting what is not said as well as reading how what is said is spoken.

19. **An account written by someone of someone else and read by yet another.**
    (a) Practical considerations – As for Convention 17.
    (b) Impact on students – Very subtle. There is a mushrooming effect and a very tight focus.
    (c) Some implications for learning – This one is very complex. The information presented to students is layered. Overtly there is one bit of information: an account of a person. Covertly there is the potential for: (i) the attitude of the writer towards the person, (ii) the attitude of the reader towards the person, (iii) the attitude of the reader towards the writer. The permutations of these can be made very complex. How do students decode all this?

20. **A story told about another, in order to bring that person close to the action. For example, 'I saw him open a safe once. It was an incredible performance. I'm not sure if he would assist us, though.'**
    (a) Practical considerations – Teacher in role or another role present. There will be a need to consider what will be foreshadowed by the story. This is different from Convention 16, as the emphasis is on bringing the person close to the action. Therefore the focus of the story must be specific.
    (b) Impact on students – Immediate contact with the role – telling the story. Limited to story, with a tight focus.
    (c) Some implications for learning – The reality of the person is established, because somebody knows him/her. There is the opportunity to build a reputation and layer in status for the person. Students may observe how they react to and are influenced by other people's opinions.

21. **A report of an event but formalized by authority or ritual. For example, an account of bravery in battle on the occasion of the presenting of posthumous medals.**
    (a) Practical considerations – Teacher in role or another role present.
    (b) Impact on students – It needs to be carefully controlled so that it is contained and dignified.
    (c) Some implications for learning – Through formalization, the event is given social significance. This is the first step towards the mythical element in life. What is selected from reality to honour or vilify the person? How do solemnity and formality transform feeling? How are responses conjured from the sense of occasion? The way

events are given social significance is a tremendous power that can be used for good or ill in a society. This convention opens up a very important area.

22. **A letter read in the voice of the writer. This is an emanation of a specific presence, not just any voice, communicating the words.**
    (a) Practical considerations – As for Convention 16. If role is used, the auditory quality must be preserved.
    (b) Impact on students – Auditory, intimate, insightful, direct.
    (c) Some implications for learning – A letter is a particular kind of writing, as it is an attempt at communication from one person to another. It is one-way, because response is always delayed. Thus a letter comes close to a person's thoughts. However, it is most important to remember that a letter is always written with the reader in mind. A letter to a bank manager will be very different in style and content from a letter between close relatives or friends. When it is read in the voice of the writer, we are brought closer to them as they were when they were writing it.

23. **The same, but the letter is read by another with no attempt to portray the person who wrote it, but still expressing feeling.**
    (a) Practical considerations – As for Convention 16.
    (b) Impact on students – Auditory, more indirect.
    (c) Some implications for learning – This time the overlay of feeling does not belong to the letter but is evoked in the reader *by* the letter. Thus we may get information about the reader: for example, a love letter read by the lover would sound very different from the same letter read by a disapproving parent. If the letter is read by an 'empathetic outsider', that is somebody quite uninvolved with the contents of the letter, the students have an opportunity to decide that person's attitude to the content or to judge whether the letter has been read truthfully.

24. **A letter read without feeling. For example, as evidence, or an accusation in a formal situation.**
    (a) Practical considerations – As for Convention16.
    (b) Impact on students – Auditory, cold and impersonal. The impact of what is not there.
    (c) Some implications for learning – The emphasis is very much on the words in the letter. Lack of emotion can sometimes throw things into relief. This demands that the students are able to read significance and meaning behind words. It demands more projective imagination on their part. It can be used to show that emotion is often a purely personal thing – an emotional empathy is something that is in our gift to others.

25. **The voice of a person overheard talking to another in informal language, that is, using naturalistic tone.**
    (a) Practical considerations – A recording is much better than a role here because it focuses attention on the voice.
    (b) Impact on students – Auditory, intimate. Limited to what is on the recording.
    (c) Some implications for learning – Students have no interaction with the roles (another reason that a recording is better), but the conversation opens up the possibility of observing how the person on the recording interacts with others. Obviously information can be fed in. The students are listeners. This convention can function rather like Convention 2 (film) except that it is only a voice. It is to Convention 2 as audio tape is to videotape.

26. **The same, but in formal language.**
    (a) Practical considerations – As for Convention 25.
    (b) Impact on students – Auditory, distant, limited.
    (c) Some implications for learning – Formal language, as opposed to social or personal language, indicating an interaction of functional roles rather than personalities. For example, an assistant manager reports to a company director or a monarch congratulates a minister. There may also be an element of ritual here, as in a coded exchange that gives entrance to a criminal's den or a secret society.

27. **A conversation overheard, where the people are not seen. Deliberate eavesdropping, as in spying.**
    (a) Practical considerations – Role is more suitable here, as it allows the element of 'Don't let them know we're here.' However, in order to maintain auditory focus it is important that the visual impact is curtailed, either by having the role behind a screen or students with backs turned.
    (b) Impact on students – Auditory, limited, direct, non-interactional but immediate.
    (c) Some implications for learning – The emphasis is on what we learn from what we hear. What judgements do we make about persons from their voices – what they say, how it is said, tone, pauses, hesitations, chuckles, signs etc.? What is heard is memorable, because it is not meant to be heard.

28. **A report of a conversation, written and spoken by another.**
    (a) Practical considerations – A recording, a person in role, or the teacher in role.
    (b) Impact on students – Auditory, indirect, distanced, limited.
    (c) Some implications for learning – Here students are hearing what somebody else is reporting. Again there is this second layer of the reporters' attitude to what they are reporting. Writing adds authenticity to what is reported, as it is slightly more formal than a purely verbal report. What is written is fixed; what is said can change with each telling.

29. **A reported conversation with two people reading the respective 'parts'.**
    (a) Practical considerations – A recording or two readers.
    (b) Impact on students – Direct, auditory and possibly visual, limited.
    (c) Some implications for learning – The fact that the conversation is reported means it is removed or distanced from students as in Convention 28 (above). Readers give the impression 'as if' it were really happening; 'as if' they were really overhearing (as in Convention 27). But they are not. It is important that students are aware of this. This awareness gives them the opportunity to judge how the parts are being read. The readers obviously put their interpretation on the words. The students can decide how truthful this interpretation is, act as directors or maybe even take over as readers.

30. **A private reading of a conversation, reported as overheard.**
    (a) Practical considerations – If done with a role, it is important to have another role present to listen.
    (b) Impact on students – Direct, visual, intimate.
    (c) Some implications for learning – Similar to Convention 28, except that the private nature of the report allows for more blatant interpretation of what was said in conversation. Because it is not written down word for word, the general tenor of the conversation and occasional phrases that stick in the mind can be reported.

31. **The finding of a cryptic code message. For example, from tramps or spies.**
    (a) Practical considerations – The preparation of the message.
    (b) Impact on students – Puzzling, visual, intriguing; demands action of solving.
    (c) Some implications for learning – Mystery. Students can either be framed to be 'in the know' or, more productively, have to decode from outside. This taps students' natural inclination towards solving puzzles and bringing meaning to things. Having to work to find out information brings commitment and investment for further developments.

32. **The signature of a person found. For example, a half-burned paper.**
    (a) Practical considerations – The preparation of the signature (and the document to which it is attached).
    (b) Impact on students – Visual, tactile – can be passed around. Direct.
    (c) Some implications for learning – What can you tell about somebody from the way they write? What attitudes and judgements are formed by seeing a person's signature? What sort of document is the signature attached to? What does that tell us?

33. **The sign of a particular person discovered. For example, the special mark of the Scarlet Pimpernel.**
    (a) Practical considerations – Preparation of the sign.
    (b) Impact on students – Visual, tactile, can be passed around. Speculative.
    (c) Some implications for learning – Secrecy/mystery allows students to speculate about the person who left the sign. This can inform the teacher about whom the students would like to meet. It also invites comments on the effect of the sign. Is it scary/exciting/disturbing/irritating/etc. to have this enigmatic contact with the person? What is the person trying to do with it? What does the sign represent?

# MEETING DR LISTER

*The chapter 'Material for Significance' in* Collected Writings *presents an interesting example of the use of conventions in teaching the history of science. This is an edited version of that chapter.*

*In Heathcote's useful phrase, the fictional world of drama provides a 'no-penalty' area where ideas and situations can be isolated, examined and acted upon, but where we are relieved of the burden of the future arising from our actions. These constructs of reality are available for examination by the spectator who exists in each of us. Heathcote warns us that stories and drama operate in different kinds of time. The 'now' time of drama generates productive tension, as situations demand resolution. The challenge for the teacher is to engage the students not with the action alone but with the meaning of the material under investigation. The teacher controls the quality of the experience but enables the students to construct their own meanings from the event.*

*Originally published in 1980, the work described here is analysed in detail in a booklet,* The Treatment of Dr. Lister: A Language Functions Approach to Drama in Education.[1]

Drama depicts life. Teachers can choose just how much of the material of any drama class will provide context for the curriculum, either as work or play, which is undertaken in the no-penalty area of art. That is, participants will be able to test out their ideas, try them over again, and generally examine them, without necessarily having to fulfil in actual life situations the promises they have tried out in the depicted situation. The material of drama consists of, first, our ability to make 'another room', a fictional world in order to examine something. You can call this plays, or playing, or the theatre, or make-believe: its name doesn't matter, so long as it takes the burden of future responsibility temporarily out of the picture. It becomes a 'no-penalty area' in which the two parts of people can have equal status, the spectator part, which allows us to stand back and see what we are experiencing at any moment, and the participant part, which has to deal with the event in a practical manner. So the immediate environment with its classroom contents can be transformed into the environment a teacher might need for teaching purposes and it can be done with a minimum of fuss.

There is no need to fuss because of the next ingredient of drama. This is our ability to identify 'as if we were' in the place of another, in a specific situation. This is of paramount and far-reaching importance, because it involves a shift in time. Placing yourself in the shoes of another suddenly brings you into a time pressure that is a key feature of dramatic activity – the need to do something now. It becomes imperative to take decisions, because the event you portray or explore demands immediate response. It involves you in trying to ease the situation, and in the eternal time-present of drama. People in drama are now, here, and under pressure to act. That is the tension of drama.

Here is another feature of drama. It is a social art and demands consensus from participants, and this makes it extremely difficult for teachers to 'make it work'. This is partly because consensus is not easily achieved with modern children, for they are no longer in awe of people called teachers. Teachers also lack training in the necessary negotiation skills required to achieve consensus in large groups. So drama is a no-penalty area, using people in groups, in immediate contextual time that generates the pressure to act in an event. This is the contribution that drama could make to the school curriculum.

The materials of drama now need scrutiny. There is a tendency for people to think that the materials of drama will be stories, because they seem like events in which people will have to act. Stories suggest diachronic time and seem to follow on in a logical way, so teachers are lured into a false situation by stories. Be warned! Learning through drama demands synchronic time, the web of interaction within the frame of a selected environment and event. The act of dramatizing is the act of constructing meaning, which may also involve the interpretation of meaning. Play makes constructs of reality that are then available for examination by the spectator who exists in each participant – that part of us which observes what we are doing. We take up a position from where we can look at something from the outside. Art does the same, but for others. As the art form that most closely resembles actual living, drama more than any other art has had to create a special frame. This frame is called theatre. Theatre is life depicted in a no-penalty zone. It looks like, seems like, but is not actuality. Drama is a social art where people are and do, and other people may see them doing and being.

## Tension

Drama involves groups, small or large, sharing in some immediate occasion. The material of such occasions is always people under conditions of tension. Tension is not conflict, such as occurs between people. Tension introduces 'another' element, usually above and beyond people power. The existence of tension in actual life is often disturbing and non-productive. In the depicted world, because of the no-penalty zone, it can be used productively, because participants can be free of worry about the outcome and so become concerned in the process of resolving the situation. Because drama explores social situations, participants employ the actual laws of social living. One aspect of these laws is that persons have to manage to pay attention to others who are also present in the circumstances. In a social situation every person is an initiator and a responder, and every person fluctuates between participating and being a spectator of others. This law of actuality must also apply in the depiction of the drama.

Society has developed rituals and symbols to be used as messages of meaning – the syntax of signal and response – and these change in intensity according to the type of communication required, in order that all present can construct meaning out of the event. The teacher, in using the no-penalty area of drama, must employ the messages of meaning used in real living. The theatre frame relieves us of the burden of the future arising from our actions but employs the communications structures of real life.

## Significance

Drama depicts matters of significance. School exists to make matters significant to the child. In the actual world outside both theatre and school, social events are endowed with different degrees of significance. Each social event demands variable and selective kinds of ritualized and symbolic behaviour. These different levels, as we acquire understanding of them, become the language of social competence by which individuals construct meaning when amongst others.

Let us examine a situation in which drama was used to construct meaning. A woman teacher of nine-year-old children wanted them to learn about Lister the surgeon and in particular to realize that his life, together with that of Pasteur, caused a watershed in medical history which is still affecting our world.

The story of Lister is gripping, so in selecting a drama approach it is necessary to be quite clear as to why the actual story of his life was set aside. The story would have placed the facts in clear order, and dates and events could have been precisely laid in. There is no doubt that the story would have helped the class to be interested, for a while, in the man Lister, and some of them might have wanted to learn more about what he did. But this approach doesn't provide the opportunity for the class to have a synchronic experience of Lister. That synchronic element is an important one for the teacher, because she wants the class to experience simultaneously two periods – the time of Lister and its relation to our time.

In order that this can occur, the teacher has to find a system that allows the children to be in their own time, looking *with* Lister, not *at* Lister. The story looks at Lister and keeps him out of our time, as it should. That is what stories can do well. To make stories in the 'now' time of drama, we have to use conventions. The teacher could have done this as she told the story. She needn't have used the classic 'Once upon a time', but she would have had to say something like 'Now I'm going to take you into another place and another time – the time of a doctor called Lister.' This often works for a while, but the ending of a story leaves the listener outside the immediate event, once the words have ceased. The participants have been subsumed in the spectator. Sometimes that is exactly what is needed to arrest the attention of classes. Teachers know that the grip of a story will give them a respite from the constant battle to gain the undivided attention of a class. The problem however remains – that of getting the children deeply involved with the outcome and meaning of the material, not the action. To be involved in constructing meaning, during the act of getting acquainted with Lister in one form or another, was what she wanted, in order that it might lead to concern and engagement.

Furthermore, the teacher wanted them to take over her power. Not the power to control the quality of the experience (no teacher can abdicate that), but the power to influence their own construct of the meaning in the event. Telling stories places the power of the form and the unfolding pattern of the event firmly in the hands of the teacher, who selects the style of telling and the relationships of facts and opinion. Acting out stories does the same. The outer skin of stories lies in the events and the way they unfold, one from another. The inner part of stories focuses upon the attitudes of persons, which then causes response from others, and, out of these, events are brought about. It is through this kind of ordering that drama produces the opportunity to make constructs.

Piaget in *Structuralism*, quoted by Peter Caws[2] argues that 'structures can be observed as an arrangement of entities which embody the following fundamental ideas; (a) the idea of wholeness, (b) the idea of transformation, (c) the idea of self-regulation'. By wholeness is meant the sense of internal coherence that can be seen in drama work as in all the other art forms. Structure is not static. The laws that govern it behave so as to make it not only structured but structuring. In other words the structure is self-regulating in that it makes no appeals beyond itself in order to validate its transformational procedures.

## Construct for learning

Do you see now why drama makes a unique and important contribution to school? We must learn to set up the work so that children construct reality, so that a careful teacher can monitor the quality of the experience, by insisting that the form of the experience is suitable for the construct required for the learning. It must have internal coherence, be a process and exist in its own right, using the power to self-regulate. This latter is usually absent in school. Teachers regulate the behaviour of their classes. The teacher in the Lister experiment has set herself these tasks, which in turn will force her to select the kinds of interaction the children must experience in order to enable them to make the constructs necessary for them to learn what she wants them to understand.

1.  Lister must be seen to have really existed and to
2.  Have affected his own time radically, but he must also be seen to
3.  Be still affecting the present time.
4.  He must be recognized as belonging in the twin medical fields of micro-biology and surgery, and these must be seen as
5.  Interdependent upon each other.
6.  He must be seen in the context and environment of his own time, but
7.  Cause the present time to be closely examined, in order that
8.  Comparison can be made between the two.

So no fewer than eight constructs will have to be made by this class, if they are to fulfil the teacher's intention, which can be briefly stated as 'I want Lister to be seen as having influenced modern medicine, and we should honour him!' Choose the 'story way', and it takes you about half an hour; choose this system of constructing meaning, and you're going to be involved for much longer than that. Your choice is not whether you are prepared to spend such time: it lies instead with the kinds of meaning you want children to make from Lister and his history. It also requires some very precise thinking about how to set the whole thing up.

This teacher chose to create an examination of doctors in the subject of 'The History of Medicine'. In the context of an important examination, the class worked an hour each day on two aspects of Lister. In their drama time they solved problems of medicine and later wrote up the process and their results under examination conditions. The drama provided the context for bothering to do it, that is, the no-penalty area – the 'as if' part. After it was set up that way, other depictions, such as pictures (modern and old-fashioned), were used to inform the class about hospitals, medication procedures and so on. Also used were real surgeon's tools of the time, desks and chairs were placed correctly for examination procedures, and children searched into books for information. The classic experiments of Pasteur and Lister, which doctors and teachers of doctors have performed ever since, including the classic agar experiment and the growing of moulds, were carried out by all the class. They used the science curriculum in fact. So what, then, can be said to be different about the construction of meaning through drama?

Well, the first matter has been to make *time* important. They came into the time of an imminent examination. They lived in the actual time of the rituals of written examinations. They were addressed as potential doctors and endowed immediately with the responsibilities of would-be doctors. The first meaning to be constructed was the dialogue between the examiner and the examined – the seriousness of the responsibility.

Next they saw Lister as if in a portrait. A teacher was seated, dressed to give an authentic impression of the man, alongside an authentic microscope and surgeon's tools. He was not precisely authentic as to dress. Teachers don't often have those resources, and anyway, good pictures can correct errors of that kind. The placing of the microscope beside surgical instruments is a classic example of the power of drama to synchronize information. As would-be doctors, accepting the yoke of responsibility, they examined the possible contribution this man 'has made to our chosen careers'. That is significant. Read it again: 'our careers' – that is, the present; 'this man' – that is, of the past – they can see that, from his old-fashioned air and his old instruments.

The children were then invited to place the evidence of their eyes together with their historical sense and write an examination paper on 'what they thought was the contribution of this man's work to his own time and our present medical scene'. They knew his name, because it was on his medical degree, which lay alongside his tools. This was correct as to the headings of Glasgow and Edinburgh Universities, though the name of the candidate was changed to that of Lister.

During the other drama sessions, each lasting an hour, they constructed more understanding, always in the context of modern doctors, facing examination of the following topics:

1.  What made Lister struggle with these problems when it was so difficult to convince his colleagues about the urgency of antiseptics?
2.  What were the hazards of the working and home conditions of his day in regard to medication processes?
3.  What developments have occurred since then because of Lister's work?

The children taught Lister about these developments in practical demonstrations. They explained kidney machines, blood banks, Band-Aids, plasma, aspirin, and a host of other matters they thought must interest and amaze him. A modern stethoscope and white coat were used to introduce Lister to modern medical practice. Finally they explained to him that

> There is no need to feel downhearted that you only managed to change things a little in your lifetime. The old listening-tube is only a step on the way to the present stethoscope, which is always being transformed by practice and new discoveries.

Lister explained to them how he felt when he received his permission to start on a medical career, and they received their first certificates in the historical study of medicine. Please note they were not certified as doctors! That is the pretend world, and this drama has no part in the pretend world. It must preserve its inner consistent truth.

From here on, the class will conduct experiments related with Lister's time and with modern medicine. For this they do not need a very dramatic environment, because that has already done its work. They now work in the context of medical personnel thinking from within the circumstances they require to explore. They will construct meaning about the health service, or do more microscope work, or, maybe, paint pictures of the conditions under which Lister worked, and compare them with modern photographs. They will meet a real practising doctor or a medical-school lecturer who will form part of another construct where they can look at how doctors today study their subject. Whatever they do, it will have no 'dummy run' aspect. It feels real, though everyone knows it isn't actually going to teach them to be doctors. It will, however, change them into serious students.

It is possible to see where the balance of power to affect and share outcomes lies in each different convention.

- **A Meeting Lister 'as portrait':**
  **Convention No. 8:** The role depicted in picture: removed from actual life. This looks like teacher power, but the teacher cannot move, so the power is equally shared. The teacher has the power to provide focus; the children have the power to respond.
- **B Listening to Lister worrying** about his new system of setting bones.
  **Convention No. 5:** The role as portrait of a person. As he shares his concern 'as if' with fellow doctors, the class and the teacher build the construct equally.
- **C Questioning Lister** about his problems with other surgeons and his life's work.
  **Convention No. 5:** The class and teacher equally build the construct together.
- **D Showing Lister the health hazards** of working people in Glasgow, in Lister's own time, by making waxwork scenes.
  **Convention No. 5.** The children take the lead, working as demonstrators using strongly symbolic behaviour. Lister is a spectator. The children have the power to show another, who affirms their power.
- **E Working with Lister** in his operating theatre – preparing for an experiment with antiseptic spray machine.
  **Convention No. 6.** As they foreshadow suitable behaviour as doctors, the class and the teacher build the construct equally.
- **F Teaching Lister** about modern medicine and innovations developed since his day.
  **Convention No. 4.** The children actively take power over their teacher and teach him as they explain, demonstrate and show.
- **G Receiving certificates** from Lister.
  **Convention No. 3.** The event holds the power as they allow it to regulate and modify their behaviour. Both the teacher and the children accede to its demands.

This is the kind of contribution drama makes to the curriculum of schools, and it is capable of being varied to suit the processes of making meaning.

## Notes

1 Carroll, J. (1984) *The Treatment of Dr. Lister: A Language Functions Approach to Drama in Education*, Bathurst, NSW: Mitchell College of Advanced Education. A videotape accompanies the booklet.
2 Caws, P. (1968) 'What is Structuralism', *Partisan Review*, 35 (1), Winter.

# THE AUTHENTIC TEACHER
# AND THE FUTURE

*This is an edited version of the inspiring paper specially written in 1984 for inclusion in* Dorothy Heathcote: Collected Writings. *It was provoked by the state of education at the time – when teachers felt disempowered and the curriculum was being restricted by increasing government control. Heathcote was aware that teachers working towards authenticity in that climate would inevitably be in conflict with the system – a system in which students often saw little purpose in school work in a society that could not guarantee them employment and in which they were not permitted to assist in the fabric of culture-making. But, as Heathcote insists, for these students, the future is now. This paper is an impassioned plea for schools, teachers and communities to think more inclusively and globally about education in our culture and to begin to allow students to share responsibility for the future. Unfortunately, Heathcote's arguments and proposals for change are more relevant and even more urgent now than they were thirty years ago.*

## Authenticity

In the earlier chapter, 'Excellence in teaching', I now think I meant authenticity when I was referring to excellence, because a central notion of excellence as outlined in that paper is the capacity to behave in an authentic way. For a teacher of drama, a subject often perceived by society as the most artificial and therefore the most inauthentic art form, it seems a bit paradoxical to strive for authenticity, except that good art is its own authenticity. We often consider the creations of scientists as being more authentic than those of artists, because artists' products are related (and relegated?) to the enterprise we call play whilst those of scientists are deemed to be of more serious intent.

## Authentic teacher power

In my paper on excellence I listed these factors which I now relate to authentic behaviour:

- seeing students as they really are demonstrating themselves to be;
- being interested in students as they represent themselves to be;

- having a personal 'something', a philosophy, a belief, a creed, whatever you call it, to stand for, from within yourself or derived from the establishment you relate to;
- defining tasks in a realistic manner; setting about their accomplishment from within the realities of the situation: working conditions, student attitudes, time, numbers, standards and forms of achievement demanded by the task;
- openness to others' ideas, ways of working, possibilities for improvement, change, reorientation and preparedness therefore to take *considered* risks;
- sharing of informational strategies and knowledge, trusting people's capacity to grow in response;
- realization and recognition that because *one feels* that one is behaving with authenticity, it does not mean that others perceive it as such whether they are participating or observing: any teacher who has taught in front of others knows this one!

## Drama's impact on society

All my teaching life I've been bothered by two things which I think relate to this matter of authenticity. First, while being labelled as a 'teacher of drama' and functioning as such overtly, I have been irritated that people have perceived the work as related only to play, fiction and pretence. Not that it isn't related to these, but that it has so much more potential for society. Second, that so many people have seen it either as a separate subject in schooling situations or as a rather 'special' affair. This has led me latterly *apparently* to neglect the art forms of such activity and to discuss it in relation to other forms of *productive depiction and distortion* such as diagrams, maps, sketches, photographs and so on. I emphasize 'apparently', because I've always been careful to stress the laws of the form as being seminal to the meaningful use of drama in class. There can be no useful impact on society if those laws are ignored or not understood. That they are not understood by a large number of teachers is beyond question and it is time we tackled this problem. This becomes more urgent every day. But we are bedevilled by polarization of opinion instead of humility in examining an art far bigger and more ancient than any of us.

The power available to society through authentic experiences in school has been touched upon in my paper 'Signs and portents', so I won't reiterate that here; suffice it to say again that theatre and society are akin except for one aspect which radically differentiates them. This is the depictive aspect: in art we reflect upon nature, people's affairs, ideas and behaviour. What a force for a nation – apparently to stand aside, but in reality take an inward look at events!

It's interesting to think that the 'antiseptic' and often sterile behaviour demonstrated in school tasks, languages and interactions can be authenticated by another apparently unreal mode of communication in order to make school and society come into some form of power for good influence.

## Schooling as prevention

It can't be said to be so at present, for, to put it at its worst, most schooling keeps children from under the feet of most adults for six or seven hours every day, and it prevents them (those who conform at any rate) from having much opportunity to ask awkward questions about society, morality, values, purposes and laws. It makes certain that the tasks accomplished in the main inside the establishment can't seriously affect what goes on outside, in society. So long as the study is undertaken as 'exercise for' and not 'practice of', with the debilitating emphasis upon the assumption that 'one day you'll be good enough to really do it', there's not really much danger of the young's interference. We stress student incapacity, hesitation and error rather than personality, exploration, process of recovery from error, and input to society. And yet, the amazing and irrefutable factor of all this is the numbers of would-be authentic teachers there are still around – teachers who struggle daily to create conditions in which students can be honoured and respected as people and personalities rather than be patronized. These teachers often work all day with their groups of thirty or more in barren rooms, designed by architects who frequently work in lovely airy offices or renovated Georgian houses. I know cost and education allowances come into this but it doesn't say much for a society that provides for the induction of its young some of the appalling buildings many students have to learn in. Many teachers care passionately about their subjects – literature, languages, music, science, needlework, geography, art; but unless they have 'stumbled upon authenticity' sufficient for their needs, they are unable to take their students into their subjects through the doorways of attraction – attention, interest, involvement, concern – to investment and, hopefully, productive obsession which thoroughly engages them for a period of time, sometimes for life. Such teachers carry a terrible burden of ineptitude, fear and heavy spirit, and that's no help with youngsters. We need mentally strong and wholesome people to work alongside our future adults.

I've always been uncomfortable pushing art rather than, say, science, as if one were more or less imaginative or in need of brain power than the other. I'm obsessed with all the marvellous knowledge collected through our time on earth, whether it be in art, objects, ideas or skills and I also believe that the 'big' people use the same qualities of imaging and crystallizing into suitable forms, whether they be called artist or scientist, doctor or writer. Likewise, I believe all persons require the same skills as social human beings, though they may use them with different powers and for different reasons, and in different circumstances. We seem to have progressed better in study skills related to object knowledge than to experience knowledge, which often is the basis of our developing world view.

## What can a teacher do?

It's all very well, you may say, to write all these things. These points have been acknowledged for years. But what can a teacher *do* about it to get things actually changed? Well, let's begin with a private individual who is also a teacher, with a teacher's individual tasks to accomplish, and work on from there.

The first question obviously has to be, 'Do I want to be an authentic teacher?' If the answer to that is yes, it's possible to see what then is required. It will mean:

- devising more systems of approaching work and tasks than transmission and direct approaches;
- learning to present problems differently to students;
- discovering more subtle forms of induction and communication;
- encouraging student interaction and decision-making processes;
- giving more leeway to students to discover other ways of tackling situations;
- imagining and carrying into action a greater variety of tasks;

- engineering a greater variety of feedback techniques;
- taking more risks with materials;
- tolerating more ambiguity in classroom set-ups, because people may choose a variety of speeds and systems to work at the same tasks;
- apportioning time differently, not necessarily slicing minutes in an orderly chronological sequence;
- when it's all put together, and I haven't mentioned the half of it, constant attention to detail.

William Blake said a marvellously apt thing for teachers. He said, 'If you would do good to anyone, you must do it in minute particulars.' And that goes for authentic teaching behaviours too. It means facing the basic fact that in devising fruitful encounters between self, students, ideas, knowledge and skills we have to become process-orientated. Process orientation means devising programmes and tasks which induct through first intriguing, then engaging and interesting our pupils. A lot of such strategies exist and are in use in school and university classrooms, but they don't get communicated around enough. We still believe the mythology of 'that something extra that good teachers have', and in that way we perpetuate the notion that teaching skills are related to personality. I don't believe this. I believe that style and personality need to find a fit, but beneath style can be a sharply honed range of skills which can be separated from the individual way of carrying out ideas, without being lost internally in the teaching situation. For example, any teacher knows that different experiences will happen to a class when consensus is being sought among the group and when differences in approach are being explored. The personal style a teacher uses will not interfere with the basic premise and internal structure. In fact, the more we could honour in our training programmes the *need* for personality, plus the need for internal structure, the more quickly we might get authentic relationships in learning situations. Those teachers with 'that something extra' could teach or be helped to analyse what they are doing when they're in action. The inspectors, the tutors could start putting the news around in practical ways. We could teach each other through Blake's 'minute particulars'.

## Meeting the pupil's needs

A basic aspect for consideration, and one in which drama can help, is that of the ways in which teachers learn to create focus and significance, so that the *needs* of students are harnessed (not overindulged or repressed) in order that the interest in externals – object-interest – (Surely by this stage in human development, object-interest has become instinctive also?) can be fostered. The school curriculum is devised on the assumption that children (especially in the upper age-range) are ready for, and equipped to deal with, object-interest. Yet pupil behaviour in school often, and most uncomfortably, demonstrates that their need-interests are not being satisfactorily met, so that object-interest can begin. The great range of interactive tasks which a drama approach – or indeed any real laboratory atmosphere – can provoke can make a match between the need-interests and the way object-interest can be developed. The 'good' student in our classrooms is either one who can subdue his or her need-interest in the presence of the object-interest put forward by the teacher, or one who has already enough need-interest satisfaction. The 'difficult' student is the one who insists upon, or who cannot help, demonstrating need-interests in class. And the same may be said of adults. There are many need-interest-orientated teachers around in schools and higher education, and some days I belong to those ranks! The more helpless we feel, the more our need-interests surface.

I am not suggesting here that it is only the arts that marry need-interest with developing object-interest. It is not the subject area, but the laboratory atmosphere, the reality structure of the tasks, and the degree of value to be placed by the person in carrying out the tasks involved in the subject/object-interest area which bring need- and object-interest into balance. That, and the opportunity for a sense of worth and responsibility in the participants' work. The productive tension which real laboratory-style teaching engenders can be seen in some classrooms in most schools – in the art rooms, the science labs, the engineering and cookery workshops, where very real objects generate concern for outcomes. But for those rooms in which ideas are the tools, we need better teachers who can create meaningful tasks around less powerful or outwardly appealing subject matter, often subject matter which needs certain developed skills to penetrate. This is where drama may make a large contribution, because under the cover of the 'simulated' situation, object-interest can grow out of need-interest that is to some extent satisfied by the outer activity levels of the work. But the present barren halls and empty spaces which are often employed for drama study – here teachers are often their own worst enemies – are not suitable. To make a laboratory atmosphere out of barren openness or worse, a junk room full of dirty cast-off objects, needs teachers of brilliance and enormous energy.

I am often confronted with such ridiculous resources, deprived of all image-making materials such as blackboards, paper, reference books and pictures. It goes back a long way of course, to the notion that children will be as committed as actors to 'being stared at', and this has been thoughtlessly taught in colleges by tutors who have become out of touch with either the real laws of art or the different generations of children in a fast changing social scene. I am not without blame in this in that I cannot say that I have ever carried the 'drama teacher's load' of short lesson periods, often removed from the body of the school for long periods of time. This is why people like me must keep on engaging with need-interest dominated classes in order to be of authentic use in training.

## Pupils' awareness of authenticity

One factor brings me a lot of comfort and faith that what I am saying about laboratory teaching could happen, and that is the recognition children have of authentic teachers, and their generosity in forgiving inauthentic teaching. When I work with a class using authentic approaches in a climate of inauthenticity, I am often confronted by two responses which are embedded in each other. These two aspects of pupil response have to be dealt with immediately, and cannot be shelved or ignored, because either evasion technique condones and reinforces the children's behaviour.

The first response is that the class tries to make me behave inauthentically by provoking the authority stance of using teacher power to coerce my tasks into action. The second is that beady-eyed, rat-like spectatorship which classes can demonstrate so well. I refer to the deliberately revealed double signal which presents a bland face of innocent conformity to the teacher whilst making certain that the privately shared sign intended for peers is also seen by me. I have then to choose to ignore it, in which case I have been manipulated to behave inauthentically, or to respond with teacher power to coerce or threaten. If I do either of these things, I will have proved that 'I'm like all the others'. The wonderful thing is, though, that when young people get through this relationship problem, and I'm not suggesting that it's easy, for I have to be at my most subtle and face it with more courage than I need at other times, they are so generous in the ways in which they will respond. It's sometimes like a miracle and I'm sure it is to do with their own understanding, which at that stage is probably instinctive, that I am using need orientation to breed object-interest in the work.

## Helping yourself to authenticity

So, let's suppose you decide you want to be an authentic teacher. What can you do to start helping yourself? Let's take four things for a start.

1.  *What do you stand for?* You can easily clarify this by taking note of what you find yourself teaching, no matter what the lesson seems to be about, because the inner structure of the work is related with your need-interests, which in teachers has to be controlled and made usable (not suppressed – that way madness lies), so that the interests and needs of the class and the subject can be activated. Now my inner need-interests go something like this. I'm only naming a few because we only need examples here. Your own list is more important than mine. I find I need to stress form in everything. I'm obsessed with it – pattern, shapes, colour, line and design. So I'm always finding a reason to satisfy that interest and draw children's attention to it. Not overtly – I'm too clever for that. But inductively in the way I use tasks to create interest in form. I also stress the relationship of past, present and future in any given moment. I stress symbols, implications and language, that is, not only word but gesture and space. The dark side, in teaching, of all these is my need; the light side, my object-interest The object-interest in teaching is first the student. Understanding and naming need-interest, then, can assist you to use it as relevant to the children's needs and the needs of the subject you want them to get interested in. If we look at what I've just said above, it would appear that the teachers most able to be 'creative' and interesting teachers would be those in the high schools able to teach the subjects they love. And conversely, the hardest teaching would be that of primary school teachers who have to have object-interest in many areas of the curriculum. Paradoxically, we often find the enthusiastic teachers working with the younger age range, but there are other factors at work there which are not the subject of this paper. Knowing what you stand for, then, is the first step towards personal authenticity.
2.  *When you look at your class what do you actually take note of first?* Energy? Features of clothing or physique? Mannerisms? Spatial behaviour or interactions? And when you take note do you place them against some judgemental line bred of your expectations? How do you accommodate when you are uncomfortable with what you see? Inauthentic behaviours make us want it our way now. Authentic behaviour presupposes in the teacher two skills: first, to withhold judgement, and second, to get a task started that employs what is perceived by the teacher about the class. I think those skills can be taught.
3.  *What does your working environment have to contain, or lack, for you to find it productive to work in, alongside your class?* And can you compensate from within yourself through methods of accommodating, for example, realizing that the class may not share your views and it may be right for their needs? How much variety can you find in the reorganization potential of the environment?

4. ***How many kinds of power must you hold on to and which can you give away?*** This is not being self-centred: it is more centring in self so that you can be wholesome to be with, understanding the needs of yourself and the needs of the work and the class. This enables you to structure assurance and stability for students so that you are free to be as authentically responsible for mutually 'stretching' outcomes as possible. It permits realistic risk-taking.

## Teachers in groups and authentic behaviour decisions

So far, we've been considering the individual in his or her own teaching space with reference to personal drives, perception of students, space and working conditions and control of communication and interaction, so let's move on to teachers in groups and authentic behaviour decisions. One of the disturbing things about a look at oneself is the way it makes one perceptive about others' behaviour and it sometimes works destructively, as we all know. We may notice many aspects of inauthentic practice before we can label the examples of authentic action. We might more readily notice the way the art in the corridors is teacher-dominated, or the empty conversations we overheard. Phrases like: 'That's nice, dear', or 'What a clever girl/boy you are', or just 'OK, put it on my desk.' We will notice the stereotyped dismissal phrases where student and teacher both acknowledge that it is the teacher's right to terminate any encounter: 'Right then, you run along.' It's so easy and dangerous to spot all the failures and so hard to take up the successes in personal encounters, because it looks as if we are commenting on people's private affairs. But these encounters *are* the breeders of the climate of inauthentic and authentic behaviours. It is somehow hard to accost a teaching colleague with statements like: 'I did admire the way you upgraded that child's contribution in assembly today', or 'You are so clear to understand when you explain things to your class', and even 'You seem very tactful when you mention the coffee fund is getting low, and people seem to respond by paying up quickly.'

We can help each other in groups by overcoming this natural reluctance to name and specify productive task-orientated and organizationally based behaviour. Society functions on this. Perhaps, if the natural reluctance of head teachers to start stressing productive establishment behaviour prevents it, individual teachers will have to start moving. Or maybe courses for heads and teachers could help it start. In one school in Cumbria they have made a beginning with staff seminars led by their counsellor colleague.

## Working with parents

Many teachers are also parents, so if they can be authentic parents, they might be authentic teachers. Can authentic parents get together with authentic teachers? Recently, I had the privilege in a Newcastle junior school of using materials which children of eight years old had worked on in the role of sociologists examining child-rearing practices in an invented tribe of seafaring people 'somewhere in the world'. The parents came in the evening to carry on with the work their children had started earlier in the week, so they of course faced the same problems as their young children. One parent said she was realizing, because of it, that she never really talked *with* her son. She tended to interrogate and tell. When others joined us, I was really impressed by the ability of those present to be self-examining and to use one process- and task-orientated situation to refer to another one, their real child-rearing practice.

We do not have to be afraid of associating with parents in the mutually responsible task of teaching children and 'growing' adults. Once perhaps they did seem to be mutually exclusive – when those who could read took over the teaching of the young, for example. In some parts of the world, England included, that is still true, but society cannot afford to neglect the mutuality of interests. We can make a start by using what parents have to offer to the school. An authentic society finds ways to do this when it wants to.

But some of the best kinds of help I've received have been when parents can come along to work alongside me in the process of teaching. Drama is particularly useful here because of the way it can employ adults in role. The role work often permits parents to feel part of the situation but at the same time to perceive the realities of teaching second by second and the areas of arousal of interest and concern the teacher is engaged in at that time. One recent example of this was when a high school class doing computer studies became interested – because of their teacher's need-interest – with the problems of privacy of the individual and the record-keeping systems employed, for example by business, the police and banks. The two parents concerned were in role – that is, they behaved as the ordinary citizens they are – but within a specific social circumstance. They were parents searching for a missing relative, so all the student tasks with regard to the computer potential to assist and their skill potential that was being used in action *now* related to their need to find their son. Any parent can identify with that. They don't have to engage with the emotional behaviours – they don't have to portray anguish, pain, or loss. But they can make it necessary to be assisted. And they can sit there awaiting results of the student's work. And their responses can be those of anyone who comes to a source for immediate help. So the skills of reading and collating, which had been approached in theory and through some practical use of computers, were employed in the 'now time' of drama, enabling dead knowledge to be activated in practice. But more than that I think what became possible was that the world of information, skills, knowledge (the object-interest) was melded for a time with the need-interest of humanity. The parents saw something of the problems of creating authentic tasks and responsibilities that teachers face, but they also shared with another generation a common need-problem, in circumstances of truthfulness, to the benefit of both generations and that of the school in its tasks. I don't think parents can make this move easily, for it smacks of interference, but teachers do have the power to invite help.

## Bringing schools and society together

Our society is recognizing that schools and cultures need to get together more. And that it is *urgent*. How much longer have young people, even the academic ones, to go on 'getting fed up with school'? But the doors of academia are becoming more and more tightly shut. Rigidity is dangerous, especially so at this time. One of the tools against rigidity is authenticity. It is not only the academic aspects of culture which are getting more tightly shut but the other skill groups are becoming more difficult to join because they often insist on the wrong qualifying processes which are, when you get right down to it, irrelevant to the skills which will really be needed. I am not discussing here the skills of reading, numeracy and writing – the lubricant of society – but the skills which the practical life requires so that complex new structures, tools and functional objects can be maintained. The second-class citizen of the future – though God help us if we continue these feudal ideas much longer – is likely to be the theorist who cannot practise and the thinker of high contemplative skill. Both will be unemployable. This is not just likely to happen. It is already happening, because even now we have doctors who are unemployed. That was unthinkable in my young days.

It is on record that a letter exists from a father to his son in the time of Ptolemy (I don't know which one), which cautions him to 'not become a maker of objects. Become a go-between.' I should say of course that at present the doctors are becoming unemployed, not because they are not needed, but because we have begun to price necessary skills out of the market. The reason for this is that we are basically an inauthentic society. We do not charge the price things cost to make — we invent a price relative to what we can cynically educate people to pay for things. The world is full of things which need doing — all kinds of interesting activities for the good of all. And we make it impossible *for* all to have their rightful opportunity to work. One of the forces in this is inauthentic schooling.

I mentioned the parents who came into school to put a human focus into computer studies, and I'm thinking of all the unemployed parents at present in the north-east of England who might help in schools, either by tutoring individuals in some skills, helping get the need-interests of children satisfied enough to get their object-interests flowing, being taught by the children, making things alongside their children and studying beside them and sharing in problem-solving, I can't see that it's dangerous, but of course it needs to be subtle and authentic. If we just invent little jobs for parents as well as for the children, we'll be in an even worse position. Local teachers could create local associations with parents on matters of local concern. I know it means dealing with matters of insurance, timetables and general openness for it to happen. Some teachers won't want it to happen because it means too much change, and we may after all be a peculiar psychological breed who are best working as the only adult in the room. Well, if that is the case, and it's something I examine in myself regularly, we may have to start pockets of quite different teacher functionaries. There's plenty of room for manoeuvre.

In addition to harnessing parent power, there's also all the student power which could be utilized, for example students writing works which are useful for others. As I write this article, seventy primary teachers in Cyprus are going to create a history archive for slow-learning children to work on seventeenth-century Cypriot life. I'm doing this sort of work with teachers, because we are examining mixed-ability teaching of difficult historical concepts, but there is no reason why a high school class studying these concepts could not make the preparation of such archives and help other children to employ them, either as reading skill material (reading *into* things), as historical material, or as problem-solving material. ('What would you have done to help the 100 young prisoners if you had been there with some power to operate?') This way we can occasionally make an attempt to get rid of the 'dummy runs' of school learning.

You can see why the first question we must ask ourselves is whether we *want* to be an authentic teacher. It means an awful lot of change, but it can be started in localized ways, not small — nothing like this is small — but cautiously based upon *will*, not doubt. We can't begin with huge legislation or large signs upon head teachers' doors exhorting us to 'be *authentic*'. André Gide has observed that no man can be sincere at the same time as he is explaining to us how sincere he is being, and likewise the same is true of authenticity. Authenticity is practice informing theory.

## Building an authentic climate

If the idea of individual teachers agreeing with colleagues on what they need for an authentic climate in which authentic behaviours can occur eventually leads to more shared teaching, more links and associations in class with colleagues, using parents and joint consultations with the community, including students and young school leavers, it must 'start a shift' around the local area. It won't touch everybody at once and there are bound to be those who prefer to work from doubt rather than change, but it could make a start. One problem is of course that it takes will and energy, and often a trend which is long established has to be reversed. And somehow doubt is always more convincing than hopeful caution.

We've got computers, photocopiers, overhead projectors, video machines and films and books and typing courses in some of our schools. All the children learning to type could be collating information, working as secretaries to groups, making demands on themselves to improve their skills because of the public nature and responsibility of their work contribution. We have teachers' centres, schools and homes to meet in, as well as local community centres and church halls. Teachers who can think in this way can be 'lent' to groups, or seconded. Teachers and parents could share the information they pick up about experiments; people could share their ideas. Groups could research specific interest areas with the help of research students in higher education or primary schools! And these research efforts could use local expertise or be just happy chance discoveries where people have to learn how to do it by themselves.

Then it might be possible for staffs to take a close supportive look (using children as well, because they are the clients after all) at the different styles of teachers and their inclinations as performers in the classroom. For example, I'm quite a useful group teacher because I'm comfortable and imaginative in devising ways of either getting class consensus when necessary for the study or tolerating a fair amount of variety of levels and speeds and types of work all in process at the same time. Some teachers are better at small group teaching, others as private tutors. The same applies to children. At some stages of study we all need private tutors. Student and teaching and parent power should be able to supply all the various kinds of help, and this division in style between school and home needn't continue. Recently at the Friend's Centre in Brighton after a day's teaching of children and teachers, I was very impressed with the work which started immediately after on a reading programme for the community members who for various reasons need reading instruction and support. And there must be a lot of this kind of activity around which never gets discussed. We urgently need to think more globally about education in our culture. Then all the people can share the responsibility for the future.

The teaching force could do a serious study of the different styles of teachers available, so that all types can be usefully employed in any school or small community. 'Enabling' teachers don't like using strict instructional methods if they can avoid it. But good instructors are unhappy when they are employed in 'enabling', especially if they have to pretend they are natural enablers. Teachers with no vocal projection, even when they try, are not helpful to themselves or the class if the numbers are too great. We need all kinds of teachers who can be authentic, because they don't do the damage which inauthentic teachers do. I don't think one is a 'failed teacher' because one can't handle the statutory size of classes. Local authority inspectors and head teachers might do a good supportive service in helping staffs take a close look at their social skills in regard to style and group size.

I really think too that students can assist in this close look at teachers and styles. They have a sense of honesty about the teaching they experience, especially when they are given responsibility for their opinion. One of my ex-students, working in a high school in Washington, DC with 'low achievers' taken from their classes for special studies in the basic subjects, gained their support by commandeering all the school video equipment (it wasn't being used much at the time, but it is now) and planning projects with groups that made them responsible for further outcomes. One of the questions discussed was 'why do we fall a bit behind in lessons' and some of the videos were made on the basis of different teaching styles. It needed tact to enable the students to learn to enter classrooms, and it needed trust and generosity on the part of some teachers. It also needed careful consideration from the students about good, bad, hopeful, and productive teaching methods, so they had to be very discriminating and most careful of the 'weak' teachers when they convened meetings with individual staff members to discuss the lessons they had put on video. It was hard work, and some teachers wanted it stopped, but it had very helpful effects in practice both for some students and some of the teachers.

If pupils can use their capability for recognizing authentic behaviour in teachers and in themselves, it seems to me that they can begin to discuss this matter of need-interest and object-interest for the good of all, because we need student energy in school. Often when I'm teaching a high school class, sometimes one that shows difficult behaviour, I'm always interested when someone from the class will approach me and start talking about 'What's different about this, Miss?' and my heart lifts. This begins a process of real pleasure in learning and teaching together.

## Teaching for the future

When I consider the examination systems we may be getting, the cynic in me wonders if we are just once again going to paint the shop instead of examining and improving the goods. I heard talk about the 'different levels' that will be available, but nothing was said about the minute particulars of teacher skills and detailed student, teacher, society interaction and responsibility. We can't take it for granted any more. There isn't an alchemy of teaching: there is a craft which in some people works like an art, but we can raise the numbers of high level achievers both in teaching and learning if we set our minds to it.

Our profession is either unable or unwilling to share and name and specify skills of social action, practical knowledge-getting and social science. Most of the high-level teaching skills are based on common sense – by that I mean the inner understanding we all have about 'what is going on here'. For example, we know that part of the problem of 'discipline' is that the students often have no context in which the work they do has any purpose other than some vague future possibility. But the future is *now* for people with need-interest-dominated behaviour. Also, long-term future goals may have to give way to more flexibility. Society shift and pressure are running ahead of behaviour patterns.

## Inauthentic schooling

This brings me to a further point of authenticity for society – the dead knowledge that is still being taught. I did not say *deadly* knowledge. I mean the ways in which the collected and useful knowledge that expands the world for us is still being served up as if we'd only got books and writing to learn from, and teacher telling-talk. This makes school seem inauthentic because the work of school – the learning-getting – seems to bear no relationship to the learning-getting systems operating outside. The child laws passed to save children from exploitation in mines, sweatshops, and up chimneys have reaped a whirlwind which any adolescent recognizes, at least by instinct if not by cognition. We have also successfully 'protected' our young from influencing society in any way which seems to matter. We have made them toys of society when small and exploited them shamelessly as consumers when large. We have not permitted them to produce, however, or to assist in the fabric of culture-making. In spite of this, of course, they do, but not in ways which can assist the necessary cross-fertilizations of young and old.

The final insult to their energy is, of course, to remove the last initiatory ceremony into adult life – a place to work, and work to do which is recognized as a contribution. Yet the world is crying out for tasks to be undertaken: dirt cleared to make way for imaginative development; the lonely visited; the helpless to be given inventive technical aids as well as love; the handicapped used in society by clever patient tutoring; the waste recycled; the tender and rare preserved for all, and the problems of this transitional age tackled with fresh minds.

## The danger of the status quo

My own despair at not being able to find ways in the classroom to make work feel 'real for society in action' led me to develop the system of drama which I call the *Mantle of the Expert*. I can't think of a more 'normal' name which expresses the ideas behind it, namely that a person will wear the mantle of their responsibility so that all may see it and recognize it, and learn the skills which make it possible for them to be given the gift label 'expert'. It enables me to create context for school work. The gift of drama is that it makes micro-societies and micro-skills and micro-behaviour and endeavours available to the teacher. I needed a structure for authentic learning, even in an inauthentic establishment situation.

This kind of approach can be used to create dynamic learning and cross the boundaries of subject divisions when it is necessary to do so. I am not suggesting that drama teaches everything. Drama teaches people by demonstrating interactive social behaviour and encouraging critical spectatorship, because art releases the spectator/action possibility in people. Art can isolate one factor from another, reveal something of infrastructure and give people a no-penalty testing zone, so that contemplation in flux is possible. So we have this paradox that art could be a vehicle for changing the work of school to make reality-usable outcomes.

Teacher power seems very small when we consider the power of cash and more tangible energies, and teachers as a breed are probably more often viewed as those with long holidays and not much responsibility and 'nothing much to see for it at the end'. But the product at the end is society in action – thinking, knowing, living – and affecting single human beings engaged with their culture. The teacher should be part of recognized cultural power to influence. In a vain attempt to be seen as such, an examination system has been evolved, which seeks to evaluate the milestones of information which have been passed. But they do not examine the relevant factors for our age. Teachers tell me that they would like to work in the Mantle of the Expert way if the examination system gave them time to do so.

## The enormous potential of teachers

In this paper I am suggesting that teacher power has enormous potential for these changing times, and I believe that one of the keys is authenticity. It can make connections in a realistic way between the present work of schools, which is based on entirely laudable skill and information areas, and society, which is creating new models, systems of work and behaviour and new exciting technology for work and study. Between these energies, the school curriculum and changes in society, stand a collection of individuals called teachers, who are freed in the main from 'hewing of wood and drawing of water'. What a privilege and awesome responsibility. They could function at present as a kind of stabilizing or holding energy, for they are the older generation dedicated to developing the younger generation into citizens of power, use and value.

## The contribution of drama

1.  *Dramatic work is first of all a social art,* in which the interaction of people comes under scrutiny in a specific encounter or a matter of concern in which they are trapped. It spans all time, race, social strata, faiths, behaviours and feelings. Thus it is a mirror of society. As a teacher I can use it to create a reflective element that can assist the young people to perceive modes and forms of communication and interaction and the effects on private individuals and in groups: that is, people's humanity to each other. This includes the development of processes of communication, private and public language, listening skills, avoidance of polarization in social encounters, respect for the quality of language choices in such encounters, toleration of others' ways of doing things, and, because it is an art, application of critical thought to these processes. No two teachers need agree on the outward forms they choose to achieve any of these skills for students, and they have plenty of devices they can select from and employ. Art is rich in offering a variety of ways to do something. Some teachers are better when they work through scripts, some are better in non-verbal modes, and some prefer simulation work or improvisational approaches. The outer form can vary, providing it is used to promote inner revelations and reflections about the human condition.

2.  *Drama is a detailed art.* It precisely examines at any moment the 'minute particulars' of a situation, using sign as its basic component of expression. It therefore permits participants to perceive the complexity of communication during the actual processes of its occurring. It can therefore enable the learners to transfer this understanding to their living community. It trains them to notice first what signs are being used. Are those signs intended to inform, illuminate, obscure, engage the feelings, or merely have an effect in a social situation? Are they being helpful to society in their use? Baby food manufacturers at one time became very clever in using sign in their films for the Third World, ostensibly to suggest the values of breastfeeding whilst carefully undermining that in favour of made-up feeds. Even doctors taking part did not at first spot what they were supporting. All those nice white-coated sincere people being seen around the production of such foods and talking about them to the viewer. Because we now have television, we are already very efficiently teaching children to read signs in the real world, but the real world does not always yield to us the power to recognize and employ the skills it develops in us.

3.  *Drama is a progressing art.* As opposed to the frozen time of the painting, the photograph or the drawing, drama activity demands that each action or sign produces a result – some change in understanding. Each sign processes and generates outcomes from the past, and creates the future in the present. It does this in a 'no-penalty zone' of agreed depiction. By using this truthful but artificial environment, students can face up to emotional, affective 'people' responses before finally having to practise them in society. So again we see the paradox of the artificiality of drama and its potential for real accountability in society. We can see this clearly in the work of the theatre, where the ideas of playwrights

are forged into action in the real conditions of audience presentation. The work I am discussing requires an extra dimension to be placed in it — that of knowing we are all engaged in the making of any encounter as well as the inbuilt scrutiny of it, in order to be responsible for its outcomes.

4. ***Drama engages the affective zone.*** It deliberately engages and explores emotional field forces. Resistances, moods, power ploys, submissions, denigrations, heroic acts, tremulous and bold ventures, daring and dangerous exploits as well as tender and delicate situations come under examination by definition and restriction of circumstances so that they can be explored in detail. Schools at present function as if they have no mandate for affective learning — the deliberate engagement of what has been called 'the celebration of the affairs of mankind' — along with the cognitive and analytical thought which is also necessary. Teachers have great freedom in selecting their methods and their materials. They can have a mandate to make learning interesting and useful. They do *not* have a mandate to teach without reflective processes and responsible outcomes.

5. ***Drama uses the person to bring it into being.*** Conversely, the person is brought into possible new being by the same process. The child enters the zone of circumstance permitted by the drama situation, and in shaping the circumstance's future, the child's future is shaped, ready to be available in the real society which at present seems cut off from school.

## In conclusion

Because of these five aspects, it seems to me that drama is a seminal force in our developing social processes. Teachers who choose authenticity cannot afford to ignore its specific potentialities for good. I leave you with the statement of Alvin Toffler, who speaks more eloquently than I. Toffler in *The Third Wave* says:

> The responsibility for change therefore lies with us. We must begin with ourselves, teaching ourselves not to close our minds prematurely to the novel, the surprising, the seemingly radical. This means fighting off the idea–assassins who rush forward to kill any new suggestions on grounds of its impracticality while defending whatever now exists as practical, no matter how absurd, oppressive or unworkable it may really be. It means fighting for freedom of expression … if we begin now, we and our children can take part in the exciting reconstitution not merely of our obsolete political structures but of civilization itself. Like the generation of the revolutionary dead we have a destiny to create.[1]

I salute any endeavour, however small it feels, and each day when I enter a classroom of adults or children I seek to use my art of teaching and the art of drama in the service of a process for change.

## Note

1 Toffler, A. (1980) *The Third Wave*, New York: Bantam Books.

**PART III**

# Mantle of the Expert

# INTRODUCTION

In 'The authentic teacher and the future' (1984), the final chapter in the previous section, Heathcote's increasing concerns about the ways in which schools disenfranchise young people and deny them any means of being effective in the world outside school is already apparent. Heathcote sees school as a sterile waiting area, where students are isolated from all matters of importance in life. Instead she wants young people to reach out to the community and to begin to take responsibility for their own learning. Her proposals for ways in which real links might be created between the school and the community clearly anticipate the development of Mantle of the Expert, her most innovative and influential approach to teaching and learning.

Mantle of the Expert arose from her profound dissatisfaction with schooling and built on all her previous practice. It is essentially an approach to the whole curriculum and a rare example of truly integrative teaching, and it developed from her search for structures that would deliver authentic learning and create real connections between the school and the real world. It is a dynamic and effective method of cultivating a love of knowledge in students, as well as an attention to detail, a respect for research, and training in a wide range of skills.

> My own despair at not being able to find ways in the classroom to make work feel 'real for society in action' led me to develop the system of drama which I call Mantle of the Expert. I can't think of a more 'normal' name which expresses the ideas behind it – namely that a person will wear the mantle of their responsibility so that all may see it and recognize it, and learn the skills which make it possible for them to be given the gift label 'expert'. It enables me to create context for school work. The gift of drama is that it makes micro-societies and micro-skills and micro-behaviour and endeavours available to the teacher. I needed a structure for authentic learning even in an inauthentic establishment situation.[1]

This section includes several papers that focus on Mantle of the Expert and its associated approaches – Rolling Role and the Commission Model. Mantle of the Expert frames the teacher and students in fictional roles in a context in which the students are 'endowed' as experts in a specific field. It sets up a supportive, interpretative, and reflective community through a pattern of relationships and a network of tasks, all embedded in a flexible context. This approach allows students to access power within the classroom, as the teacher becomes an 'enabler' rather than a 'transmitter'. Heathcote reminds us that this factor changes the way in which students engage in learning, because information is being communicated in a very different manner. Students are not merely passively receiving knowledge but actively constructing it. This is an active, urgent, purposeful view of learning in which knowledge is operated on, not merely absorbed.[2]

The most obvious change to her previous ways of working was that now the *setting* helps to generate the fiction – as Bolton puts it 'the classroom takes on a role'.[3] It becomes the location for different kinds of 'establishments' indicated by careful signing, where a variety of enterprises may be engaged in. Instead of taking on roles in a drama, the students become co-workers in an enterprise as they undertake tasks for 'clients'. Mantle of the Expert may appear less obviously 'dramatic' than previous approaches, but it includes a variety of theatrical elements. The fictional setting dictates the roles, tasks and functions of those within it, whether they are teachers or students, the work is still in 'now' time and the challenges and crises that arise from the fictional context must be dealt with as they occur. Conventions may be used as a means of encountering 'others' who are connected with the enterprise, and even the formal, presentational mode of Chamber Theatre may be included.

In this approach to the themes and materials of the curriculum, Heathcote proposes a paradox. The teaching is authentic, and yet it achieves its authenticity through 'the big lie,' since it operates within a powerful fictional context, created through the inner dramatic rules of time, space, role, and situation. Its effect is purposeful and empowering. Students who accept the mantle and its responsibilities are in an active state of attention to a range of projects and plans of action. Thinking from *within* a situation immediately forces a different kind of thinking from the students. They begin to generate their own knowing and, most importantly, this knowing is always embedded in a fertile but fictional context.

In Mantle of the Expert, this contextualization is the key to its effect, and the problems and challenges that arise within the context are both motivating and comprehensible. Everything that takes place within the work is elevated into significance. This significance is achieved through situation, role, and task, but above all through the language initially modelled by the teacher but gradually claimed by the students as their own. This 'language' includes not just discussion but also written language and the reading and interpretation of a variety of sign systems. There is a growing sense of audience, both within the work and through the wider community to which the students become accountable. The students inhabit their roles as experts in the enterprise with increasing conviction, complexity and truth. They grow into their roles in a way that goes far beyond the functional as they experience the enlargement of both identity and capacity within the tasks they undertake and the challenges they encounter. Their involvement is always tied to the immediate task, the demands of the enterprise and their responsibility to the client and the community. Although the quality of the students' imaginative encounters as they engage in these enterprises may appear less intense than that in 'living-through' drama, they are operating with *social* imagination – the kind that promotes cooperation rather than competition and invites membership of a community endeavour.

> Without the encouragement of the social imagination, of freedom to imagine the
> world being other than it is, we are left without hope for society as a whole.[4]

The development of the other two approaches included in this section also arose from the
need to make links between teachers and students within the school and between the school
and the community. Heathcote developed the complex system she called Rolling Role in an
attempt to alleviate the isolation of subject teachers within the secondary school and, if necessary, to provide drama teachers with a curriculum for purposeful exploration. This approach
recognizes the restrictions of the limited time that is likely to be allotted to each lesson and
allows students to carry the same context with them from lesson to lesson. It promotes a
realization that the disparate and disconnected subjects of the curriculum have essential links
with each other. This approach promotes communication, and planning the work and sharing
skills and information are paramount for both teachers and students. In the Commission
Model, the actual community beyond the school becomes the setting for the work. The key
difference in this approach is the absence of any kind of fiction. Tasks and functions are all
undertaken in the context of the real world.

The social dimensions of this kind of teaching are extremely significant. Learning is known
to occur most efficiently within a supportive and collaborative community where, instead of
sterile competitiveness, everyone's level of achievement is elevated. In these approaches,
students work in the kinds of teams and collaborative environments which anticipate the
challenges that will face them in the real world.

Working in Mantle of the Expert, students are required to question, negotiate, compromise, take responsibility, cooperate, and collaborate, all in the service of something beyond
themselves. Their energies are focused less on these interactions than on the tasks to be
accomplished as they develop an awareness of their own knowledge and competencies. They
are motivated and empowered by the knowledge that they are learners as they become active
in the learning process, not just cognitively but socially and kinaesthetically. They express
their understandings in their response to the variety of tasks demanded of them, and they
reflect on their perceptions from both inside and outside the context.

In each of the approaches included in this section, responsibility for the learning is shared
among the students and includes the teacher, who is admitted as a member of the learning
community. The key function of the teacher is to maintain the momentum of the learning
experience and support and challenge the students within it. As teachers work with this
method, they begin to understand more about their own learning processes; as a result they
are likely to become more sensitive and knowledgeable about their students' ways of learning.
All successful learning depends on the capacity of the learner to bring relevant background
and information to bear on a problem and to accumulate further experience as a result of
encountering and resolving the problem. Here, the students' prior knowledge and experience
are validated and their frame of reference is enlarged.

These approaches challenge some basic ideas about the nature of teaching and require a
new way of thinking about education. As Bolton points out, if Mantle of the Expert is to
become part of the curriculum structure of schools, it cannot be left to drama teachers alone
to take it on. Educationalists need to acquire a vested interest in fundamentally revising current
conceptions of education. They must be prepared to inspire politicians, advisers, head teachers
and their staff, and Mantle of the Expert must be included in teacher training.[5]

In recent years, an encouraging number of primary schools in England have accepted this challenge and successfully placed Mantle of the Expert at the heart of their curriculum. As one teacher puts it:

> Over the last year it has been a major part of the children's learning and we have watched our classes become transformed by the powerful thinking, speaking, listening, and freedom of imagination that happens within Mantle of the Expert.[6]

Many educators recognize the flaws in our present approach to education – the multiplication of decontextualized 'skills' and competencies, the obsession with measurement, the lack of challenge, the reliance on a transmission mode of teaching – practices that are visibly failing even where students themselves collude in these practices. In contrast, Heathcote, in developing Mantle of the Expert, Rolling Role and the Commission Model, assumes that education can go beyond the pre-packaged, bite-size, fragmented, and highly disposable facts with which students' genuine appetite for knowledge is too often assuaged. In these approaches, the students are empowered, not by giving them a spurious 'freedom', but by encouraging them to accept constraints within which they will work and through which they will encounter challenges and take decisions from a position of increasing authority and knowledge. From the firm foundation provided by the teacher, the students gradually begin to take control of both the fictional and the actual contexts, a control they have earned in contexts they have helped to create. They become experts – experts at learning.

## Notes

1 Johnson, L. and O'Neill, C. (eds.) (1984) *Dorothy Heathcote: Collected Writings on Education and Drama*, London: Hutchinson, p. 192.
2 Heathcote, D. and Bolton, G. (1999) *So You Want to Use Role Play?* Stoke-on-Trent: Trentham Books, p. 32.
3 Bolton, G. (1985) 'Changes in Thinking about Drama in Education', *Theory into Practice* 24 (3).
4 Kohl, H. (1995) *Should We Burn Babar? Essays on Children's Literature and the Power of Stories*, New York: The New Press.
5 Bolton, G. (2003) *Dorothy Heathcote's Story: The Biography of a Remarkable Drama Teacher*, Stoke-on-Trent: Trentham. p. 177.
6 Quoted on the website: www.mantleoftheexpert.com.

# MANTLE OF THE EXPERT

## Key elements

*This paper, published in the Turkish* Creative Drama Journal *in 2010, gives a particularly clear account of the key elements in Mantle of the Expert. In this approach, the instinct to pretend – to play – is harnessed to the specific learning goals that schools are designed to achieve. The teacher sustains the 'as if' behaviour of the students, modelling behaviour and attitude through selective language and signing. It is this 'as if' stance that changes the familiar classroom stance of thinking and learning about* things to thinking *from* within *the situation. A distinguishing characteristic of this approach is that all students work from the same point of view – the perspective of people running some form of enterprise that serves fictional clients. Students accept responsibility for responding to their clients' needs and they become engaged in the research and skills essential to making the enterprise truthful, even though teacher and students all realize that they themselves are the creators and sustainers of the developing enterprise.*

*In her paper* 'Mantle of the Expert – Establishing Procedures' *available on the website www. mantleoftheexpert.com, Heathcote covers similar ground, occasionally developing her ideas in greater detail. Where she has expanded on some of the key points, I have included her remarks here.*

*In that paper she lists the elements that are essential to generating and sustaining Mantle of the Expert:*

- *Behaving 'as if' produces the 'now time' of theatre and the drama elements of deep play.*
- *The particular enterprise has been selected to provide access to the curriculum.*
- *The enterprise starts in the middle so that the historical background of the enterprise is available for exploration.*
- *The work progresses through relevant tasks.*
- *The teacher's language sustains the fiction.*
- *The teacher may work in different roles as well as a colleague in the enterprise.*

I have a special interest in exploring a system now known as Mantle of the Expert. This rather fanciful title involves two elements, both of which are equally important. 'Mantle' in this context is not a garment to be worn but expresses the responsibility or authority by which people carry out their duties. This means that they must carry out their work so that their colleagues recognize their integrity and trust is built amongst all with whom they come into contact. I want schools to function in ways that nurture this community learning, and drama can foster this.

Students are taught according to the way in which their teachers perceive them. These perceptions generate the attitude teachers take when in contact with their classes. Let us consider some of these:

Child as 'flower' – 'I will give you time and care.'
Child as 'candle' – 'You can rely on me to light you up.'
Child as 'echo' – 'No, do it the way I've shown you.'
Child as 'friend' – 'If I'm nice to you, will you …?'
Child as 'adversary'-'The trouble with you is …'
Child as 'clay' – 'In time you'll turn into the students I want.'
Child as 'crucible' – 'You and I must keep stirring our understanding around.'
Child as 'machine' – 'By the end of the course everyone should be able to …'
Child as 'vessel' – 'My knowledge will fill you up.'

We will all have experienced some of these paradigms, and at different times each viewpoint may serve the learning process. Problems arise when one organizing principle dominates, because each paradigm determines how teachers expect children to behave in class. Mantle of the Expert presumes that teacher and children associate within the 'crucible' paradigm, where knowledge is formulated through the process of action, social participation and ethical standards. 'Drama' means that we explore what it means to be human in an active community association, considering all the affairs of interest to humankind. So it seems to me that it is an essential element in schooling.

The roots of drama are embedded in play – the ability to imagine different places and behaviours that most children possess. Mantle of the Expert exploits this ability by deliberately creating circumstances in which everyone assumes adulthood as well as spheres of responsibility *towards clients*. This latter element is of supreme importance, because clients create a serious purpose in the playing out of ideas. So the instinct to pretend – to play – is harnessed to the specific learning goals that schools are designed to achieve. This is common sense, but it is not easily achieved, because it challenges many of the established mores and conventions of schools, not all of which are negative.

Teachers themselves are challenged if they wish to operate in this way. They must:

1. negotiate learning in a different relationship with their students;
2. relinquish the power of 'knowing best' in favour of everyone learning alongside each other; they must not withhold knowledge;
3. invent relevant contexts to service the social health of the children and the curriculum that is to be studied;
4. create contexts that have parameters, as the theatre does, enabling detailed exploration and exploitation of the potential of the context. Everyone must become responsible for taking charge of some establishment. These invented parameters create the need of *clients*, and it is the client aspect that raises the children's engagement, begins the process of independent thinking and erodes their dependence on the teacher.
5. An establishment has to be consistently 'signed'.
6. Some 'signs' will be location and orientation signifiers, such as notices indicating the presence of objects – for example telephone 'signs', not actual telephones. These objects must be found in the mind and expressed in behaviours. Or electrical connection signs

to locate business tools – for example, sewing machines, computers, power tools, depending on the particular enterprise.

7. Working associations are 'signed' by the suitable placement of furniture. All classrooms require this, but the fictional establishment may call for a change in such arrangements, depending on the nature of the particular episode. It cannot be assumed that chairs will always be needed or that tables will be seen as desks. The teacher has to consider the classroom as a shape-shifting laboratory that will be made suitable for immediate and varying purposes. Display space will become important. A noticeboard space is not the same as a 'questions we need to answer' space. Some filing and record-keeping space must be made so that, as the establishment develops, the work is preserved and documents can be created as required.

8. The establishment is 'signed' in process by the range of *voices* open to the teacher/manager.

## Voices

The 'voices' the teacher uses in Mantle of the Expert are mainly in three styles:

The *colleague/manager* voice – always using the collegial 'we', 'us', 'our' vocabulary, never the 'you' or 'I' of separateness.

The *mentor* voice that enables information to be injected without sounding like the voice of authority – the one who knows, patronizing others who know less, which is the more familiar teacher/student style.

The *role* voice that allows 'others' to enter the establishment. Some roles may be played by real people, for example colleagues, friends or other students who are not involved in the enterprise. Some 'others' are brought into existence by letters or recorded messages on tape or video, by fax, emails or telephone calls.

In Mantle of the Expert the same point of view is sustained throughout: 'We work in and are responsible for maintaining this establishment.' This is the huge difference between Mantle of the Expert and all other ways of working in drama. There is no casting of parts, no storyline to follow. The establishment is parallel to life in that episodes are encountered. These emerge because of the lifestyle, duties, responsibilities and attitudes of the participants. The teacher plans the episodes to serve the learning within the establishment.

## Enterprises

The establishments fall into a number of categories, so teachers have a wide range to select from:

*Social enterprises* – for example a bank, a hotel, a library, a restaurant, a hospital, a travel agency, a veterinary surgery, a shop, a fire station, a funeral home. No goods are produced.

*Manufacturing enterprises* – for example a factory, a bakery, a fashion house, a herb garden.

*Charitable enterprises* – for example Oxfam, heritage sites open to the public such as the National Trust in the UK, the Salvation Army, Greenpeace.

*Nurturing enterprises* – for example homes for orphans, hospices for the sick, play groups, a gene bank for plants or rare animals, a national park, a nature reserve, social services, a home for the elderly.

*Regulatory enterprises* – for example an immigration office, police stations, prisons, justice departments, the armed services.

*Maintenance enterprises* – for example skilled artisans, plumbers, electricians, stonemasons, join-
ers, restorers of antiques or art treasures.

*Arts enterprises* – for example a photographic studio, an art gallery, a craft centre, an opera,
ballet or theatre company.

*Learning enterprises* – for example sports centres, museums, zoos, university departments such
as archaeology or history.

Any one of these enterprises is bound to nurture the 'Mantle' element, because ethics, standards and responsibility to clients are common to any invented enterprise. All will draw on
curriculum skills and knowledge. All will make demands on language-speaking, reading and
writing in a variety of forms and styles. All will require numeracy in a variety of ways, including mathematics and computing skills. All will demand social collaboration. In making the
choice of enterprise the teacher will consider short- and long-term learning goals, the present
needs of the class as they embark upon developing their enterprises, and the variety of
strategies to be used that will best serve the learning. Each enterprise will reveal the social
health of the class. Some students will need to participate in situations where they can learn
to help each other. Sometimes dealing first with *things* helps the students to collaborate –
assembling something, or making labels or badges to be planned together and worn. The
teacher is usually in a position to judge where students can begin to work from their strengths,
and what attitudes dominate during other kinds of work.

There will be differences in the way the teacher prepares to launch the learning. The
initial preparation must include evidence that the business is already established. This follows
a basic law of theatre – all human actions and behaviours are already in process and arise
from what has gone before. All plays 'begin in the middle'. Hamlet is already in the grip of
his dilemma. Juliet's parents are already planning her marriage. There is no play that begins
at the beginning – the audience meets the actors at a point when a specific episode is already
under way and must be resolved. Theatre and Mantle of the Expert share this common
purpose, that of doing, in now and immediate time, that which it is imperative to achieve.
There is one radical difference. The playwright begins from a feeling or psychological basis,
whereas Mantle of the Expert begins with organization and tasks. Thus, a talent for acting
is never a factor. Feeling and emotional involvement grow through caring for and commitment to the clients and belief in the enterprise. It is this that opens the gates of study, research,
mastery of skills and the dignity of responsibility. Thus a natural affinity for self-regulated play
emerges, and students can enter the enterprise at individual levels of skills, information and
social health.

In Mantle of the Expert, students engaging in an enterprise must feel as if 'we've been
working in this establishment and now we must deal with a new client'. In starting the enterprise, then, one strand will be chosen that can set off the chain of all the other episodes.
Throughout Mantle of the Expert, students are functioning actively in iconic, symbolic and
expressive modes. It is *not* desk-bound, nor is it merely pen-and-paper work. A variety of tasks
is created, because the client, the type of audience, and the purpose of the work generate
constant shifts in presentation, research, and the type of occasion that requires the material.

In order to progress and deepen the work the teacher constantly selects from the curriculum
possibilities of the chosen enterprise. The students' concern drives the study forward and the
teacher sustains challenges and feedback and assists in keeping a record system of all the work.
Written work of varying lengths and styles is generated and there must be constant 'client'
pressure for clarity in language, appropriate presentations and forms of spoken communication.

It is the teacher's responsibility to devise the kinds of active tasks that enable students to explore and learn in ever-increasing and challenging ways. These tasks will be many and varied, some using small groups, others needing all students to plan and collaborate as one large team. There is an excellent palette of choice that can be tailored to each student's capacity and level of skill. The range and vitality of the work grow as students take on more and more responsibility for decisions and become engaged with accuracy, layout, presentation in many forms, and above all, feel that they care about their enterprise and their clients.

A word of warning. I notice that teachers are prone to telling their students that they are experts. The students know that this is not the case, so pretence is introduced inappropriately. The word 'expert' is irrelevant and should never be used, because it presupposes points of arrival and peaks of achievement. Mantle of the Expert calls for steady progress through a series of challenges. These are encountered at the pace and intensity that the teacher deems suitable for the social and academic needs of the students.

Research shows that when working under Mantle circumstances, students reveal skills and aptitudes in advance of those that have been predicted and evaluated in transmission and enquiry classrooms. The healthiest teacher stance is that of 'Let's see what happens' or 'How best can we deal with this?' rather than predicting or pre-judging what the children are capable of. These skills and aptitudes emerge as a result of very rigorous planning and subtle negotiating on the part of teachers. This has profound implications for the training of teachers, not only in resourcing materials but also in using these materials within the Mantle. Fortunately, teachers today have access to a rich variety of resources – colour printing of works of art, photography, the Internet, films, and books provide a mine of resources. Using them within Mantle of the Expert requires discretion and appropriate presentation.

## Frame

An important drama element that supports the laboratory aspects of the classroom is the way in which the Point of View of the students is consistently preserved, but which allows concerns and issues to be explored through different 'frame' distances. A teacher can set an episode within the 'frame' distance most appropriate to the learning experience. Frame distance is like a ladder moving from closeness to distance in exploring the event. Each step in the ladder demands changes in how to think, act, express and hold power in the exploration. At each step, language is forged from a different mindset. The following steps in the ladder move from the frame of immediate involvement in the event to increasingly remote perspectives:

1. We participate: we are involved at the time of it happening.
2. We guide others: we were there. We can show, tell or explain the event.
3. We are agents: we must re-enact the event so that it can be understood.
4. We are authorized: we must reconstruct the event because it has occurred and everyone should know about it.
5. We record it: it must be clarified so that in the future the truth will be available.
6. The media: we were not at the event but we consider why the event happened and we comment on it.
7. The researchers: we examine the event carefully so that it can be seen clearly in hindsight.
8. The critics: we scrutinize the events and records and interpret them in relation to other such occurrences.
9. The artists: the event can form the basis of transformations into other art forms.

Because Mantle of the Expert needs 'others' – sometimes real people who represent a particular point of view – it allows the teacher to create this range of frame distances. Because the students consistently sustain their responsibilities and point of view in regard to the establishment, they can keep returning to an event from within the enterprise when circumstances require it. For example, an episode in which a serious accident occurs in the workplace can be examined through the descending levels of nearness and distance to the event.

Level 1. The group agrees with the teacher to create the episode. 'We are here. It is happening.'

Level 2. The guides. 'We have to explain what happened to a medical team who are dealing with the victim.'

Level 3. The agents. 'We have to show them exactly what happened.'

Level 4. The authority. 'We must meet the insurance representative.'

Level 5. The recorders. 'We must write a detailed report.'

Level 6. The media. 'We must submit to the event being made public and ensure that the press represent the event accurately.'

Level 7. Research. 'We must consider how the accident occurred, what caused it and what precautions must be taken so that it does not happen again.'

Level 8. Interpretation. 'We examine the records and interpret the event in relation to other accidents.'

Level 9. The artist. 'We must produce a textbook of rules and illustrations for publication, or we must make a film as a teaching aid for training purposes.'

Each of these degrees of distance from the event will involve workers in the enterprise – the students – having an investment in preserving the truth, but at each level their thinking, speaking and behaviour will be generated through a different frame. What generates their engagement is the responsibility to the clients who may cease to bring their needs to us if we are perceived as having no integrity. I have seen eight-year-old children interviewed by the press – myself in role – about their enterprise who then demanded that before my account was published I should submit it to their scrutiny. I typed my report, revealing some bias. The students studied my account extremely carefully and identified every subtle bias. They demanded changes – modelled by me – otherwise they declared that my newspaper might expect to hear from their lawyers. Such thinking does not emerge from textbook curricula!

This paper can only touch upon the elements that can be incorporated into the system of teaching I have called Mantle of the Expert. In *Images of Man* Shotter[1] has a view of humankind living in a world in a state of exchange with other agents both like and unlike themselves, forming communities so that together they can do more than they ever could by themselves. As agents immersed in the world with other agents and in community with them, they face the task, not just intelligently but intelligibly and responsibly. This view of humankind lies at the very centre of the Mantle of the Expert system of teaching children how to learn.

## Note

1 Shotter, J. (1975) *Images of Man in Psychological Research*, London: Methuen.

# CONVENTIONS IN MANTLE OF THE EXPERT

*This paper deals with an episode used by Heathcote during a workshop on Mantle of the Expert in 2008. It revisits some key elements of this approach, but also describes ways in which the 33 Conventions listed in 'Signs and portents' in Part II can be used to develop encounters with an 'other' – a role introduced to deepen the work of a Mantle of the Expert 'enterprise' – in this case a firm bottling and marketing spring water.*

*The chapter is edited from Heathcote's account of a workshop she gave with teachers in Ankara in November 2008, published in* Creative Drama Journal *in 2010.*

Two elements are essential in launching enterprises in Mantle of the Expert. I teach these deliberately to all classes.

| *Drama Eyes* | *Implications* |
| --- | --- |
| There are eyes that see real things and eyes of the mind that can imagine things. We know they are not actually real, but we can use these to help us feel as if everything we do is very truthful. | Every act will mean more than just the doing of it – every act carries implications. For example, a fastener for a bottle of water. |
| When students ask 'Is this true?', my reply is, 'Not true like real but truthful because we can all agree to keep it feeling truthful'. Children always comprehend this. | Possible implications: it keeps contents in; it preserves contents safely; someone made it; it used materials; it has been designed for purpose; it must be capable of being opened and closed after use; it must have cost money to make, etc. |

Once students comprehend these, teachers can use them as brief reminders regarding quality and to preserve the social entry into the fictional enterprise – 'We'll just put on our drama eyes and work in the bottling company now' and 'We're going to have to look really carefully at the implication in this situation.'

I want to demonstrate the many different ways there are for a teacher to create the presence of 'others', who are required as the enterprise develops. There are at least 33 ways of manifesting 'others'. Remember, in running any enterprise the class of students and the teacher/

manager keep the same point of view throughout all the work. In this example we are workers in a firm that collects, processes, bottles, sells and delivers pure spring water to clients. Such enterprises have to interact with clients or other persons who might be interested in the firm, so these have to come into existence through our agreement. To do this a teacher can use what I have called 'conventions'. All the people involved will agree that however an 'other' will be represented, they will be accepted as affecting the situation.

Remember the 'voices' available to the teacher:

- The first voice is that of the manager, who works alongside the staff of the enterprise. In these situations no actual things are being made. It all exists in the drama mindset, so by agreement, it feels real. What makes it feel real is the way we talk to each other about the details of the preparation. This does not involve acting as actors in the theatre behave – it means behaving *as if* all is real. Some teachers find this way of working embarrassing at first, because it changes the normal teacher behaviour. This is the most important change in the teacher/class relationship when Mantle of the Expert is used.
- The second voice is the helpful colleague, raising issues, suggesting possibilities and avoiding telling. The talk is 'we', 'our', 'us', but the vocabulary is as accurate as the teacher has available to serve the period and the nature of social behaviour.
- The third voice is the teacher providing 'others' for students to encounter. It is the third voice the teacher needs when 'others' are required to deepen the work and challenge everyone through specific episodes the teacher may devise for or with the class so that the ethical and social elements of the work are explored. Conventions can achieve this. If you bring in the presence of an 'other', it means that the students need to understand that person. Matters depend upon it. It is never casual. Everyone must recognize the significance of the presence of 'others' as part of the enterprise.[1]

All encounters with roles – teacher in role representing others, or different persons who enter the work for short periods, such as colleagues or others represented by the conventions – happen in specific episodes for discrete learning that the teacher decides the class is ready to deal with.

In Mantle of the Expert the teacher *never* uses guile or surprises the class unless there is an agreed contract to do so. The teacher is always frank and open about why such an episode is chosen. In that way the children really participate in recognizing all the learning content of the action. Antisocial behaviour falls away and self-discipline and cooperation develop. The social and academic learning develops in a seamless way.

The participants all selected the tasks they would be responsible for in the spring water firm. When they had settled to their work, I made a contract regarding what might happen if an elderly person came to apply for a job. So first we created a job description based upon a fairly skilled job requiring a degree of strength. Thus the social problem was the unsuitability of the elderly person – 'Dorothy' – for the advertised position. The workers demonstrated a variety of responses. Some were brusque and dismissive, other more sympathetic. They avoided the issue by telling 'Dorothy' that if a position arose, they would let her know about it.

This is an example of how a contract can be made so that the class can deal with a very complex and awkward situation. This is Teacher in Role. Immediately the lady left, Dorothy, now in role as teacher/manager, asked 'Has anyone responded to our advertised position?' The manager was immediately told about the encounter the workers had experienced with

'Dorothy'. Children are never confused by such shifts in teacher behaviour. They recognize how useful it is.

So 'Dorothy' – an 'other' – came into being in:

> *Convention 1: The role actually present, naturalistic, yet significantly behaving, giving and accepting responses.*

Now see how *Convention 4* may deepen and widen considerations:

> *Convention 4: The role present as in 'effigy', but with the convention that the effigy can be brought into lifelike response and then returned to effigy.*

The teacher now stands as 'Dorothy' as an effigy – that is with her back to the wall, dressed now in hat and coat with handbag. She silently watches as workers continue their work in the bottling plant. As they work, they begin to think individually about the previous encounter and start to put their thoughts on Post-it notes and place these on the floor around 'Dorothy's' feet or in her open handbag. Lunch break arrives and all the workers now sit to eat lunch with their backs to the effigy. During this time, they hear 'Dorothy' reading and replying to their Post-it notes so they can widen their understanding of her point of view. The teacher as 'Dorothy' may have an agenda – for example, she is a widow, needs work, has little formal education, her children have married and gone away.

But she must respond honestly to the Post-it notes from within those parameters in order to help them consider other aspects and possible resolutions that are suitable to the bottling firm and perhaps useful to 'Dorothy'.

As a result of the Convention 4 episode they decided with the teacher/manager that perhaps employment could be found so that 'Dorothy' could join the workforce. Together the group looked at other conventions they could use.

'Dorothy' wrote a letter discussing her wedding twenty-five years ago. Together they composed the wedding photograph using the description in the letter. They are still workers in the bottling factory but are so interested in 'Dorothy's' story that they want to recall her life experiences in action. The teacher/manager and all the group now build 'Dorothy's' life story in still pictures, while at the same time they begin to realize that old people may have interesting and unusual stories to tell. Had this been a group of children, it would be an opportunity to for the children to have a genuine relationship *in the drama* with an older person.

Making the photographs is:

> *Convention 5: The roles as portrait of a person. Not three dimensional but in all other ways the same as effigy.*

To move to a very different kind of convention the teachers tried out:

> *Convention 15: Objects to represent a person's interests. More intimate things can indicate concerns as well as interests.*

The participants created 'Dorothy's' work locker and put inside it all the things in her life they considered to be important to her. It could be arranged that small groups make 'Dorothy's' locker – the 'objects' need only be drawings or paper cut-outs. Working on the lockers allows them to understand the importance of memory and to realize how objects can become symbols to their owners.

The 'Dorothy' role can also be used to examine bullying, which is now of concern in schools. The class can decide who might bully 'Dorothy' in the workplace, *but not enact it*. Then they might use:

> Convention 17: *An account of a person written as if from that person, but read by someone else. For example, a diary.*

They might find 'Dorothy's' diary or letter on a day when she has not come to work. Being concerned, they have looked in the pocket of her work overall and discover she has been bullied. What might they do?

One of the conventions we tried in the workshop was:

> Convention 8: *The role depicted in picture: removed from actual life, as in a slide, a painting, a photograph or a drawing of the role. This includes those made by the class, as well as prepared depictions.*

They made greetings cards and drew pictures of her as if they were photographs taken when she worked in the bottling factory. They 'sent' these to her 'address'. So 'Dorothy' existed through conventions:

- as a living person looking for a job: *Convention 1*;
- as a memory when the group told the teacher/manager about the work interview: *Convention 16*;
- as an effigy to be thought about: *Convention 4*;
- as a voice reading their Post-it notes: *Convention 25*;
- as a letter describing her wedding: *Convention 17*;
- as photographs of 'Dorothy's' life: *Convention 8*;
- as the contents of 'Dorothy's' locker symbolizing her interests: *Convention 15*;
- as 'Dorothy' existing through her diary: *Convention 17*;
- as 'Dorothy' existing through greeting cards with photographs: *Convention 8*.

The workshop group did not actually include all these episodes but I include them here to show how useful the conventions are in exploring many dimensions of events using 'drama eyes' and 'implication' to deepen the work. I find that in Mantle of the Expert, conventions are the least used and understood of drama strategies.

Mantle of the Expert is an alternative to transmission teaching. It is organized around the twin motifs of reflection and action – language as a means of reflecting on things and language as a means of acting on things. In the collaborative system of reality building in Mantle of the Expert the students participate in constructing a 'world'. But they are also endowed with the power to change the world through their own agency and to link the enterprise world of Mantle of the Expert to the community in which they actually live. In the sequences with the 'Dorothy' role the participants use in action what they comprehend about being human but also venture into new channels of understanding.

Drama, like all of the arts, takes us *into* reality rather than giving us an escape route from reality – a much more potent reality than the culture of transmission teaching. Mantle of the Expert cannot flower in the conveyor belt system of learning where the textbook reigns. It needs the casebook represented by the clients and the mentoring student–teacher collaboration, plus the best resources that leadership education requires. Bringing our schools into the 21st century may seem a frightening prospect, but not so dangerous as continuing to function with 19th-century attitudes. Technology is already breeding a will to change and a frustration in our young people regarding their schooling. Consider Shaffer's *How Computer Games help Children Learn*:

> School is a game about thinking like a factory worker. It is a game with an epistemology of right and wrong answers in which students are supposed to follow instructions, whether they make sense in the moment or not. Truth is whatever the teacher says is the right answer.... School is a game in which to know something is to be able to answer specific kinds of questions on specific kinds of tests. Back when a high-school degree led to a good manufacturing job, usually for life, this version of school may have made sense, however manufacturing jobs are somewhere between going and gone.[2]

In Shaffer's view, rewarding jobs will increasingly be those that require something beyond the traditional high school education. They will be jobs that address problems with many possible answers, jobs that require creativity and reward innovation.

If society wants to leave no child behind, the education system needs to change its game. Shaffer wants more learning by doing. He wants students to learn by making them participants in simulations of real-world challenges that are faced by engineers, urban planners, journalists and other professionals. I would add to this list parents and all those who support our communities by the work of their hands, backs and muscles. They also have minds, ethics and empathies to influence humanity. They also deserve better schooling than the conveyor belt system. Let us free our teachers into the same creative risks.

## Notes

1  For a full list of conventions, see 'Signs and portents' pp. 70–78, this volume.
2  Shaffer, D. W. (2006) *How Computer Games Help Children Learn*, London: Palgrave Macmillan.

# STORIES AS CONTEXTS IN MANTLE OF THE EXPERT

*In this paper, first published in the* Journal for Drama in Education *(2007) 23 (2), Heathcote considers whether it is possible for stories to provide contexts for Mantle of the Expert. Can such a task-based approach be used to discover the meaning of a story, while remaining truthful to the purpose of the tale? She reviews the basic elements of the Mantle of the Expert approach and insists that the notion of 'pretend' is not appropriate when one is working in this way. Although the commonly agreed context of the enterprise and the client will be fictional, the participants will stay in their own mindset – the real children will remain present as a self-spectators of their own behaviour.*

*As one possible way of exploring a story though Mantle of the Expert, she proposes the exciting notion that an enterprise might involve responding to a commission to design an opera. This kind of approach might help to place the heart of the story at the centre of an enterprise without distorting the story's true form.*

Is it possible for stories to provide contexts for Mantle of the Expert enterprises? At first glance the two seem incompatible. Stories tell of real or imaginary events and plot lines in which people move towards some resolution of their circumstances in a satisfactory way for the reader or listener. These seem a long way from the enterprise context demanded by a Mantle of the Expert approach. This polarity has made me think again and this paper is my attempt to see whether story and enterprise can operate one within the other, and if so, how.

My first challenge was to incorporate the book of *The Crane*.[1] This is a complex tale involving mythic elements. A solitary young boy is driven by his ambition to be in charge of the largest crane in the town. His companion is an eagle which uses the crane as his nesting eyrie. Mythic time is invoked: wars, floods, and changes of government occur. A friend is sacrificed to war. The crane changes its function as events overwhelm the town. In turn, it becomes a lighthouse among the invading seas, a nemesis when pirates are thwarted as they attempt to steal the corporation gold plate and mayoral chain, a Save and Rescue engine when rampaging zoo elephants run amok. Finally, when the town officials decide that the great crane must give way to a taller more modern device, there is the mysterious silent departure of the driver and the eagle. You can see the dilemma.

I want to examine the process I undertook in finding an approach to the events in the tale that were also in accordance with what I have begun to understand as the laws underpinning Mantle of the Expert. I realized that both story and system have mandatory guidelines for me:

- The story themes must be preserved.
- The elements of location, period, people and bondings are sacrosanct.
- The truth of the story's meaning must be discovered by whatever means that Mantle of the Expert can provide.

In the process of action the children must care about the story so much that it feels 'normal' to be dealing with it through a Mantle of the Expert approach. Trying to find my way through all this has given me some insights into the way my mind works as a planner of Mantle of the Expert learning. These insights are as yet raw, but others may benefit from my trying to set them down.

Let us review the basic elements in Mantle of the Expert:

(a) An enterprise is selected, so children are responsible for building the entire social structure, patterns of work and the culture of the enterprise.

(b) This will begin with the first task involving each individual and from this small shift in perception all the culture of the enterprise will emerge in process.

Remember Christopher Fry has said 'The Mud Hut contains the first imprint of the Cathedral, so the first grunt foreshadows King Lear's outpourings.'

Thus the first task, while seeming simple, must be at the very centre of the imminent enterprise. Every simple aspect of potential curriculum (expert) and life style (mantle) should be launched by the first task which should involve individuals at the level at which they can begin.

(c) The enterprise is selected to induct participants into the curriculum areas selected by the teacher as essential to be learned, practised and understood.

(d) The language shift summons the enterprise culture and establishes the context from which the Mantle of the Expert will develop. From this point all behaviours will arise from relevant circumstances. Two styles of talk are used, neither of them akin to the talk that usually takes place between teacher and class, which is often regulatory and instructional. Both styles of talk in Mantle of the Expert create opportunity for discourse, conjecture and enquiry.

The most important element is inclusiveness. 'WE'. This element is used in two ways. First it creates the social culture. 'We are all in this together' as we fulfil the work of the enterprise. The second 'We' is that of being decision-makers about our developing enterprise. We live in it and we design it and cultivate it by the way we take decisions about it. Usually there is little need for teacher regulatory talk, once classes have experienced the power they may take hold of and exercise. A potential responsibility develops which replaces dependence on the teacher. If the enterprise tasks are at a level that first engages, then absorbs, challenges and rewards participants, they rarely wish to avoid the behaviour demanded by the context and the study that is required to develop curriculum skills.

In my experience regulatory language is the one that teachers find it hardest to relinquish or subdue. Certain words are best avoided: 'you', 'where', 'what', 'how', 'when' are all disempowering. They question. They have within them a demand element, one that assumes that the answers that are already in the mind of the questioner, and students are forced to try to guess these answers.

(e) The changing of all other signs in the environment. This means creating locations for objects or events, providing spaces for encounters of different kinds, and altering the body language of the teacher who is engaging with the class. 'Sign' here is a noun. Signs are placed to be read. They are selected for purpose and agreed upon by making contracts with the class to use them in specific ways. Shakespeare gives us a comic example in *A Midsummer Night's Dream* when Quince, Bottom, Snug, Flute, Snout and Starveling meet to plan their play plot.

> *This green plot shall be our stage, this hawthorn brake our tiring house: and we will do it in action as we will do it before the duke.*

Sign is a factor in our real lives. We read it constantly in order to interpret our environment and our social and bonding encounters. But sign is also an invocation to the muse of theatre. In Mantle of the Expert it summons the environment, which becomes believable so that the context can become more and more tangible.

(f) Banish the word 'pretend' from your mind in Mantle of the Expert work. Pretending is about making an interior contract with yourself to enter a persona that is not yourself. Mantle of the Expert begins from an entirely different basis. It is a *social* situation demanding selective behaviour which will contribute to supporting a commonly agreed context. Demonstration and modelling amongst peers creates social reading of sign for purpose. These signs are not born out of characterization or psychological differences of personality.

Mantle of the Expert demands that participants stay in their own mindset but inhabit unfamiliar places and contexts for action. Behaviour is selected in order to be relevant to the circumstances the group has contracted to explore. This is what happens when children play. It is what Bottom and his companions undertake when they make their play in *A Midsummer Night's Dream*. When I am working with children in Mantle of the Expert mode I want the real child to stay present as a self-spectator of what s/he is contributing, sustaining and enjoying the power of making, in the act of behaving within the context. Each task will vary the kind of thinking and behaving as it imposes its different discipline, but all will take place as social events.

Pretending is at the psychological pole of social events. Demonstrating behaviour in social encounters enables people to learn together and read others' signals. This is in the field of sociology and is much safer for children to engage in, as they explore what society and being human is about. The same factor will be present when they practise curriculum skills. Most schooling organizes children into 'tribes' but their work is rarely based in learning together, where minds are meeting minds and ideas are being bounced about.

At the highest level of theatre, the muse (one of the nine goddesses of the arts) is summoned by skilled actors using both polarities. I enter the mind of an 'other', and *I* show by my behaviour to others that I have done so as I share in the circumstances and style demanded by the plot and genre of the play. Some children have such instincts and sometimes they are exploited because they seem talented. Mantle of the Expert creates contexts that empower them to bring what they know to the social worlds made for purpose by teacher planning.

It is here that my dilemma of Story and Mantle of the Expert arises. Stories explore motives, desires, urges, personalities, and dilemmas brought about by circumstances, the individual responses to these circumstances and a desire that all will be brought to some satisfactory conclusion. Different genres impose levels of behaviour and subtlety of character and motive. Everything is embedded in personality.

Mantle of the Expert is created around the context of serving a client – an 'other' generated in our heads and mutually agreed upon to make demands upon us. We remain in the mindset of ourselves as makers and sustainers of the enterprise and client simultaneously. It is ourselves as we actually are who reflect upon, design and behave appropriately as we decide, or the culture we create imposes on us. That is why children are safe even when creating dangerous ideas to explore. The context and the client cradle us, while challenging us to be independent within the culture we are in process of bringing into being. My psychology colleague at Newcastle University observing Mantle of the Expert enterprises in action used to muse that 'schools may not be safe places but drama can be'. Mantle of the Expert should ensure it should always be so.

How can the complex story of *The Crane* provide the curriculum of study through a Mantle of the Expert enterprise? Solving this dilemma has caused me to unpack an instinctive process which I have never been able to explain to others satisfactorily. I am still only in the first stages of understanding how I make a bridge between curriculum study and a perfect enterprise to form the working context. The challenge of the story basis, being unfamiliar, has alerted me to something of the process.

## The Crane

*The Crane* was my first story challenge.

*The Crane* raises the questions:

(a)  What can make the enterprise workers care about an old crane?
(b)  And how can they be made to be curious about the crane driver? His ambition draws all events to him.
(c)  How will the workers in the selected enterprise learn about the crane driver's personality and psyche? He never communicates directly with the world he observes from on high as he works the crane for the community below.
(d)  That community changes with time and crises, and the crane adapts to the its needs because the driver is more than a technician.
(e)  The crane story is ultimately a tragedy of ennoblement. The young driver is at first ambitious, self-willed and obdurate. His ending is born of that. Through trials he learns to be servant to the crane's formal power. Submitting to that power is what ennobles him. When the crane's time is reaching its end (brought about by the vain ambitions of smaller men), it is time for the companionship of eagle and man to leave the canvas of events. Anything less is to demean the high stature of the tale. How can a Mantle of the Expert enterprise serve such a telling in literary form? Should it?
(f)  What may be gained by such a transformation?

The first problem to be solved is c) above. How can the workers learn of the crane driver's life? What enterprise can possibly serve this? And how can the mythic time changes become a natural element, thoroughly integrated into the story? It is at this point a flash of realization occurs to me. I marvel that I didn't realize it before. Of course the destruction of the crane by thoughtless power seekers is the very means by which the symbiosis of the driver, crane and eagle companion will be discovered. And the story will become forever part of the historical inheritance in the archives of the town – classic rebirth for future generations.

The literary version of the story tells of practical everyday matters. The trumpet the driver plays rather badly, the peppermints he loves, the perch he makes for the eagle, his garden and the hut he fashions to shelter them both. Others can be invented, because logic tells us they would be there. His toilet and systems of storing and hauling up food and necessities of survival. So long as these fulfil the nature of the crane design, they fulfil the mythic elements of the story. But the teacher's dilemma is how to provide the minutiae of his life but reveal his growth as a hero. This evidence, left behind, must be detailed and in a form to enable a large group of people to have to sort it out and make sense of it. It will require an archive to be prepared in advance.

But who then shall be our client? Could the undertaking be launched by a commission from the townsfolk who have folk memories of the crane and the driver?

And what shall be the enterprise? Well of course if a crane is to be broken and eclipsed, then where does it go? To the town refuse disposal site.

## Alice

At the risk of confusing you yet further, here is another story to form the curriculum basis of a Mantle of the Expert. This one relates the life, in so far as it is known, of a real person who lives the life of an anchorite or hermit in the woods near Derby. Her name is known and her story exists mainly as folk memory in the villages around Little Eaton. She was born in 1867 and after her parents died, she was evicted from the family cottage and became a beggar for a while. She occupied various shelters belonging to people in the area – an empty stable, a shed, and finally a large wooden bacon box donated by a local butcher. She set this up beside a vestigial stone cave – more of a storage shelf – in an area close by. Thus she became an object of charity, of pity and finally earned a reputation as a wise woman offering advice. Later she earned respect because of her knowledge of plants. There are two authentic photographs of her amongst her metal buckets and cooking pans and a little information about her life. So what context will create *our* context, client and curriculum? And what enterprise will drive it?

We design operas. Let's examine how designing an opera (and why not a play?) will fulfil the learning opportunities of Alice's folk history. What clients would commission such an enterprise and to what purpose? I find it difficult to understand and explain why an opera rather than a play text might be more suitable. In either form Alice can exist as she did in her time and either theatre form can explain all the kaleidoscopic events of her life as orphan, vagrant, beggar and wise hermit. The factor missing in the play text is that of her being set apart from the people who were linked to her by curiosity. So the opera form permits many kinds of encounter to be expressed in classically formal ways. It moves it from the domestic study of her life to the classical. The arias, the choruses, the recitative passages, the formalized settings, all demanded high selection of line and colour. And of course an opera creates many more aspects of theatre design than a play text would. It can move out of naturalism and the dramatic unities into a range of conventions. I feel more satisfied for having recognized these richer aspects.

The question arises, why could the crane driver's life not also be treated as an opera? Is it because the crane becomes a mythic object and the bacon box retains its domestic purpose?

The life of the driver must span time far more than a 'lifetime', whilst the time of Alice's life is of our own more mundane measurement. Both stories might share individuals who stand out from their peers and become objects of curiosity and conjecture, and might share clients who are alike citizens in the community. Both stories involve elements of reconstruction. The difference lies in the story's telling. One is detailed, one fragmented. One explains and clarifies motives, bondings, relationships and actions. The other invites the filling in of all the details that are merely shadowed in. This is what has caught my attention.

Here we have two stories. A myth seemingly mundane and practical and a folk memory about the unusual life of an actual person whose 'place' is now remembered by people walking their dogs, those making pilgrimages of curiosity as well as those seeking to understand 'how it might have been to live like that'.

I am certain now that story forms are not alien to or outside the scope of the Mantle of the Expert form of curriculum learning. In fact, the more I think about it, the more useful Mantle of the Expert can be in coming to understand stories. They do not take the place of the ancient attention good tellers of story evoke in listeners. But at least Mantle of the Expert places the heart of the story at the centre of the enterprise and it never need interfere with the form of the story's telling as the dramatization of stories may do. We all know that theatre and literature are quite different art forms. Both forms engage us differently.

What a Mantle of the Expert approach always offers, whatever the enterprise, is that it is never a 'dummy run'. It is rooted in deep play, the concentrated sustaining of responsibility and tangible outcomes of high quality.

## A final note and warning

This paper cannot cover all the actual detail of preparation involved in starting these enterprises, nor list the many tasks and very varied dramatic opportunities each story provides. Each teacher will have to tease out the curriculum potential of each tale and set in the tasks accordingly. As with other enterprises starting from curriculum rather than story, all the same principles apply. The enterprise is well established, the work of the client's commission arrives as the establishment is busy about other work and there must be a tangible outcome plus a celebration of presentation as a closure to the Mantle of the Expert enterprise.

Story will perhaps help those teachers who feel more comfortable if there is a plot line to anchor the curriculum, but it is a somewhat poisoned chalice in that every tale is unique. It exists to fulfil itself. It requires very close analysis if the enterprise chosen is to be truthful to the tale's purpose and existence. If this does not happen, the tale is ruined by the treatment and will be best left to a telling of it.

## The warning

Mantle: I earn by my work the right to be seen to be capable and responsible in upholding the stature of the mantle which others may recognize as valuing and expressing what I stand for.

Expert: I attend to the necessary study and acquisition of skills and knowledge required to uphold the quality of the learning I undertake.

When addressing your class do not use the label of 'expert'. This is shabby and I hear it often spoken thus: 'Today we're going to be experts.' It is a journey, not a label. I understand the reason why this happens. It is because Mantle of the Expert is being considered as an alternative to present systems of teaching, and it can be very valuable in changing the way schools provide learning interest. It invokes sacred time, which is diachronic, as opposed to monochromic profane time, the time of clocks and timetables and curriculum divisions retained from past models of schooling. Remember, 'expert' is a gift word, as is 'mantle'. These words are like 'teacher', 'poet', 'artist', 'writer', 'physician' and 'healer'. You cannot award them to yourself.

## Note

1 Zimnik, R. (1978) *The Crane*, translated by M. Koenig, London: Macmillan Education.

# CONTEXTS FOR ACTIVE LEARNING

*In this final paper Heathcote reflects on her professional life and summarizes four stages of development in her theory and practice. Inevitably, there is some repetition here, as she restates the key characteristics of each model. In the first model she sums up the phase of her practice that has become known as 'living-through' drama. Although she moves on to working through Mantle of the Expert and the other models – Rolling Role and Commissions – she recalls the advantages of what she calls this 'pure form' and analyses it very precisely. She emphasizes the need to use role in very subtle ways and explains the significance of focus and tension in driving the work as well as the importance of developing a group point of view among the students. As we have seen in the previous chapters, Mantle of the Expert also employs these elements but is built on task situations and develops a powerful sense of self-spectatorship in the participants.*

*The idea of Rolling Role was Heathcote's attempt to reduce the isolation of subject teachers and to allow students to carry the same context with them from lesson to lesson while sharing skills and information. An example of Rolling Role is Heathcote's description of the way in which students might create the life story of a house. A family who owned the house is invented and a diary is created about some important events in the life of one member of the family. Further recycling might be developed if a class used the diary and the history of the house to create a television programme about the family 'story'. The invented family might be developed further by another class tracing the historical family trees and names and relationships over the period of history that the teachers are interested in exploring. Natural history could be incorporated by using the house environs and the plant life, animals, and weather. Architectural and detailed drawing might be another 'recycling', as well as 'furnishing' the house to reflect the dominant period of the building's existence. These documents could become an archive which might be used to advertise the house when it comes up for sale.*

*Heathcote takes both of these models further in the Commission Model, which carries the social element that is present in the other models right out into the community beyond the school. For the first time, there is no fiction involved in this approach. The fictional clients of Mantle of the Expert exist in the actual world with which the Commission Model becomes concerned.*

*Heathcote recognizes that the special virtue of the theatre as an art form is that in ideal circumstances it is inseparable from the community and describes how each model has the potential to forge links between school and society.*

*Because of space limitations, this is an edited version of the paper published in the* Journal for Drama in Education, *Dorothy Heathcote Special Issue, Summer 2012. It is well worth reading in its entirety, and is available on the Mantle of the Expert website: www.mantleoftheexpert.com.*

## Four models

I propose to examine four models of teacher/student activity using what I've always thought of as a drama approach. But in reality the base building block of all four models is that of agreeing to work through an invented and agreed fiction. Fiction contains the word drama. It widens the possibilities for action and necessarily blurs the genre. This broader spectrum of action has earned much criticism, because I wasn't able to explain my vision of fiction being more overarching than drama.

These four models forge links between schooling and society:

Model 1 – Drama used to explore people
Model 2 – Mantle of the Expert
Model 3 – Rolling Role
Model 4 – Commission Model.

### *Model 1: Drama*

The first model will be very familiar. It occurs when drama is used to explore people, their behaviour, their circumstances, and their responses to events that affect them. The art form of theatre, like play, is a self-fulfilling activity. It fulfils its own future by the actions of the makers. So at one level teachers and classes quite legitimately make theatre and use audiences.

But around this 'pure' form a network of other forms of exploring people and events has developed, invented by teachers to serve their own interests and beliefs. Certain elements must be present if these forms are to be linked with drama work.

- It works through social collaboration.
- It will always involve exploration in immediate 'now' time where participants engage with events in the first person. That's the drama element.
- It must involve participants considering one of the three levels of social politics: the psychology of individuals to drive the action, the anthropological drives of the community, and the social politics of how power operates. These three provide the lubrication and friction that give the work the kind of meaning for participants that goes beyond the ordinary and mundane.
- It will always require some modification of behaviour so that the fiction isn't mixed up with the usual way people behave. It needs some selectivity, however limited.
- The event must have focus, usually through productive tension, which has to be injected deliberately. In the early stages the teacher usually provides the focus, like the first stitch in a tapestry around which all the other elaboration will naturally develop. At this level the teacher has to do the play *wright's* job – as maker collaborating with the nature of the material. I prefer the concept of 'wrighting', because it performs its intention in collaboration with the readiness of the material to receive the stimulation.

All craftspeople instinctively temper their incursions to the nature of the materials they work on. But what the about the teacher and the social and academic level of the class? This is the heart of the problem and the reason that such a wide range of strategies and negotiation skills are needed. The soul of the artist protects the wood or stone, and the teacher's strategies must defend the class from feeling threatened, being stared at or exposed in negative ways. I always knew that this kind of exposure must at all costs be avoided and this is why I began to develop strategies that made some observers think that I spent most of a lesson in not getting started. Consensus and interest has to be won. Hence my drawings, or being in role, or discussions about how a situation might be resolved. So my lessons at this stage looked static in so far as the children first moved in their heads but not immediately off their bottoms.

In hindsight I realize I was preparing the material to meet the productive tension, so that by the time the children were intrigued nothing would fail them, no matter how inexperienced they were. It was ages before I met and instantly recognized Bruner's particularization of *iconic* (get the picture) and *symbolic* (shape it in familiar ways of writing and talking it through) before you embark on the *expressive* (do it now). The imperative of taking the group through those stages caused my strategic vocabulary to grow. Hence my attention to 'voices', the use of paper, and all the conventions I developed to protect the class, and above all my work in subtle kinds of role. There was, however, one element which seems to have come from nowhere but which I used in my very first teaching encounter. I knew how to develop a group point of view and not to cast children in roles in the way that actors are organized.

## Model 2: Mantle of the Expert

I perversely insist on using this name because I cannot find a more precise way to express the full meaning of the work. The phrase carries two layers of meaning, both precious and to be preserved.

'**Expert**' means the opportunity to work at knowledge and to master skills.
'**Mantle**' means 'I declare my calling and live up to what is expected of me in the community.'
  It encompasses style, attitude and dedication, all of which take time to build in fiction as well as in the real world.

Mantle of the Expert carries forward the elements of Model 1 except that the group point of view is taken into *task* situations where a fictional client is involved. It operates rather like the trades guilds of earlier times. A master oversees the work of apprentices, but everyone shares in the tasks that must be accomplished for the client. In my head I think of myself as a working 'maister', responsible for providing, overseeing and maintaining the momentum of the work.

**Model 1** shifts the shape of the human explorations. **Mantle of the Expert** shifts the shape of the episodes as the complexity of the enterprise and the curriculum demands are brought into focus by the 'maister'.[1] This model is designed to be built around all curriculum study but is lifted from the drudgery of mere task enforcement by the control and power to serve the client, which are given circumspectly and generously to the 'apprentices'. The control and power are mainly delivered by the teacher's language, which, in the 'maister' role periods, uses a restricted code. Two ways of servicing this work are available to the teacher:

- *Inside* the 'mantle' the Maister regulates behaviour, offers information in restricted code, and builds belief in the ongoing tasks of the enterprise.
- *Outside* the 'mantle' the teacher operates as helper towards the success of the enterprise. The task then helps everyone to 'think about' some aspect of the work. The teacher never uses the voice of the expert instructor. The form of the communication will be as a 'helpful colleague', or what Chris Lawrence has called an 'enlightened witness', which exactly embodies what I have in mind.

An example of the two voices negotiating the same situation could be useful here. This situation arose when Broadwood Junior School children were running a shoe factory and unemployment was affecting many workers in the north-east where they lived.

> The maister's 'voice': 'I don't like having to say this but you know people aren't ordering handmade shoes like they used to. We're going to have to think of other sorts of leather work. … I wondered about Roman leather buckets for Vindolanda?'
>
> The teacher's 'voice': 'You know when we did the shoe survey and saw how many shoes nowadays have synthetic soles and uppers? I wonder if we could think of other things our factory might make in leather so all the workers can be kept busy. We could tell the maister at the next meeting.'

I introduced Mantle of the Expert when I was trying to help teachers who didn't understand how to create tension, and to eliminate the need for children to 'act', or behave 'like other people'. It seemed easier to start from doing tasks, and all enterprises can begin with very unthreatening activity. A name for the enterprise can be chosen, or a drawing of the place where everyone works, or a job that everyone would do together so long as it doesn't demand too much expertise. I recently started a brewery stables of 1836 by all of us deciding on the name of the horse we drove when delivering barrels. When the names were written and placed round the hall, we could then all clean out the dirty straw. From that one task all the complexity of a working brewery could be launched, *because we knew where 'our' horses were*.

Mantle of the Expert fulfils a very important function very easily. It develops the watcher in the head – the self-spectator. It achieves this because our enterprise includes our client, and this makes everyone aware of why these things have to be done. The client in the head in Mantle of the Expert is akin to the artist's position in working on materials. They not only do what is necessary but they examine the materials. They not only do what is necessary but they examine the nature of the doing. It is the 'maister' who invokes this for each individual as well as for the whole group as a community of workers. *Community is essential in Mantle of the Expert*.

Mantle of the Expert has strong links with play but protects students from feeling 'babyish'. In play a world is made by the will of the players who control that world and live in it as long as they are intrigued by it. This also happens in the enterprise. Everyone is 'grown up', carrying the responsibilities of adults and facing up to the results of their decisions. A feature of this approach has to be faced and can have repercussions when colleagues first see it in action. At first it appears to be a muddle with the teacher apparently having lost authority to shape the lesson. This is because, as in play, the children enter the first tasks at their own level of socialization, imagination, and information. The teacher can readily diagnose the dropouts, the copiers, the watchers, and the leaders during the early stages, and especially the 'actors' who start inventing crises at the drop of a hat. The maister's voice has to regulate the latter. For example in the stable there was an outbreak of lameness among the horses. 'If you're telling me you've neglected the horses' feet to this state, I can't believe the boss is still going to employ you. Later on when we have to get them between the shafts, you'd better have another look.' – Hence my reputation 'Bully Heathcote'.

This apparent chaos invites the question of what exactly is a 'properly' organized lesson. In Mantle of the Expert, imposed external organization has to wait a little until the children develop belief in their responsibility to the common enterprise. The 1836 stable took fifteen minutes before a full class of ethnically mixed Year Six children started worrying about the shortage of hay, and that belief was never lost, because children quickly feel the power of their position.

In **Model 1** the tasks in the stable would form the background to working out people's lives in their work and their 'story'. **Model 2 – Mantle of the Expert** – has no story, for it is an invented lifestyle working its way forward into more and more complex cultural and societal circumstances and situations that mould the community values, labours and world viewpoint.

To return to my own development. The Drama model taught me a very large range of strategies that I justified because they won children to the work and protected them from feeling stared at. Because I took part in role, it allowed them to gang up and acquire a common point of view in developing the event. When it was necessary for an individual to represent an 'other', we negotiated it using protective devices like the conventions I developed. The Mantle of the Expert model employed all these strategies but in addition became a developing saga that could be manipulated to serve any curriculum work by using episodic shifts. Both of these models fulfil my need as a teacher to create positive social communities outside schools.

## Model 3: Rolling Role

I have called this model 'Rolling Role', because the base work can roll from teacher to teacher and many classes can share in the common context. This seems particularly useful in high school, where teachers are often subject-based and meet classes for relatively short periods of time on a weekly or two-weekly basis. Teachers often feel isolated as they have a discrete area of curriculum responsibility. If there are drama specialists, they have to invent their curriculum and are frequently seen as teaching a 'soft' subject, however much they try to service other subject areas. So I invented Rolling Role to try to alleviate the isolation of subject teachers as well as help students to carry the same context with them from lesson to lesson and to begin to realize that subjects have links with each other. Sharing skills and information is paramount in the work for teachers and students alike.

Rolling Role can be used either by one teacher working with all the timetabled classes s/he meets or by teams of teachers who want to feel they are in touch with the work of their team colleagues without disturbing their regular timetable too much. To do this the team must develop a common context that will provide a 'bank' of work designed to meet the curriculum areas for which the team members are individually responsible. So every member of the team ensures that the bank will sustain what he or she needs to draw out from it in order to make relevant contexts for their class work.

In Rolling Role participants explore different facets of a community. They are not members of that community but they have access over time to many aspects of how the community has been in the past and in the present, and they certainly wield power over how the work may develop. So the team of teachers creates a community in a place and with features that they all agree will be mandatory as they develop the affairs and concerns of the community. This model allows lessons of different lengths to be incorporated. Sometimes a very brief circumstance that relates to the subject area of the individual teacher will be explored. Work can be left incomplete so that another class takes it forward, or products arising from one group can be recycled to serve another curriculum area.

For example, a school in Birmingham organized a team from the departments of art, history and drama with English. Each member of the team had mandatory studies to teach that term. The history colleague was interested in some classes learning about Saxon culture, particularly the laws relating to social hierarchy. The teacher of art and technology was interested that term in some classes experimenting with pastiche painting and studying different period styles. Technology ranged between three-dimensional model making and computerized modelling. The drama teacher had a strong interest in helping children to examine how people lived before consumerism dominated their lives, as well as encouraging them to become involved in reading. When the team has invented the context (in this case a town, but it need not be such a large social structure), they must together decide upon a 'disturbance factor' that will trigger changes for the modern citizens to deal with. This is akin to the playwright's point of tension and any changes should relate to curriculum study.

The team devised the town of Leyford, existing since Saxon times, currently in receipt of a public gift. The town map they made showed the small Reeve Library housed in a barn, now a listed building. There was a (now disused) cinema in a central position and a Saxon manor house and stables in private ownership at the edge of the map. The map presumes and informs students that Leyford exists, has a history and that people still live there now. It has a future. The teachers also devised specific artefacts and materials to serve their teaching goals. The history teacher made a 'damaged' manuscript that told of the memories of a citizen who in his youth had seen what we now call Halley's Comet. His memories incorporated detailed information regarding Saxon life, and yet appeared to be a remarkable tale of a day when huntsmen discovered two green children and brought them into the manor and reared them.[2]

This story of the hunt formed the basis of fragments of a fresco discovered on a wall of a manor house during renovations. Because the fresco painted by the art teacher was all in pieces (plaster of Paris protected by brown-paper backing), it would enable her students to study the style of the painting and content and paint in all the missing parts, just as restorers of frescoes do today. This was the pastiche element. The Reeve cruck barn[3] housing the library was defined by a series of architects' drawings so that the Saxon imprint was carried throughout. The drama lessons would involve children in inventing shelving (for a listed building) to house more books and filling the shelves with 'recent additions and acquisitions' and so invent storylines and build the classification system. These children were in the main reluctant readers who needed to feel important and take initiatives.

The work on Leyford town began when a letter headed by a drawing of the cruck barn and a logo of 'The Old Reeve Library' indicated

> that they had been contacted by an ex-resident of Leyford, living now mainly in America who had a successful career in leading a pop group. The person wished to show their gratitude to Leyford, their birthplace, by endowing a new library etc., etc.

So the citizens were given a large gift from a grateful member of the town who had become rich and currently had a prominent and successful career. S/he was a pop star born in Leyford and was since much travelled but had relatives still living in the area following their usual lifestyle. The star wished to build and endow a new and larger library on the site of the derelict cinema and to buy the Saxon manor house and stables in order to develop it as a school for blind children (a special charity interest for the star) and also to house a school for guide dogs in the stable.

So exploring the map and its implications and finding the various locations was the work of the class needing to read, and lead, in the first decisions. This group discussed the feasibility of the project and wrote an advertisement for the local paper to call all interested citizens to hear of the proposed gift and to examine the proposals thoroughly. All classes received this missive at their normal lesson times and consulted the Leyford map, placed so that it was always available. And so the town was launched. The curriculum opportunities were taken from this common pot of possibilities. Everyone in the teaching partnership was free to select work around the central context.

These three factors – library, guide dogs and school for the blind – were selected to serve quite specific ends: The school for the blind would require audio tapes of books. This would involve students summarizing stories and reading them on audio tapes, which would then be reviewed by other classes. The story tapes would be positively criticized by blind people, who could also suggest other materials and tapes made with backing sounds or recorded in different locations. The guide dogs provided animals to be cared for in unsentimental ways. The genuinely blind would be 'invited' to visit and learn about the dogs and their training. This aspect of the work provided animal interest for younger classes.

In Rolling Role the drama element lies in building belief in the lives of the people and the events they encounter in the current time. The mandatory evidence demands interrogation of various kinds, depending upon the teachers' choice of engagements with the town's matters of concern. Teachers never use the drama word and certainly don't introduce the work as a drama project. However all work produced by classes is publicly open and available to stimulate further work. The outcomes are enormous. Some will be rough notes or sketches inviting recycling. Some will require more additions, such as illustrations for a text, or critical study needing a report. The teachers with a vested interest in the opportunities provided for specific curriculum teaching introduced the frescoes and ancient texts but these artefacts were available to other classes for different learning experiences that became immediately obvious. It will be seen that an area available to all the groups and the team had to be set aside for displaying and keeping all the mass of materials properly catalogued.

Sadly, it has been my experience that when this collection is viewed by colleagues it is often seen as showing off or, as one headmaster said to me in scathing tones, 'It looks more like an infant school.' He made no comment regarding the large number of children and a very few staff who regularly visited the site to see 'how Leyford was getting on'. What a website opportunity Rolling Role provides.

So Rolling Role becomes a soap opera of sorts, as many people add to the complex developments that arise from servicing the story of Leyford. The children become like gods developing the culture of the town and the lives of the people they create. We soon had an archive of the community – a kind of Domesday collection. The past, the present and the future were available for attention. The teachers narrowly focused each session (as does soap opera) and milked each opportunity as much as it was deemed necessary for the curriculum work. The Rolling Role was drawn to a kind of conclusion when the team of teachers considered it to have served its purpose. The archive need not be thrown away – it could be collected and kept as Leyford's Domesday Book, or to help with teacher education!

You can see now the central thread that is consistent through all three models. It is social politics so easily introduced through systems where 'people' business is central. In **Model 1** I developed the strategies that bred *common points of view and a shared impulse* to resolve social events. In **Mantle of the Expert**, I created *working communities* with concern for others – fictional clients. In **Rolling Role** I discovered the power of children to *build a whole community*, although this need not necessarily be a town. It could be a commune, or a Marks & Spencer's management team, or a cathedral or a health centre – any group with aspirations that is facing change.

In Rolling Role the children do not actually do the work of an enterprise. Like gods, they oversee and decide how best to work things out on a variety of levels and with many varied aspects requiring attention. All classes will become familiar with some elements more than others. The whole picture will be explored only when they visit the display of incremental and ever-changing work. The emphasis is on a socially maturing community.

You can see now how my main teaching drives have never changed – to present children with ever-increasing webs of information and skill within a framework of social and cultural awareness. You can see also that what I thought was a new paradigm, my fourth model, is only a continuation of the first question I ever asked a class: 'If you were captain of a ship, what qualities would you look for in choosing a crew?' The question is ill formed. I could certainly never ask it in that way now. But it carries me like an arrow to my present teaching stance and my new paradigm for running a school.

## Model 4: The Commission Model

Until I discover a better term it shall serve. It can involve a whole school, or, as with Rolling Role, only a proportion of children and staff may be involved. Then it would work like a school within a school. The Commission Model cannot accommodate to school timetabling as Rolling Role can.

It operates like this. The work of the staff and students will be that of responders to commissions sent to them from the community. The commissions will make precise demands and will have a built-in time structure so that when the commission has been accepted, an allowance of time and resources will be decided. The work and the results of the commissions will always culminate in a publication that can vary according to the nature of the commission. This builds in standards and quality, because the publication will be submitted to the original commissioners.

The class work will be related to three teaching values that will be built in from the very start with all the participants. These are *rigour, responsibility* and *realization*. The last is very significant, because it embodies a factor often omitted from schooling – realizing what we have learned, can understand, and put to use in our lives, which previously we had not recognized. Publishing carefully organized results provides the necessary culminating point of realization.

The Commission Model carries the social element that is present in other models right out into the community beyond the school's interests and environs. So there will be a need for teachers to search out commissions actively and use their imaginations about institutions that might like to become involved. There are many instances of sponsors becoming involved in school work, such as the Gateshead Domesday Book with which the NatWest bank collaborated. I get the impression that as schooling and partnership becomes more and more debated in the media, there is varied opportunity and a wide range of business interest in collaborating – if only at the lowest level of publicity!

Not all commissions need to be sought from outside the school, especially in the early stages. Teachers can invent commissions which are curriculum-based and can be tempered to suit any group and time span suitable to their needs. A simple commission may be a request for a story mat or collage to be used by a preschool class. This would have to be introduced in a realistic and believable way to a group of children who need to develop measuring, designing and vocabulary skills, as well as an opportunity to share and collaborate. Such a commission would entail a collection of old worn-out clothing. Then the designs would have to be prepared based upon who will use it, and what is available from the fabrics as to colour, weight and texture. There will be the need of a rug frame – easily made – and blunt wooden pushing tools. Then come the choosing of canvas, marking out the design and sorting out working teams to cut and classify the different fabrics. There will be reports of progress to prepare and send, photographs to show progress from start to finish, and finally the completion and presentation of the mat for use during story time, or the collage to be mounted for use.

You don't need a lot of imagination to see how this commission will yield curriculum work in number, measuring accurately, designing textures, designing, cutting with a minimum of waste the garments that are likely to be contributed, talking about procedures, inventing stories about the mats and visiting places where they can be seen. The work will involve curriculum and timescales so that the commission achieves the teacher's intentions. And remember, a commission is NOT A PROJECT!

Imagine then a building in which commissions dictate the groupings of staff, children and timetables, where spaces are booked according to the need of specific kinds of work and materials are drawn with discrimination from the general supply. Staff, parents and children must be involved, especially in the early stages, in deciding precisely what terms like 'commission' and the three Rs mentioned previously – rigour, responsibility and realization – shall mean in their school/community. A crash course in specific areas of knowledge will be essential (as they are in society at large) and these will be instigated when a commission requires them. Times can be also set aside for practice periods, such as when new information or research or library skills or penmanship or whatever comes to the teacher's mind are needed, but these are always linked with an upcoming commission or an interest triggered by a completed one.

It is important that the formal structures of timetable, peer-group classes, allocations of staff to specific groupings, etc. are not all discarded at once. I know one high school that is consulting staff to see who might be interested in trying a commission first with their own class, to be decided upon consultation with the parents who may be involved but who certainly will be informed at every stage. These commissions will need to be related to the skills and expertise of the teacher, but all the teachers taking part will be prepared to move around different commissions, helping as best they can.

The three processes, of accepting a commission, accomplishing all stages of the work it requires and bringing it to a published usable conclusion must in my view be integrated into a teaching philosophy which is agreed upon by everyone concerned. Usually the philosophy is embedded in a mission statement. And I do not mean the type of pamphlet being produced by schools that makes promises that are frequently not fulfilled in process. The mission statement must be mandatory and always incorporated in the work of each commission. For my mission statement, I choose that 'All work undertaken shall be in the spirit of stewardship not exploitation.' This statement encapsulates economy, service, respect, detachment of scrutiny and observation, care for quality and fitness for purpose. That would be my baseline for all the work of all the people for all their commission days.

This way of working falls into what Fritzof Capra calls 'the emergent design of human organizations'. Designed organizations become rule-bound and difficult to change, because they tend to form the 'establishment'. He offers a word of caution, useful when considering bringing changes to social organizations:

> The two types of structure – designed and emergent structures – are very different, and every organization needs both kinds. Whereas designed structures cannot grow, emergent structures are adaptable, develop and evolve. They are expressions of the community's collective creativity … the challenge for any organization is to find a creative balance between designed and emergent structures.[4]

He goes on to consider leadership, which is of prime importance to teachers and teaching.

> The organization's mission is generally the result of a design process. The traditional idea of a leader is that of a person who is able to formulate it well. The other kind of leadership would be the facilitation of emergence. This kind of leadership is not limited to a single individual but can be distributed. It consists in continually facilitating the emergence of new structures and bringing the best of them into the organization's design.

He suggests that emergence is facilitated 'by creating a learning culture, by encouraging continual questioning and by rewarding innovation … by creating conditions rather than giving directions'.

He could be commenting on Ofsted[5] when he states that 'organizations are still judged according to their design structures, not according to their emergent structures' and further, that 'one of the important implications of the new scientific understanding of life for the management of human organizations is that more attention should be paid to emergent structures and to the leadership that facilitates emergence'. There's something in there that might be considered in planning teacher education.

A recent example of an emergent structure happened on Tyneside when a piece of derelict land was transformed. A head teacher out in her car 'collecting up' children who should have been inside the school saw the site as a possible play area where none had existed. She consulted the unemployed people living around the school and together everybody started hauling out the detritus with which wind and fly-by-night dumpers had cluttered up the area. Then they tackled the dog dirt, the bits of glass and plastic bags and finally consulted parents and the council at a school meeting about how the land could best be put to use. During the clearing period many youths without jobs began to 'muck in', bringing their mates 'for the heavy stuff'.

This area is now a children's playground and low-maintenance gardens with contributions from gardeners, benches made with local gifts and a dog-walking area and dog bins. It was interesting that during a night of riotous protest about a youth joyriding in a stolen car who was killed when being chased by the police, the youths stopped their vandalizing when they reached the newly dedicated area, walked quietly through it, only resuming the calculated vandalism after they were clear of it!

There are many such examples where someone sees a need and facilitates change based upon local ideas and energy. This makes me think a commission model would be timely, provided all the participants are drawn in to collaborate. This means parents and children as well as teachers. As commissions reach out into community matters, it will be necessary to involve many kinds of organizations, both designed and emergent.

This then incorporates what Capra calls 'feedback loops':

> The feedback phenomenon is important for all living systems. Because of feedback, living networks can regulate and organize themselves. A human community, for example, can learn from its mistakes, because their effects will travel and come back along those feedback loops. So the community can correct itself, regulate itself and ultimately organize itself. Because of feedback, a community has its own intelligence, its own learning capacity.[6]

He quotes Niklas Luhmann, who has described a human community as a network of conversations. The results of conversations give rise to further conversations, which generate self-amplifying loops. Thus an offhand comment may be picked up and amplified by the network until it has a major consequence. The closure of the network within the boundaries of the community results in a shared system of beliefs, explanations and values, which is continually sustained by further conversations. The Institute for Research on Learning in Palo Alto, California came to the conclusion that the most powerful organizational learning and collective knowledge-sharing flourishes through informal relationships and personal networks – in other words through working conversations in communities of practice.

This last idea is exactly borne out in the four models I am discussing. It is very obvious in Mantle of the Expert and Rolling Role. And it becomes so in the conventional drama model when the teacher uses role, whether by facilitating a guest role or working in role herself. Also, each model I have suggested fulfils Capra's philosophy of emergent organizations and feedback loops. Drama permits organizations to be inaugurated and teacher in role is a powerful feedback loop when subtly and generously used with the children.

Now what about the staff and divisions of labour? So long as commissions remain 'domestic', invented by staff from within the school to serve specific necessary purposes related to the curriculum, they need not require 'delicate' ventures involving people outside. Parents and all service staff will have been consulted and are usually pleased to be involved as listeners or in visiting roles – the sort of thing we are all familiar with. Certainly commissions work does not tolerate 'gawpers' – spectators – who pop in just to take a look. This applies in Mantle of the Expert and Rolling Role, because the invented communities lose authenticity when spectators arrive.

I envisage commissions growing in complexity of knowledge, research and interaction, so someone has to take responsibility for facilitating community contacts and seeking out those who can best be usefully (and challengingly) involved. This means someone with status and authority, so here is a whole new job description for a head teacher. I envisage them working outside the school much of the time, sometimes at the behest of busy staff, to locate the kind of knowledge and advice (and resources!) a commission will require. But also in surveying and cataloguing the human and facility resources available and making unthreatening contacts, generally introducing the school to the community. And now someone can have a lot of interesting encounters through websites and email.

Staff must pool and use all their talents and be completely honest about what they can't do. Some teachers are excellent tutors and hopeless at giving lectures where people must be caught up by the speaker's style so that content becomes of absorbing interest. Commission work is no soft option or 'go-as-you-please model', but then teaching through drama systems was never a soft option. Teachers have to learn to build up group belief in the commissions, especially in early 'invented' ones. Later, more complex commissions may be believable in the sense that they are real in relation to community matters. The dilemma here may lie in convincing a group that a current commission is really relevant to their lives as young people, linking school work with their needs and interests. I have never found children to reject any Rolling Role community, and they will work to their limits to 'get things right' once they care about the people whose lives they facilitate.

I have never possessed an area of knowledge I could call a subject, so I have always operated in aspects of social politics and relied heavily upon the expertise of subject teachers or skilled workers in the community. Social politics, however, as any drama teacher knows, makes positive entry to subject enquiry, as it relates people to information. Thus gateways are made to a surprising range of interests and skills. But this gateway always incorporates the homely words our politicians, unfortunately so glibly, say — society, morals, work, family, concentration, courtesy, clear communication, imagination, standards, having initiative. These are the lubricants of society in forging productive social health.

The metaphor of a hot-air balloon best illustrates for me a commission model: the basket supports the human energy that produces the power to sustain and guide the enterprise; it contains and limits but clearly defines the destination. There are literally thousands of commissions waiting to be taken up so that schools and community become more and more interdependent. I have this dream that if that could ever be possible, children would not have to spend thirteen years of their lives being denied protected responsibility and without power to influence how they spend their time in school. Neither would they be expected to suddenly emerge at eighteen like Pallas Athena out of Zeus's head, as mature responsible members of their community. Mantle of the Expert and Rolling Role work allow them to test their capacities as maturing human beings and certainly to demonstrate their interests and abilities. A commission school would make a seamless link between the two worlds of work and active participation in learning together.

So long as teachers come to school to teach pupils and students come 'to be taught', the energies of both are deflected and neglected. Paradoxically, if teachers can find a way of not needing to teach students, they will become doers and creators exploiting opportunities so that their knowledge and skills are needed and welcomed. Then Shaw's insulting statement that has always offended me (and I fear has become one of the myths absorbed by our culture) that 'those who can, do, and those who can't, teach' will at last lapse into the obscurity it deserves.

The perfect model I keep before me of a commission engaging students and staff, and serving the world community is the one in the science department of the school that tracked and identified the first Sputnik in space before even NASA knew it existed. Let that encourage us.

## Notes

1 'Maister' is a dialect word for 'master'.
2 The story is known as 'The Green Children' in Hayes, B. and Ingpen, R. (1987) *Folk Tales and Fables of the World*, London: Dragon's World Ltd.
3 A 'cruck' or 'crook frame' is a curved timber which supports the roof of a building.
4 Capra, F. (1996) *The Web of Life – A New Synthesis of Mind and Matter*, London: HarperCollins.
5 Ofsted is the UK Office for Standards in Education, Children's Services and Skills. It inspects and regulates services providing education and skills and reports directly to Parliament.
6 Capra, F. (1998) 'Creativity in Communities', *Resurgence* 186, January–February.

**PART IV**

# Epilogue

# ENCOUNTERS WITH POWER GIVERS AND POWER TAKERS

*Dorothy Heathcote MBE was born in the West Yorkshire village of Steeton in 1926. She left the local school at the age of fourteen and was employed at the local woollen mill as a weaver. In 1945, after auditioning for a place at the Northern Theatre School, Bradford, Heathcote trained as an actress. Her fees were paid by the manager of the mill where she worked. In 1950, at the age of 24, she was appointed as a lecturer at the Newcastle upon Tyne campus of Durham University, the start of a career that was to last for 60 years and during which she was to travel around the world sharing her practice. In 1974 a BBC film about her practice,* Three Looms Waiting, *brought her to the attention of a wider public and she became an inspiration to generations of teachers. She retired from full-time lecturing at the University of Newcastle upon Tyne in 1986, but continued to teach, write and contribute to courses and drama conferences throughout the world.*

*Her significance as one of the most influential drama teachers of the twentieth century was recognized when she was awarded an MBE in the Queen's Birthday Honours list in June 2011. She died on 8 October, 2011, a week before she was due to collect her award at Buckingham Palace on 18 October. After her death many obituaries were published in newspapers and drama journals throughout the world.[1] These mentioned both her personal and professional life and included heartfelt tributes and reminiscences from the many students and teachers from around the world whose lives she touched and whose practice she influenced.*

*The most complete account of Heathcote's life and work is 'Dorothy Heathcote's Story' by Gavin Bolton, who was her close friend and colleague.[2] He paints a vivid picture of her background and upbringing and traces and analyses her professional growth over forty years.*

*Heathcote tells the story of her life in her own vivid and memorable words in this edited version of a talk given in Ankara in October 2009 for the Çağdaş Drama Derneği Organization. She gives us glimpses of some fascinating and unexpected episodes in her life and honours all those she encountered whose trust and belief in her helped her to develop into the remarkable person she became.*

I thought long and hard about my approach to this occasion because I did not want to tell you a wearisome tale of my experiences over a span of eighty three years. And then I remembered how I helped my daughter Marianne when she was in high school studying English Literature and encountering very long classics by authors such as Jane Austen and the Brontë sisters. I used to ask her to find the main central characters in each book and examine the relationships they encountered as their story unfolded. Each of these encounters would bring both benign and positive influences or negative and harmful attitudes, each one affecting the heroine differently. Victorian novels usually are concerned with heroines! I used the terms power givers for those who helped in some way, however slight, and power takers for those others who caused trouble and a degree of powerlessness for our heroine. And I thought if I used this approach, it would make it less tedious for you to listen to.

I have had a most fortunate life in that I have met and been helped on my way by many and various power givers and very few power takers. We are programmed to associate with others, and our characters and personalities are formed partly by encounters with our fellow humans and partly by the social events we participate in.

My mother was widowed very young and it was not an easy birth. My mother would, I think, still be grieving, and the doctor who delivered me asked whether he could adopt me. His wife could not have children and he would have known all my family and the background I came from. My mother, however, supported by her sisters and brothers and parents, could not give me away to another couple, even though the lives of the doctor and his wife would certainly be more comfortable and prosperous than my mother's prospects. My people were all factory workers – weavers, wood workers, spinners, with little schooling gained in the village school which educated me in my turn. Like so many of their generation they were intelligent but not necessarily intellectual – such people formed the bulk of British society – good artisans and skilled craftspeople working for factory owners. My family did not feel themselves to be poor, because all our neighbours were like us, earning the same wages, sharing the same ambitions and being as independent as they could in their circumstances.

My grandparents left school aged eleven years and went to work. My mother, aged twelve, spent mornings in school and the afternoons learning to weave. Then at thirteen she was a skilled weaver making fine woollen cloth for men's suits worn by the wealthy folks. I left the same village school aged fourteen and joined the weaving force in the same mill where my mother and her sisters and brothers were working. I worked as a weaver till I was nineteen. During those years I encountered people I was to regard as power givers.

The first power giver was the daughter of the mill owner. Realizing my love of reading, she let me use her collection of books, which were housed in the billiard room of a large Victorian mansion. This collection ranged from children's classics, through playwrights past and current, including all the works of Shakespeare, and Bernard Shaw and J. B. Priestley, both still alive and writing for the contemporary theatre. And there were the poetry books and the novels written at many periods. Part of the power she gave me lay in her trust. I never needed to ask for access. I only had to let her cook/housekeeper know when I was borrowing or returning books. She never asked me what I was reading or whether I understood everything. When she died, her house was sold with all the contents. I had by then acquired my own collection of books but I could not resist visiting her house to see the books all packed in bundles to be bid for at the auction. I hope they all went to good homes to inspire readers like me.

Between the years of fourteen to nineteen I met two power givers. One was a young girl a little older than me. She later became a television star in a very popular sitcom on the BBC. From her I took elocution lessons and learned the performance of comedy. She introduced me to a middle-aged schoolteacher of English Literature. He widened my interest in poetry and introduced me to Shakespeare and particularly the sonnet forms. What a power giver he was. He enriched my life.

Another very important power giver in my life was Esme Church, a classical actress well known in the 1930s who had played every Shakespearian heroine in the London theatres as well as at Stratford-upon-Avon. Along with Michel Saint-Denis, the influential French director, Esme Church started a theatre school in Bradford in Yorkshire ten miles from my village. She accepted me at the school, and then my third power giver emerged. He was the mill owner for whom I worked, a Methodist by belief and not a particular lover of the theatre. However, he paid my fees for the three years of theatre study and my mother took over my looms because it was wartime.[3]

So I went to theatre school with hardly a coin to spare, as I was now unemployed, but when the years of study were over, I met another two power givers. One was a well-to-do lady who ran an amateur theatre company. She paid me to produce amateur theatre. The other was a teacher of English in a high school. It was she who told me of a teaching position – a staff tutorship – advertised at the Newcastle upon Tyne campus of the University of Durham. I was now twenty-three years old and considering whether I should return to the weaving work in my village. She made me apply for the position. And to my amazement I was appointed to the position with no experience of teaching and not having entered a school since I left the local school on my fourteenth birthday. My task was to help head teachers of primary schools who were taking a three-year part-time Froebel course.[4] I was to help them understand and introduce drama for learning in their schools. There were two power endowments here. I had access to dozens of schools and classrooms in which to try out my own ideas and a young professor of Education who, having appointed me to his staff, quietly and watchfully supported me throughout.

During these early years I met my husband. He had an ancient family history behind him, collected in a family book giving family trees back to the fourteenth century right up to the entry of his father's birth in the late nineteenth century. At one time a family member, John Heathcote, in the eighteenth century, was the richest commoner in England. A commoner is someone who is not of royal blood. Raymond was born on a farm. His father was one of the sons of a doctor who had educated seven sons and two daughters through medical school. His mother was one of four children. Her father was first a master joiner, and then founder of a building business. He had designed the first revolving door and built many of the administration buildings in Manchester city such as the town hall as well as other civic buildings.

Raymond's education was a complete contrast to mine. He was a pupil at West House Preparatory School and later at Dauntsey's School, a minor public school founded in 1542 for the sons of farmers, where he developed his interest in engineering. He joined the air force on his eighteenth birthday and he didn't return to England until he was twenty-three, serving in India, Burma and Singapore, always just escaping from Japanese invasions. During these years he widened his experience of people from many backgrounds, so by the time we met he said he had learned 'never to judge others by outside appearances'. I felt I should tell him that I was from a one-parent family – my father's name was unknown to me – and remains so. He replied that it didn't matter, as he wasn't about to marry my mother.

Raymond was born in Lancashire and I was born in Yorkshire. These counties of Britain share a long history of wars and enmity, as friends frequently reminded us. We seemed like chalk and cheese but a strong bond held us. We were both obsessed with form, and fitness for purpose in the service of people, and this mutually empowered me daily. Michelangelo said 'I saw the angel in the stone and set him free.' As a teacher, my chisels for carving are many kinds of discourse with my students, and the stone is the curriculum that I am trying to interest them in becoming curious about, hoping they will remain curious all their lives and not only during their formal education.

I belong to the last generation of those who saw people 'forming' or 'making' in the streets on my way to school – engaged in shoeing horses, herding beasts to the butchers, baking bread, making useful wooden objects, blowing glass and washing and drying their clothes. So much is hidden now behind factory doors and technology.

After I left theatre school, I met two other power givers while I was attending a youth theatre event on a visit to Stuttgart with a puppeteer. Then I met the Eytel sisters, daughters of Baron Eytel who had been foreign ambassador to the German government before the outbreak of World War II. The Eytel sisters, Lola and Margaret, spoke as many languages as the countries their parents had lived in. When Hitler came to power, they lost their position in high society, as their father's government service came to an end. They became working girls: Lola worked in what used to be the Royal stables and exercised the horses of the rising young soldiers in Hitler's developing armies; Lola knew Goering well and exercised his horses, which were always 'entire', as he favoured ungelded mounts. Margaret went to work as a secretary in the American embassy in Berlin, where the family had settled in modest accommodation. Both women were violinists and when I met them, they were still playing in the Stuttgart state orchestra. I was invited to their flat to read English poetry to them and remind them of their spoken English, and a strange meeting took place. At the Northern Theatre School I was taught by Rudolph Laban for three years. He had met Lola during the time when he was in charge of the Berlin Classical Ballet company, just before the start of World War II. He needed masks for a challenging ballet called 'Motherhood versus War' and asked Lola to carve them in beechwood. Hitler was so displeased by the ballet that he ordered Laban's arrest and had all his books burned. Laban gave Lola three of the masks. When I knew her, two had been lost in air raids and she gave the third one to me. It has remained a strong link with three important power givers for me until the present time. It will finally rest with the Laban Institute, its logical place. Fortunately Laban flourished in England, and Lola and Margaret lived through the war. Margaret managed to smuggle affidavits past Hitler so that Jewish members of the orchestra could escape via the American embassy, and Lola smuggled letters to England from a prisoner of war camp where she was working as an interpreter. Power helpers come in many shapes and sizes, don't they?

At the university I had to deal with the rules and regulations of university courses. I was grappling with marks, assessments and those academic circles of 'grey men' with whom I had little in common. Fortunately I did not succumb, aided and abetted by my experienced students who joined my course to extend their abilities to use drama for learning not merely to gain more paper qualifications! My professor and the academic boards empowered my resistance to academic narrowness but of course the attitudes of the 'grey men' to a certain extent disempowered me. My confidence could easily have been wounded.

My courses were always overfilled with legitimate and sometimes illegitimate students. I was in a position where many of my students had high paper qualifications so they were happy to slip into my courses. In fact, looking back on those thirty-eight years of full employment in the university, I realized that most of my students were cleverer than me but it didn't worry either of us, for we empowered each other. On my course they were expected to teach all ages and abilities in all kinds of locations and with many professions. I owe so much to these teachers – most of them now administering schools and university departments, or working in Theatre in Education, the police, medicine and the law. Two are Catholic priests serving parishes. Three are nuns working among the American poor, and those from Canada, African countries, Scandinavia, the Netherlands, Portugal, India, West Indies, New Zealand, Australia,

Hungary, Ireland, Poland, Iceland, the USA, Greece and Cyprus are all spreading the word about this remarkably empowering experience of drama for learning. This occasion we are all sharing this evening has been brought about because of the intelligent vision of the Çağdaş Drama Derneği organization.

The range of those who have seen possibilities in drama methods for educating people are many and various, and I have been empowered by the challenges offered by lawyers, car manufacturers, the police, the punishment institutions and medicine and mental hospitals.

Each one of these presents thinking and planning challenges that are unique to their spheres of influence and the learning required of practitioners in the separate fields. These empowering challenges have allowed me to consistently test my ideas and the power of this shape-shifting activity we place under the umbrella word 'drama'. It is deeply rooted in play, sociology, psychology and anthropology and in theatre performance, its most disciplined art form. At the centre of all these is the ability of us humans to look at ourselves and the variety of relationships we experience as we go through life.

This range of challenges makes me consider myself to be a journeyman teacher, not the 'guru' title I am increasingly given, which embarrasses me. The dictionary definition suits me – 'a qualified mechanic or artisan who works for another; a reliable worker'. Sometimes I earn that gift word 'teacher' which you cannot give to yourself. I am a radical. If I were God for a day, I would change the schools so that more young people begin to recognize how to question what they are told by television advertising and subject experts, and in positive ways to find their own deep interests, skills and competencies so that they become lifelong learners.

I cannot leave my range of empowers without discussing the place of books, painting and sculpture in my life. I am an eclectic reader. I have had to be as a preparer of work for students of all ages and abilities. Novelists, poets, the professionals such as journalists, actors and playwrights have all empowered my range of thinking about the human condition, as have painters and sculptors, together with philosophers and actors. I am still dependent on those whose works I have access to. Books and a radio are essential, because they slow time into meaning. Television is my blind spot. As a journeyman teacher, I need my own images, not the rich diet of those of other creative people.

These would be my value systems so far as I can understand them and explain them in words:

- Say yes if you can, when people ask of you.
- Inclusion – relate with all races, faiths, and the place others hold in society.
- The arts and sciences are of equal importance in human development.
- The stories of the world, racial memory and myths, the fairy stories, legends, all in their way tell of truths through different lenses.
- Teachers and students must learn in partnership, feeding on each other to mutual ends.

My stance as an individual would be:

- I believe in rigour, responsibility and realizations as my path to lifelong learning.
- I follow no religious creed but I believe that spiritually is a source of energy in humans.
- My mantra would be 'Be a steward and leave all better than you found it.'

Finally, if I do have a faith, it would be like that of the Bishop of Durham, who spoke of faith as being: 'A risky commitment to a glimpsed possibility, in the face of reasonable human hesitation about whether it is really possible to live with mystery and not always have answers. This is the fate of human kind and its road to really existing.'

## Awards and Honorary Degrees:

Dorothy Heathcote's achievements have been recognized internationally by many honorary degrees, awards and citations from professional bodies such as NATD and National Drama as well as those listed here:

1958. Honorary MA degree, Durham University.
2001. The Campton Bell Lifetime Achievement Award, The American Alliance for Theatre and Education.
2005. Honorary Doctor of Letters (D.Litt), Newcastle University.
2005. International Citation of Merit, ISPA (International Society for the Performing Arts).
2007. Honorary Doctor of Education, the University of Derby.
2011. MBE. Member of the Most Excellent Order of the British Empire.

## Notes

1 'Obituary: Dorothy Heathcote', *The Journal for Drama in Education*, NATD, 29 (1), Spring 2012; Bowell, P. (2012) 'Dorothy Heathcote: A Personal Reflection', *Drama* 18 (1), Spring; Saxton, J. and Miller, C. (2012) 'Points and Practices', *RiDE: The Journal of Applied Theatre and Performance* 17 (1), February; Taylor, P. (2012) 'Dorothy Heathcote: 1926–2011', *TYA Today*, Spring.
2 Bolton, G. (2003) *Dorothy Heathcote's Story: The Biography of a Remarkable Drama Teacher*, Stoke-on-Trent: Trentham.
3 Heathcote gives a vivid account of this episode in her life in the award-winning BBC film *Three Looms Waiting* (1974).
4 Friedrich Froebel (1782–1852) was a German educator who developed the idea of the kindergarten, a holistic approach to education, where young children learned through first-hand experience, play, talk and reflection.

**PART V**

# Resources and references

# RESOURCES

## Websites

www.mantleoftheexpert.com is a comprehensive website designed as a central location for information and resources on Mantle of the Expert. It presents an overview of Mantle of the Expert and gives access to a large number of articles on Heathcote's work. Resources include a catalogue of books, articles and videotapes.

The site also contains details of training courses for schools and teachers in Mantle of the Expert.

An official tribute site has been organized by Heathcote's daughter, Marianne Heathcote, and can be found at www.dorothyheathcote.org.

## The Heathcote Archive

The Dorothy Heathcote Archive and its index were constructed and developed by Dr Sandra Hesten as part of her 1994 PhD at Lancaster University. Later, the materials were relocated to the Faculty of Education at Manchester Metropolitan University (MMU). The archive contains a large library of Heathcote's collection of books, teaching notes, plans and papers written for individual students. It also includes work for advanced diplomas, master's and doctorate degrees written by Heathcote's students, mostly dating from Heathcote's time at the University of Newcastle. It has been supplemented with her personal library and with regular boxes of material relating to the various projects on which she was engaged between 1986 and her death in 2011. The computerized index to the archive has been updated and made available online at www.did.stu.mmu.ac.uk/dha, where Dr Hesten's PhD thesis is also available to download. This thesis contains a great deal of invaluable material, including an interview with Heathcote and her analyses of various lessons.

The archive contains hundreds of documents, films and other materials, including more than 200 hours of unedited videotapes of Heathcote working with students.

In partnership with the website www.mantleoftheexpert.com, key materials from the archive have been digitized and are available online. However, the ever-expanding collection needs to be recatalogued and conserved so that the potential of the archive as a research resource and a testimony to one of the most remarkable educators of our time is safeguarded for the future. There is free access to all researchers by arrangement. Enquiries via email to John Rainer at j.rainer@mmu.ac.uk; www.did.stu.mmu.ac.uk/dha/.

## Films, DVDs and videos

DVDs and videos of Heathcote at work have been made by drama associations, schools, colleges and other educational establishments throughout the world. Many of these remain unedited. Those listed here are probably the best known and most easily accessed. The website www. mantleoftheexpert.com also contains a catalogue of the many videos of Heathcote's work made during her time at Newcastle University.

### *Building Belief* (colour, 60 minutes)

Dorothy Heathcote works with a class of ten- and eleven-year-olds in America. Together they explore the concept of the strength of a nation as they become a nation in its first struggling days in a hostile land.

### *Dorothy Heathcote Talks to Teachers*

### *Part 1* (colour, 30 minutes)

A lecture about teaching drama. Dorothy Heathcote compares the formal lesson, where the teacher starts from where she or he is, filters the information and sets the pace, with the informal approach of starting where the children are, and drawing out their own ideas. (USA 1974.)

### *Part 2* (colour, 30 minutes)

Dorothy Heathcote talks about finding material for drama and how this material can be used to expand the children's experience of life and relate to universal concepts. Questions are extremely significant but must never suggest that the teacher already knows the answers. (USA 1974.)

### *Three Looms Waiting* (black and white, 50 minutes) DVD 1976

When Dorothy Heathcote decided to go into the theatre, the mill owner she had been working for paid her fees at the acting school and told her there would be three looms waiting for her if she ever decided to go back. As she works in Tyneside with young people from a secure institution, as well as in a primary school and a hospital for the mentally impaired, it is clear Dorothy Heathcote will never go back to those waiting looms. (BBC *Omnibus* programme.)

### *Seeds of a New Life* (colour, 55 minutes) DVD 1976

The film covers two weeks of drama therapy in a hospital for people with mental impairment. The course is led by a group of twenty-two secondary school teachers working under the supervision of Dorothy Heathcote. At the core of Heathcote's philosophy is her belief that the patients have a right to emotional experiences as well as cognitive ones. The film raises the question of the difference between drama as therapy and drama as education.

Available for sale or hire from Concord Media, 22 Hines Rd. Ipswich, Suffolk, IP3 9BJ. Tel: 01473 726012

## *Albert* (12 minutes) DVD 1973

Dorothy Heathcote uses drama with a group of children with learning difficulties in a special school. She confronts them with 'Albert', supposedly a derelict, who is found in their school hall. The children's reactions to someone who needs help from them are closely observed.

Available for sale or hire from Concord Media, 22 Hines Rd. Ipswich, Suffolk, IP3 9BJ. Tel: 01473 726012

## *Pieces of Dorothy* (58 minutes)

This biographical documentary tells Dorothy Heathcote's story, from Yorkshire mill girl to internationally renowned educator. It contains extracts from teaching videos recorded since 1971 by Newcastle University. DVD copies of this film can be obtained by contacting the Newcastle University Audio and Visual Department online at www.ncl.ac.uk/iss/teaching/av-services.

Newcastle University also holds a large range of teaching video and DVD tapes showing Heathcote working with pupils in schools and hospitals and with children and adults with special needs. Copies of these are also available for viewing in the Heathcote archive at Manchester Metropolitan University, England. www.did.stu.mmu.ac.uk/dha

## *Dorothy Heathcote and David Booth in Conversation* (80 minutes) Audio Recording

The conversation between Dorothy Heathcote and David Booth was one of the highlights of National Drama's 2008 international conference. Booth interrogates Heathcote about the philosophy and practice that has been the foundation of her drama teaching. This publication is a MP3 file. Available from National Drama at www.nationaldrama.org.uk.

## *Drama for Living: A 21st Century Vision for Education* (3 hours) DVD 2009

This DVD features an extended keynote address by Dorothy Heathcote and a practical workshop with children in Trinity College, Dublin. Available from ADEI, the Association for Drama in Education.

Clips of Heathcote at work with teachers and children are available on YouTube, including *Three Looms Waiting*, and several films made by BBC North East during the 1980s. These are very early examples of Mantle of the Expert. They show Dorothy Heathcote working with a class of children as they run a shoe factory. The Medical School of Newcastle University became interested in Heathcote's methods and a number of films were made of her work for use in the training of medical students.

# BIBLIOGRAPHY AND REFERENCES

## Bibliography

Articles by and about Dorothy Heathcote, as well as transcripts of her speeches, have been published in drama and education journals throughout the world. In the UK, the National Association for the Teaching of Drama (NATD) has published many of her articles and talks, several of which are included in this book. An archive of NATD's *Journal for Drama in Education* is available on the Mantle of the Expert website, www.mantleoftheexpert.com. *Drama*, National Drama's magazine of professional practice, includes a number of articles by and about Heathcote in past issues, available online at www.drama-magazine.co.uk. National Drama's research journal, *DramaResearch*, Vol. 5 No. 1, April 2014, www.dramaresearch.co.uk, contains papers from the *Heathcote Re-Considered* conference, London, July 2013. Keynote speeches from this conference are published in *Heathcote Re-Considered: Conference Echoes*, www.nationaldrama.org.uk.

The revised edition of B. J. Wagner's *Dorothy Heathcote: Drama as a Learning Medium*, published in 1991, contains details of many publications by and about Dorothy Heathcote, including dissertations and theses. This list is likely to be already out of date as more research studies are completed.

## Selected books and articles by and about Dorothy Heathcote

Abbott, L. and Edmiston, B. (1998) *Curriculum and Pedagogy in the Classroom*, available online at www.mantleoftheexpert.com.

Bolton, G. (1984) *Drama as Education: An Argument for Placing Drama at the Centre of the Curriculum*, London: Longman.

Bolton, G. (1985) 'Changes in Thinking about Drama in Education', *Theory into Practice* 24 (3).

Bolton, G. (1999) *Acting in Classroom Drama*, Stoke-on-Trent: Trentham Books.

Bolton, G. (2003) *Dorothy Heathcote's Story: The Biography of a Remarkable Drama Teacher*, Stoke-on-Trent: Trentham Books.

Bolton, G. (2007) 'A History of Drama Education – a Search for Substance' in L. Bresler (ed.) *International Handbook of Research in Arts Education*, Dordrecht: Springer.

Bolton, G. (2013) 'Digging for Dorothy', keynote address given at *Heathcote Re-Considered*, National Drama Conference, Greenwich, July 2013.

Bolton, G. and Heathcote, D. (1999) *So You Want to Use Role-Play? A New Approach in How to Plan*, Stoke-on-Trent: Trentham Books.

Carroll, J. (1986) 'Framing Drama: Some Classroom Strategies', *The NADIE Journal* 10 (2).

Davis, D. (ed.) (2010) *Gavin Bolton: Essential Writings*, Stoke-on-Trent: Trentham Books.

Davis, D. (2014) *Imagining the Real: Towards a New Theory of Drama in Education*, Stoke-on-Trent: Trentham Books.

Eriksson, S. A. (2009) *Distancing at Close Range*, Vasa: Abo.

Fiala, O. (1977) 'An Artistic Affinity: Notes on Dorothy Heathcote and Bertolt Brecht's Modes of Work', *Drama in Education Journal* 2 (1).

Fines, J. and Verrier, R. (1974) *The Drama of History: An Experiment in Co-operative Teaching*, London: New University Education.

Fines, J. and Verrier, R. (1976) 'The Work of Dorothy Heathcote', *Young Drama* 4 (1), February.

Gillham, G. (1997) 'What Life is for: An Analysis of Dorothy Heathcote's "Levels of Explanation"', *SCYPT Journal* 34.

Goode, A. (1982) 'Dancing with a Whirlwind' in A. Goode (ed.) *Heathcote at the National*, Banbury: Kemble Press.

Grady, T. and O'Sullivan, C. (eds.) (1998) *A Head Taller: Developing a Humanizing Curriculum through Drama*, Birmingham: NATD.

Heathcote, D. (1976) 'Drama as Education' in A. Davidson (ed.) *New Destinations: The Arts and Education*, London: Greater London Association for the Arts.

Heathcote, D. (1978) 'Of These Seeds Becoming' in R. Baird Schuman (ed.) *Educational Drama for Today's Schools*, Metuchen, NJ: The Scarecrow Press.

Heathcote, D. (1992) 'Stewardship – A Paradigm for Education?', *Drama Broadsheet* 9 (3).

Heathcote, D. (2007) 'Stories as Contexts in Mantle of the Expert', *The Journal for Drama in Education* 23 (2).

Heathcote, D. (2010) 'Dramatic Imagination', *The Journal for Drama in Education* 6 (2).

Heathcote, D. (2010) 'Mantle of the Expert: Key Elements', keynote speech given at the international Drama/Theatre in Education Congress, Ankara, 2008, *Creative Drama Journal* 5 (9–10).

Heathcote, D. (2010) 'Mantle of the Expert Work in Ankara: Workshop with Secondary School Students, November 2009', *Creative Drama Journal* 5 (9–10), p. 203.

Heathcote, D. (2012) 'Contexts for Active Learning', *The Journal for Drama in Education*, Dorothy Heathcote Special Issue, Summer.

Heathcote, D. (2012) 'The Fight for Drama – The Fight for Education', *The Journal for Drama in Education* 28 (1), Special Supplement, Spring.

Heathcote, D. and Bolton, G. (1995) *Drama for Learning: Dorothy Heathcote's Mantle of the Expert Approach to Education*, Portsmouth, NH: Heinemann US.

Heathcote, D. and Herbert, P. (1985) 'A Drama of Learning: Mantle of the Expert', *Theory into Practice* XXIV (3).

Heathcote, D. and Pennington, E. (1989) 'National Theatre Education Project: Model Drama/Theatre Curriculum', *Drama Broadsheet* 6 (1).

Johnson, L. and O'Neill, C. (eds.) (1984) *Dorothy Heathcote: Collected Writings on Education and Drama*, London: Hutchinson.

Lacey, S. and Woolland, B. (1992) 'Educational Drama and Radical Theatre Practice', *New Theatre Quarterly* 29 (8).

Landy, R. J. and Montgomery, D. (2012) *Theatre for Change: Education, Social Action and Therapy*, New York: Palgrave Macmillan.

Morgan, N. and Saxton, J. (1987) *Teaching Drama: A Mind of Many Wonders*, Porstmouth, NH: Heinemann US.

Muir, A. (1996) *New Beginnings: Knowledge and Form in the Drama of Bertolt Brecht and Dorothy Heathcote*, Stoke-on-Trent: Trentham Books.

O'Sullivan, C. and Williams, G. (ed.) (1998) *Building Bridges: Laying Foundations for a Child-centered Curriculum in Drama and Education*, Birmingham: NATD.

Robinson, Ken (1980) *Exploring Theatre and Education*, London: Heinemann.
Wagner, B. J. (1976) *Dorothy Heathcote: Drama as a Learning Medium*, Washington, DC: National Education Association. Revised UK edition (1991). Stoke-on-Trent: Trentham Books.

## Drama in education: select bibliography

Ackroyd, J. (2004) *Role Reconsidered: A Re-evaluation of the Relationship between Teacher-in-Role and Acting*, Stoke-on-Trent: Trentham Books.
Anderson, M. and Dunn, J. (2013). *How Drama Activates Learning: Contemporary Research and Practice*, London: Bloomsbury Academic.
Baldwin, P. (2004) *With Drama in Mind: Real Learning in Imagined Worlds*, London: Continuum.
Baldwin, P., Fleming, K. and Neelands, J. (2003) *Teaching Literacy through Drama: Creative Approaches*, London: Routledge.
Booth, D. (1996) *Story Drama*, Markham, Ontario: Pembroke.
Bowell, P. and Heap, B. (2001) *Planning Process Drama*, London: David Fulton.
Duffy, P. (2014) *A Reflective Practitioner's Guide to (Mis)Adventures in Drama Education or What Was I Thinking?*, Bristol: Intellect Publishing.
Edmiston, B. (2013) *Transforming Teaching and Learning with Active and Dramatic Approaches*, New York: Routledge.
Fleming, M. (1994) *Starting Drama Teaching*, London: David Fulton.
Gallagher, K. and Neelands, J. (2013) *Drama and Theatre in Urban Contexts*, London: Routledge.
Jackson, A. (2007) *Theatre, Education and the Making of Meanings*, Manchester: Manchester University Press.
Neelands, J. (1998) *Beginning Drama 11–14*, London: David Fulton.
Nicholson, H. (2003) *Applied Drama: The Gift of Theatre*, New York: Palgrave Macmillan.
O'Neill, C. (1995) *Drama Worlds*, Portsmouth, NH: Heinemann US.
O'Toole, J. (2002) *Pretending to Learn: Helping Children Learn through Drama*, Frenchs Forest, NSW: Longman.
Rainer, J. and Lewis, M. (2012) *Drama at the Heart of the Secondary School: Projects to Promote Authentic Learning*, London: Routledge.
Taylor, P. (2000) *The Drama Classroom: Action, Reflection, Transformation*, New York: Routledge.
Taylor, P. and Warner, C. (2006) *Structure and Spontaneity: The Process Drama of Cecily O'Neill*, Stoke-on-Trent: Trentham Books.
Woolland, B. (2001) *Teaching Drama in Primary and Secondary Schools*, London: David Fulton.

## References

Breen, R. S. (1986) *Chamber Theatre*, Evanston, IL: William Caxton.
Capra, F. (1996) *The Web of Life – A New Synthesis of Mind and Matter*, London: HarperCollins.
Capra, F. (1998) 'Creativity in Communities', *Resurgence* 186, January–February.
Carroll, J. (1984) *The Treatment of Dr. Lister: A Language Functions Approach to Drama in Education*, Bathurst, NSW: Mitchell College of Advanced Education.
Caws, P. (1968) 'What is Structuralism', *Partisan Review* 35 (1), Winter.
Danz, Louis (1932) *The Psychologist Looks at Art*, New York: Longman.
Dodd, N. and Hickson, W. (eds.) (1971) *Drama and Theatre in Education*, London: Heinemann.
Goffman, Erving (1975) *Frame Analysis*, Harmondsworth: Peregrine Books.
Hall, E. T. (1959) *The Silent Language*, London: Anchor Books.
Hayes, B. and Ingpen, R. (1987) *Folk Tales and Fables of the World*, London: Dragon's World Ltd.
Hodgson, J. and Richards, E. (1966) *Improvisation*, London: Methuen and Co. Ltd.
Hornbrook, D. (1989) *Education and Dramatic Art*, Oxford: Blackwell Education.
Jack, I. and Fowler, R. (1997) *The Poetical Works of Robert Browning*, volume III, Oxford: Oxford University Press.

Kohl, H. (1995) *Should We Burn Babar? Essays on Children's Literature and the Power of Stories*, New York: The New Press.

McCaslin, N. (ed.) (1977) *Children and Drama*, New York: David McKay & Co. Ltd.

Rugg, Harold (1963) *Imagination*, New York: Harper and Row.

Shaffer, D. W. (2006) *How Computer Games Help Children Learn*, London: Palgrave Macmillan.

Shotter, J. (1975) *Images of Man in Psychological Research*, London: Methuen.

Slade, Peter (1954) *Child Drama*, London: University of London Press.

Toffler, Alvin (1980) *The Third Wave*, New York: Bantam Books.

Van Deville, O. (2000) *A Thomas Jefferson Education*, Salt Lake City, UT: George Wythe College Press.

Way, B. (1967) *Development through Drama*, London: Longman.

Zimnik, R. (1978) *The Crane*, translated by M. Koenig, London: Macmillan Education.

# INDEX